PEL

FAMI

Jean Medawar was brou[ght up to] become a doctor like h[er father. She was] awarded a scholarship i[n science to Somerville] College, Oxford, and took a B.Sc. degree there, working under Professor (later Lord) Florey in the School of Pathology. She now lives in Hampstead, is married and has four children and three grandchildren. She was chairman of the FPA from 1968 to 1970, co-edits *Family Planning* with Dr David Pyke and is now chairman of the Margaret Pyke Centres' Management Committee.

David Pyke is a physician on the staff of a London teaching hospital and head of its Diabetic Department. He became interested in family planning through his mother, Margaret Pyke, who was chairman of the FPA for twelve years until her death in 1966 and was one of the main pioneers in its success. Dr Pyke started the FPA's journal *Family Planning* in 1952 and has been joint editor with Lady Medawar since 1959; he is a trustee of the Margaret Pyke Memorial Trust, which set up a model family-planning centre for training and research.

Family Planning

EDITED BY
JEAN MEDAWAR AND
DAVID PYKE

PENGUIN BOOKS

Penguin Books Ltd, Harmondsworth, Middlesex, England
Penguin Books Inc., 7110 Ambassador Road, Baltimore, Maryland 21207, U.S.A.
Penguin Books Australia Ltd, Ringwood, Victoria, Australia

First published 1971

This selection copyright © Jean Medawar and David Pyke, 1971

Made and printed in Great Britain by
Hazell Watson & Viney Ltd, Aylesbury, Bucks
Set in Linotype Times

This book is sold subject to the condition
that it shall not, by way of trade or otherwise,
be lent, re-sold, hired out, or otherwise circulated
without the publisher's prior consent in any form of
binding or cover other than that in which it is
published and without a similar condition
including this condition being imposed
on the subsequent purchaser

Contents

DATE AND SOURCE OF CONTRIBUTIONS		7
A NOTE ON THE CONTRIBUTORS		9
ACKNOWLEDGEMENTS		11
PREFACE	*Jean Medawar* *David Pyke*	13
INTRODUCTION	*Katharine Whitehorn*	15
1 NOAH'S NEW FLOOD or the Multiplication of Man	*Theodore Fox*	17
2 FAMILY LIMITATION IN THE PAST	*E. A. Wrigley*	37
3 THE HISTORY OF FAMILY PLANNING IN BRITAIN	*Jean Medawar*	45
4 THE KEY OF THE DOOR	*Edwin Brooks*	58
5 PLANNING TODAY		
(I) Conventional Methods	*Norman Morris*	63
(II) Oral Contraceptives	*P. M. F. Bishop*	75
(III) Voluntary Sterilization	*L. N. Jackson*	95
6 PROBLEMS AND SOLUTIONS		
(I) Artificial Insemination	*A Physician*	99
(II) Subfertility	*P. M. F. Bishop*	113
(III) Abortion		
(a) Abortion without Birth Control	*Madeleine Simms*	115
(b) Reflections of an Abortionist	*C.H.*	116
(c) Attitudes of Women Abortionists	*Moya Woodside*	126

- (IV) Domiciliary Family Planning
  - (a) One Foot in the Door — Renée Brittain — 138
  - (b) The Domiciliary Service — Frances Solano — 144

7 EDUCATION
- (I) Educating the Educators — Theodore Fox — 150
- (II) The Very Young Mother — Donald Gough — 159
- (III) What Is Sex Education? — Faith Spicer — 170
- (IV) The Sexual Behaviour of Young People — Michael Schofield — 173
- (V) A Small Experiment — Michael Duane — 178
- (VI) Brook Advisory Centres — Helen Brook — 187

8 RELIGION AND BIRTH CONTROL
- (I) The Non-Roman View — G. R. Dunstan — 190
- (II) The Roman Catholic View — Denis Rice — 206

9 WIDER CONSEQUENCES OF PLANNING
- (I) Principle and Paradox — Peter Medawar — 223
- (II) Genetic Advice for Potential Parents — J. A. Fraser Roberts — 233

APPENDIX
- (I) United Nations – the Statutory Body — George Cadbury — 239
- (II) The International Planned Parenthood Federation — Colville Deverell — 245

Date and Source of Contributions

Chapter 1	*Family Planning*, vol. 15, no. 4, January 1967
Chapter 2	*Family Planning*, vol. 15, no. 2, July 1966
Chapter 3	written specially for this book
Chapter 4	adapted from a speech given to the Annual Conference of Medical Officers of Health in 1967
Chapter 5 (I)	written specially for this book
(II)	written specially for this book
(III)	*Family Planning*, vol. 16, no. 3, October 1967
Chapter 6 (I)	*Family Planning*, vol. 7, no. 1, April 1958
(II)	*Family Planning*, vol. 14, no. 3, October 1965
(III) (a)	written specially for this book
(b)	*Family Planning*, vol. 16, no. 2, July 1967
(c)	*Family Planning*, vol. 12, no. 2, July 1963
(IV) (a)	*Family Planning*, vol. 13, no. 3, October 1964
(b)	*Family Planning*, vol. 16, no. 2, July 1967
Chapter 7 (I)	*Family Planning*, vol. 15, no. 3, October 1966
(II)	*Family Planning*, vol. 15, no. 2, July 1966
(III)	*Family Planning*, vol. 10, no. 2, April 1961
(IV)	*Family Planning*, vol. 14, no. 2, July 1965
(V)	*Family Planning*, vol. 11, no. 2, July 1962
(VI)	written specially for this book
Chapter 8 (I)	written specially for this book
(II)	based on an article in *Family Planning*, vol. 14, no. 1, April 1965
Chapter 9 (I)	*Family Planning*, vol. 10, no. 4, January 1962
(II)	*Family Planning*, vol. 11, no. 2, July 1962
Appendix (I)	written specially for this book
(II)	written specially for this book

A Note on the Contributors

Dr Peter Bishop is Medical Consultant to the Family Planning Association. He is Emeritus Endocrinologist to Guy's Hospital and Honorary Consultant Endocrinologist to Chelsea Hospital for Women and was formerly Endocrinologist to the Department of Obstetrics and Gynaecology at the Royal Postgraduate Medical School. He was President of the section of Endocrinology of the Royal Society of Medicine in 1955 and Chairman of the Committee of the Society for the Study of Fertility from 1960–63. He was Sir Arthur Sims's Commonwealth Travelling Professor in 1964 and is an honorary member of the American Society for the Study of Sterility.

Renée Brittain is a freelance journalist with a great interest in family planning. She spent some time publicizing the Marie Stopes Memorial Foundation.

Helen Brook was one of those who established the Brook Advisory Centres. She has worked for the FPA for twenty-two years and has, at one time or another, been a member of all the FPA's major national committees.

Dr Edwin Brooks was the Labour MP for Bebington until 1970, before which he was a lecturer in geography at the University of Liverpool. It was he who, as a Private Member, brought in the bill which became law as the National Health Service (Family Planning) Act 1967.

George Cadbury is Chairman of the Governing Body of the International Planned Parenthood Federation. He was formerly a director of the Technical Assistance Board of the United Nations.

Sir Colville Deverell was from 1964 to 1969 Secretary-General of the International Planned Parenthood Federation. He had previously held a number of posts in the colonial service, the final one being Governor of Mauritius.

A Note on the Contributors

Michael Duane spent a number of years teaching in secondary modern schools and training teachers. He became head of four schools, the last of which was Risinghill. He is now training teachers at Garnett College and also lectures to parents all over the country.

Professor G. R. Dunstan is F.D. Maurice Professor of Moral and Social Theology at King's College London, Canon Theologian of Leicester Cathedral, and Editor of the monthly journal *Theology*.

Sir Theodore Fox was for twenty years Editor of the *Lancet*. Subsequently, from 1965 to 1967, he was Director of the Family Planning Association. He is a Fellow of the Royal College of Physicians of London.

Dr Donald Gough is a psychoanalyst in private practice and Consultant Psychiatrist to the Spastics Society Headquarters and to a GLC residential school for schoolgirl mothers. He trained as a child psychiatrist at the Department for Children and Parents in the Tavistock Clinic and has research interest in adoption and mother-child interaction.

Dr L. N. Jackson is a general practitioner in Devonshire. He is also Honorary Director of the Simon Population Trust Voluntary Sterilization Project.

Sir Peter Medawar is Director of the National Institute for Medical Research. He was formerly Jodrell Professor of Zoology at University College, London, and in 1960 was awarded, jointly with Sir Macfarlane Burnet, the Nobel prize for Medicine.

Professor Norman Morris is Professor of Obstetrics and Gynaecology at the Charing Cross Medical School. His department was the second in London to develop its own family-planning unit, which is run in conjunction with the ante-natal clinic. His department has become well-known for its interest in developing the humanitarian aspects of obstetric practice.

Denis Rice, the Warden of Vaughan College, Leicester, is a Roman Catholic and was one of the signatories of the Address to the second Vatican Council. He has academic training in philosophy and social science and practical experience as case-worker, and education officer.

Dr J. A. Fraser Roberts is a geneticist at the Paediatric Research Unit, Guy's Hospital Medical School and Honorary Consultant in

Medical Genetics, Guy's Hospital. He was formerly Director of the Clinical Medical Research Council Genetics Research Unit, and Honorary Consultant in Medical Genetics, the Hospital for Sick Children, Great Ormond Street.

Michael Schofield took his degree in psychology at Cambridge University and has specialized in social psychology. He has conducted research for the British Social Biology Council, the Home Office and the University of London. He is the author of a number of books and is at present carrying out research on sexual development for the Health Education Council.

Madeleine Simms was for four years Editor of the Abortion Law Reform Association (ALRA) Newsletter. She is currently doing research on abortion.

Frances Solano is a nurse with wide experience of family-planning work, especially in the area of the domiciliary service.

Dr Faith Spicer was former Medical Director of the Brook Advisory Centres. She works part-time in maternity and child welfare clinics and also lectures in child care and child development, personal relationships and sex education. She is working also on projects for drifters and the unattached.

Moya Woodside is currently Senior Psychiatric Social Worker at the Royal Edinburgh Hospital. She has held a number of research posts at the University of North Carolina, Guy's Hospital and Holloway Prison and published several papers.

Dr E. A. Wrigley is co-founder and member of the Cambridge Group for the History of Population and Social Structure. He is a Fellow and Senior Bursar of Peterhouse, Cambridge, and a university lecturer in the Department of Geography.

ACKNOWLEDGEMENTS

We acknowledge permission to the Family Planning Association to print the sections that have appeared in *Family Planning* and to the authors for the remaining sections.

Preface

The idea of family planning is commonsense today. Fifty years ago it was condemned. Since June 1967 we have had an Act of Parliament which allows and encourages all local health authorities to give family-planning advice as a normal part of the welfare services.

A visiting stranger might well suppose that in a country where such an act had been passed no unwanted babies were born, that there was no need for abortion, and that newly trained doctors and nurses left their medical schools with an understanding of human sexual needs and a knowledge of how to teach all forms of contraception. The stranger would be wrong. If he consulted the Registrar General's Office or the records of one of London's large teaching hospitals, he would learn that probably only a quarter of all the babies born were planned by their parents, that there are something like 300 abortions a day, and that the cost of failed abortions receiving hospital treatment was £31,000 a month last time it was estimated; he would learn that some 70,000 of the annual crop of babies are born illegitimate, that there are 50,000 children in care and that the population of this country is increasing by about a third of a million a year. He would find that only a quarter of the councils are offering the full family-planning service which the 1967 act encourages, and that of these forty-nine doing so thirty-eight do it through the agency of a voluntary body, the Family Planning Association, which supports and administers around 1,000 clinics without any government money.

This book tries to explain how such a situation is possible. Some of the sections have already appeared as articles in the quarterly *Family Planning* and some have been specially written.

Each chapter is planned to answer the obvious questions asked by the intelligent but uninformed reader. 'Why is there so much talk about family planning today?' 'Why don't people plan?' 'How can you plan?' 'Is birth control harmful?' 'Why don't they do something?'

When Charles Bradlaugh was fighting for the right to affirm and not swear the oath of allegiance, and had been forcibly removed from the House, an amiable Conservative MP remonstrated with him. 'By God, Bradlaugh,' he said, 'what does it *matter* if there is a God or not?' In Bradlaugh's fight the casualties were principles; in the case of fertility control they are unfortunately unwanted babies – a cruel currency for a civilized country. The object of this book is to help change the currency before the human cost becomes crippling.

JEAN MEDAWAR
DAVID PYKE

Margaret Pyke Centre
London

Introduction

Why this book? You might think, with family planning now grudgingly accepted by just about all authorities, with the storm-centre of controversy shifted to abortion, and the teeming families that gave rise to the movement almost a back number, that the whole issue of family planning could be considered a dead letter. Surely the matter now needs as little discussion as toothpaste, refuse disposal or the provision of electric light: just one more good, clean, necessary, boring, modern service?

Well, no. Twenty years ago it must have seemed that, if only you could get past the barriers of prudery and vindictiveness, past the ignorance and distrust which afflicted the whole subject, there would be nothing left to argue about. But in fact as one level of controversy is smoothed out, another surprisingly appears beneath: we have to face the fact that this is an area where there are vastly more complexities than any of the original crisp reformers might have suspected.

More. Just because family planning is now so universally admitted to be sensible, there's a reaction against it, never more openly expressed than in Margaret Drabble's *The Waterfall*:

> Jane reflected on the amazing apparent control with which her mother's generation had planned their lives and their families – family planning had been a meaningful phrase to them, whereas to her and most of her generation it seemed a fallacious concept; quite out of date, a bad joke, like those turban hats that women wore in wartime to conceal their uncherished hair.

All this may seem about as logical as Pogo's 'I notice they all waits to git born thesselves before they gits so struck on this family planning'; but there it is: the Drabble girls may be a bunch of nitwits but they still have their wombs about them, and the family planning movement can only sigh and shoulder its burden all over again.

The questions remain. What is an unwanted child? Why are some people hopeless even with foolproof methods? What is the right spacing for a family, anyway? And what happens to the child who grows up with only a single parent? What are the psychological barriers against planning at all? How does the birth of babies fit into a twentieth-century life cycle, vastly longer than it ever used to be? What does family planning do to the primitive side of human beings, and vice versa? Every aspect of method, propaganda, consequences, outcome and attitude needs investigating still.

And not just to keep our mother-and-baby homes from bursting at the seams either. The problem is so much wider than what goes on here. For if we can't get family planning going, can't integrate it totally into the way people think and live in a sophisticated western society, what hope has Asia? In an appalling sort of way, we are a pilot project for the world, and what we do – or fail to do – here affects the whole hope for the world's population control. Other problems can be solved, at a pinch, by governments and guns; not this one. The world has got to stop overproducing at the rate it does; and there are still only three ways of doing it. The abortionist's couch, the traditional methods of battle, famine and pestilence – or what goes on between two people privately in the dark.

We realize now that interfering with anything so fundamental as the human instinct to breed (and not just to mate) is never going to be easy; and that if you ever so effectively quashed people's instinct to go on having children, that it *was* easy, you'd have a hundred other problems on your hands from the repercussions. This book doesn't give all the answers – but goes into virtually all of the questions. We need the discussion, and we need to gather up everything that has been worked out on the subject, which is what it does. It isn't the last word, only because there isn't a last word, and never will be.

KATHARINE WHITEHORN

1
Noah's New Flood
or the Multiplication of Man

THEODORE FOX

World population has become a problem only recently. It was not until 1830 that the population of the world reached its first thousand million; the second thousand million came in a century and the third in thirty years. At the present rate of increase the number of people in the world will double by the year 2000.

This great and accelerating increase comes not from a rise in fertility but from a dramatic fall in death rates produced by improvement in food, medicine and hygiene. All this is to the good, but the rise in the tide of population – a flood of people not water – poses great problems.

When Noah and his family came out of the ark, they were told that they would need it no more. For never again would the waters rise and destroy all living creatures. But, in obeying the injunction to be fruitful and multiply and replenish the earth, Noah and his sons started what is becoming a new flood – not this time of water but of men.

Some think that the tide of human population carries no danger, since it will ebb as surely as it flows. But others see it as threatening disaster. I want to consider what is happening and what we should do. What is happening is clear enough: after hundreds of thousands of years of multiplying slowly, man has begun to multiply fast. The reason for the sudden acceleration is not that we have become more fertile but merely that so many more of us remain alive. In the old days deaths were nearly as numerous as births; but today, for every one that dies, two are born to take his place. This is happening because immense effort has been put into the prevention, or postponement, of death, but very little into the prevention of birth. All through the ages birth has been thought good, but death bad; and man still does his utmost to interfere with nature when she would destroy human life but positively abets her when she creates it.

Because of this interference, some of nature's checks on the multiplication of our species – particularly pestilence and famine – are largely in abeyance. Death rates have fallen sharply – latterly through better medical care and mass campaigns against infection, but earlier through the improvement of law and order, of sanitation, and of food supplies. The net result is not so much that we live longer as that we less often die in infancy.

The biggest difference between the world of today and the world of fifty years ago is that, over larger and larger areas, the majority of children now survive to have children of their own. Hitherto man has had to bury many of his babies; but now he has to bring them up. Can he hope to do this properly when every minute there are more?

STANDING ROOM ONLY

What is alarming is the gathering speed with which population is rising. To work up to the present total of about 3,400 million men, women, and children has taken hundreds of thousands of years; but, as we are going, a second 3,400 million will be added in only thirty-five years. This would give us nearly 7,000 million by the end of the century – which is not unlikely. After that, if today's birth and death rates were to persist, our race would go on doubling itself at shorter and shorter intervals until the earth could offer standing room only. Everybody knows that this can never really happen – that, before it does happen, the multiplication of man will somehow cease. But how is it to cease? The alternative possibilities were stated starkly three years ago by the United States National Academy of Science: 'Either the birth rate of the world must come down or the death rate must go back up.' In other words, our problem can be solved only by an increase of deaths or a decrease of births. At the moment, an increase of deaths seems the more probable solution; but we can still hope that the people of the world will decide to limit their numbers before nature does this for them.

Some think such talk alarmist. They say that this is a problem that will solve itself. The countries now foremost in replenishing the earth will automatically slacken reproductive speed, we are told, as their prosperity and education rise towards European levels.

Let us consider then, what happened here when we were a developing country.

EUROPEAN PRECEDENT

Not so long ago, Britain was mainly agricultural; and, to people who wrest a living from the soil, a large family, though a burden, can also be an economic asset. On a farm or croft children who do not go to school can soon repay what they cost to feed and clothe.

Not so long ago too in Britain, as elsewhere, anyone who wanted descendants was wise to have as many children as he could manage; for an infection descending on the family might leave few survivors. (I lately read about a Victorian archbishop and his wife who lost four of their five children within a month – from measles.) In the old days men who could afford it often had enormous families, sometimes by successive wives. And most people probably had as many children as they could.

But I am not of course saying that families were never limited before there were handbooks on contraception. At all times and in all places parents have found means of controlling the number of their offspring – sometimes by abortion; sometimes by exposing infants on the mountainside; and sometimes by later marriage. In pre-industrial Europe, unlike today's developing societies, women seem to have married relatively late. Thus about the end of the seventeenth century in the Devon village of Colyton the average age of brides was over thirty, their husbands being in general two years younger.

ADVANTAGES OF HAVING FEW CHILDREN

The Industrial Revolution changed our world by drawing so many people into cities; and at first the age of marriage fell and the birth rate rose. But the new factory worker found that when one is a wage-earner, without so much as a garden, each addition to the family leaves less to spend on other things. Death rates were slowly falling; and as the survival of children became more likely, more and more parents saw the advantages of having only a few, and giving them better food and clothing, more learning, and more of a chance in life. Perhaps for this reason, when our death rates began to go down, our birth rates followed suit. Just how people managed to control their fertility, we do not know; but not a few remained celibate, and the age of marriage rose again. Many couples must have made their intercourse infrequent; many others must have used the oldest form of birth control, *coitus interruptus*; and many must have procured abortion, as they still do. In our present century the birth rate was further lowered by the economic depression of the 1930s; and before the war the British population was actually declining. Even today Europe is still the continent with the lowest growth rate.

Thus our European experience has been that, when deaths fall and standards of living rise, people want to do more for their children. The barefoot urchin who used to feed the calves, or sell newspapers in the street, now leaves by bus each morning in a blazer with the school crest.

EFFECT OF EDUCATION

Likewise evidence from many parts of the world shows that, as education improves, people tend to limit their families so that each child shall have a better upbringing. For example, Egyptian girls who went to a university have fewer children than those who went only to an elementary school. Similarly, when people have a chance of enjoying some of the amenities (or alleged amenities) of modern life, they are more likely to restrict their fertility – preferring a sewing machine, or even a motor bicycle, to yet another child.

So we must go some way with those who believe that our problem will solve itself. As people become more prosperous and better educated they tend to have fewer children; and no doubt the inhabitants of Asia and South America will cease to multiply so fast when they are better off and better read.

But when is this going to happen? Will it indeed ever happen? For surely the argument rests on fallacy. One cannot rely on education and prosperity to prevent birth in a country where births are preventing education and prosperity.

DEVELOPING COUNTRIES

Even if the European precedent is followed, the relief of population pressure is unlikely to be immediate. Here in Europe death rates were probably on the decline for some time before birth rates declined too; and many of the developing countries cannot now afford – literally cannot afford – to wait for so slow a process of adjustment. This process, moreover, has hardly begun: in many countries deaths have been halved or quartered since the war, but births remain at much the same level as before. This fact is perhaps the most alarming of our time.

Throughout the richer third of the world (North America, Europe, Russia, Argentina, Australasia, Japan) the birth rates are much lower than formerly – usually below twenty-five or twenty per thousand. But in the poor two-thirds of the world, though deaths have tumbled, births remain at forty or even fifty per thousand. As someone has put it, these developing countries now combine a medieval birth rate with a twentieth century death rate.

The result is unprecedented – something new in the story of man. The increases in population are already so much larger as to create a situation that is different in kind.

Here in Europe our population has never risen by more than about one per cent per annum even in the days when North

America lay open to our surplus population. But today the figure for the world as a whole is over two per cent. In some countries it is between three and four per cent. This may not sound alarming; but, if you remember those old sums about money – other people's money – accumulating at compound interest, you will know that the results were always astonishingly large. Populations likewise can increase by compound interest; and if it maintains an annual increase of three-and-half per cent a population will double in about twenty years, and go on doing so till something stops it.

That deaths have fallen but births have not is disturbing, to say the least; but we have no right to feel surprised. After all, in the old colonial days Europeans took great pains over introducing law and order, sanitation, and medical care, but they seldom recommended to other races the methods of family limitation they themselves used at home. Similarly, in the past few decades the World Health Organization and others have worked medical wonders by inexpensive programmes of death control – eradication of malaria, for instance. But these have not been balanced by the programmes of birth control needed if a big rise in population was not to follow.

We can be thankful that public health campaigns since the war have reduced the death rate in Ceylon or Mexico to European levels, but we must also think hard about the economic and other consequences of doubling their population in under twenty years.

POPULATION VERSUS DEVELOPMENT

Consider, for a moment, the case of Egypt, which has a population rise now put at 2·8 per cent per annum. To improve the life of the people, the Egyptian Government commissioned the building of the High Dam at Aswan, which with other projects is to reclaim a couple of million acres for agriculture and provide power for industries. But this scheme is already in a sense a failure. For between 1952 when the dam was conceived and 1972 when the reservoir is to be full, the population will have risen by something like thirteen million; and most if not all the produce of the extra land will be needed to fill these extra mouths.

And filling mouths is not all that has to be done: additional citizens need additional clothes, additional houses, additional hospitals, additional education. Of these, education may prove the biggest headache; for with an enlarging population the main hope of prosperity lies in some form of industrialization which more and more requires training of the workers. To say that a country will have another 10,000 children next year may seem a small matter; but, just to maintain its previous educational level, that country will have to build, equip, and staff a new school of 400 children every fortnight, which certainly will not make it any easier to reduce the size of classes and improve the quality of teaching. In India ten years ago fewer than forty per cent of children were at school, and one wonders what the proportion will be when the school-age population has risen to the 150 million predicted for 1978. These will be the parents of the next generation; and, if they remain uneducated, not only will they be too primitive to be an effective labour force but they will also preserve the traditions of early marriage and excessive child-bearing, breeding yet more people.

SHARING OUT THE WORK

Stand in a street in Calcutta and you will see thousands and thousands of people following avocations which by some miracle provide almost all of them with enough food to keep alive. But hardly more than that – because they are producing so little. For everything that has to be done there are far too many to do it; but, instead of scheduling half the population as unemployed or redundant, the eastern tradition is to share out the work so that everybody does a little and is entitled to some tiny part of the proceeds. Instead of unemployment huge areas of the world have underemployment; and their chronic poverty is curable only by reducing the growth of population or by increasing the work.

Had he been writing of the east today, Goldsmith might have

described an overcrowded village rather than a deserted one, and might have reversed his famous words:

> Ill fares the land, to hast'ning ills a prey
> Where men accumulate, and wealth decays.

How are the work and the wealth to be increased? This is the dilemma of all developing countries where population is growing fast.

To build factories requires money; and, unless it can get this money from abroad, a country has to finance new enterprises from its own savings. Only by consuming less than it produces will it have a balance to invest in industrialization. In many poor countries this would be hard enough if the population remained the same; but, where perhaps ten per cent of the national income each year is used up each year on providing for extra people, there is not likely to be much over for the investment. For a nation, as for a family, saving is very difficult if one has a lot of children.

Of course many developing countries have in fact had money from abroad, especially from the United States. With financial and technical aid, their total economic output has risen. But all too often neither generosity nor science has done much to improve the quality of life: instead of enabling the same number of people to live better, they have merely enabled more people to live in the same old way. This does not mean that foreign aid is unnecessary: on the contrary, even if the richer countries did no more than study their own interests, they would now be devoting far more of their resources to rescuing their neighbours from poverty. But obviously foreign aid cannot succeed in increasing a nation's income per head if the number of new heads each year is always sufficient to absorb it.

Some years ago, it seems, agricultural production per person may have ceased to rise. The fear is that it is starting to fall. The latest report from the United Nations Food and Agriculture Organization suggests that it fell in 1965–6; for the world's population increased by some seventy million whereas its production of food remained much the same.

ADVANCES IN SCIENCE?

So much for the argument that industrialization brings prosperity and that prosperity will prevent births. What about the other reassuring argument – that advances in science can be relied upon to provide for any number of people that may be born?

For my part, I expect a lot from science: if atomic energy were widely used, and if the sea were farmed as carefully as the land, this planet would support far more human beings than today. Indeed we shall have to see that it does; for, short of war or an appalling epidemic, nothing anybody can do now will prevent an immense increase in world population in the next few decades. But merely to say that science will solve everything is to ignore an unpleasant but important fact – namely that we are not yet living in one world in which resources are readily transferred to wherever they are needed. A mere quarter of the world's inhabitants use three quarters of its energy (the kind got from atoms, dams, coal, and oil); and the countries rich in this physical power are not the ones where population is rising fastest. The economic gap between peoples, instead of narrowing as we hoped, is getting wider.

Nowadays even the remoter tribes of headhunters have heard about our affluent societies; and countless millions everywhere, though they may not have much hope of dinner at the Ritz, are still expecting the twentieth century, with its inventions, to deliver them from the bondage of poverty. If, instead of getting better, their condition gets worse, whether through shortage of food or work, the prospects of world order will be dim. For the more fortunate nations to become sophisticated, equable, and urbane will avail little if the less fortunate, in considerably greater numbers, become more primitive, angry and combustible.

EXAMPLE OF JAPAN

Nations, like individuals, are members of one another; and the economic gap is so great and dangerous that its reduction is now an urgent necessity, not a philanthropic luxury. At present we in the rich countries are giving or lending the poorer ones (with or without strings) about one per cent of our income; and, though it could mean great immediate sacrifice, we should be wise to start sharing our resources with them on a far more realistic scale. Yet even this will do little good unless most of the countries with growth rates of two, three or four per cent see for themselves that they are heading for disaster. Probably most of them could still regain the road to economic progress if they could cut their birth rate by half within a generation – as has been done by Japan.

The reason why halving the birth rate would bring so much relief is simple: the workers would no longer have so many dependants to support. Notestein points out that, in a country with 'little more than minimal health protection' uncontrolled fertility will mean that over forty per cent of the population are under the age of fifteen. The people of working age in Costa Rica have to support far more children than the people of working age in Sweden. By halving its birth rate, such a country could quickly reduce the number of its dependent children and so regain its power to put more money into productive investment. And, instead of being called a developing country by courtesy, it would truly be one. Its children would then have some chance of getting the better deal they deserve.

Facts of this kind lead Enke to calculate that, if you are trying to raise a country's income per head, you can do a hundred times more with a dollar if you spend it on retarding population growth than if you spend it on accelerating economic output. President Johnson was on the safe side when he said that 'less than $5 invested in birth control is worth $100 invested in economic development'. But for many countries, population control without economic investment is of no more use than economic investment without population control. They are needed together.

POPULATION CONTROL

To the humanist, though 'birth control' may sound acceptable, the words 'population control' have an impersonal and ruthless ring. A population consists of individual people; and whether these people have babies is very much their own affair. Certainly I should agree that in a humane society compulsion should be a last resort. But to withhold knowledge can be as bad. I see no excuse for the kind of humanity that carries non-interference to the length of leaving people in ignorance of effective contraception – the kind of humanity that cannot interfere with incessant childbearing because to do so would be unnatural. Of course contraception is not natural, but nor is the use of penicillin to stop the mother dying of infection. Nowadays the question is not whether a thing is natural but whether it is desirable.

In every country there are men and women – sometimes millions and millions of them – who would be thankful to stop having children if they knew how. Though many of them have already had several children, a government wishing to reduce its birth rate would probably be wise to begin by helping its citizens not to have babies they do not want. But in most countries the population increase could not even be halved unless a great many people were persuaded not to have babies they do want, or babies they accept as sent to them by Fate.

Especially in societies where life has always revolved round the family, young parents are not going to take the trouble to control their fertility until convinced that this would be to their own advantage. When they can see that times have changed and that babies now survive instead of dying, they may be ready to listen to the medical truth that spacing and limitation of the family makes for healthier mothers and healthier children. When, through urbanization or otherwise, their way of life is such that each child is no longer a financial asset, they may be ready to listen to the economic truth that you can have prosperity or you can have a lot of children, but nowadays you can seldom have both.

DUTIES OF GOVERNMENT

This economic truth applies to governments as much as to parents; and I believe that any government anywhere which does not consider its population and its economy together is failing in what has become a primary duty. Any government ought to know what its population is doing; what it is certain to do; what it is likely to do; and what it might do. In the light of the definite data and of the alternative forecasts, it should consider whether there will be food and education and work for all its additional citizens, yet still a prospect of progress, economic and human. If it finds the multiplication of its people a hindrance rather than an aid to this progress, it should stop leaving everything to philoprogenitive Nature and enable parents to understand and face the various choices open to them. Population control thus interpreted is not like traffic control, requiring wardens and policemen. But when a government, knowing the facts, concludes that its population ought to grow less quickly or not at all, the least it can do is to try to ensure that all its people are able to use contraception and know how it can help them.

In lands where the public in their hearts feel that fertility is the last thing they should control, the spell of tradition and convention must be countered by explaining why what was right in the old world may be wrong in the new. And where emotional satisfactions have hitherto been obtainable only through large family groups, new social developments may have to be promoted, by which, for example, women can work outside their homes. We must not set our hopes too high: perhaps Judith Blake is right when she doubts whether the desire for larger families 'will succumb to flipcharts, flannelboards, message movies, group leaders, or "explanations" about the "advantages" of few children'. Yet I am sure that much can be done – partly because our ways of spreading a gospel quickly are improving all the time, but mainly because this particular gospel is true. In the world which we are now entering more and more people would genuinely do better to have a small family.

Where knowledge and means of contraception have been provided but the public refuse to see that family limitation is in their interest, the argument can be strengthened by taxation – by taxes that encourage later marriage and benefit the small family rather than the large one. Or even by bonuses for not producing children above a certain number. If necessary, there could of course be penalties for producing too many; but a good deal more thought is needed on how to penalize irresponsible parenthood without penalizing the children of the irresponsible parents. Unquestionably, the more dangerous the situation is allowed to become, the nastier will be the remedies.

BRITISH SITUATION

In Britain the situation is not yet thought alarming. Because most married people use some sort of birth control, the 'natural increase' of our population – the excess of births over deaths – is about 0·7 per cent per annum. Nevertheless, like any other country, we need a population policy. We need to know where we are going, and if we do not want to go there, we need to know what options are still open.

In 1965 a national economic plan was a welcome innovation; but when the planners said that by 1970 we should need another 200,000 workers, their calculation was based on employers' estimates of what they would require in order to produce twenty-five per cent more than in 1964. To deduce from this forecast that Britain needs a continuously increasing population would be premature. Is it certain for example, that we need a twenty-five per cent rise in output by 1970? Are we proposing to purchase a somewhat higher rate of growth at the cost of greater crowding in the 1980s and later? How much of the four per cent annual increase at which the plan was aimed was to go into providing additional goods and services and investment for the additional people we were going to have?

I do not know whether Britain should have 200,000 more workers by 1970, or whether we could in fact do as well with 200,000 fewer. But I do know that much besides the requirements of employers and the attainment of the fastest possible economic growth ought to be considered before anyone decides that more people are needed in this country. A modern government has to plan ahead: it should have a continuing economic policy, a continuing social policy, and (not least) a continuing population policy closely related to them. The legislative and other actions of our governments as of other governments should take account of population trends, as of economic or social trends, and should be designed to strengthen them if they are desirable or weaken them if they are not.

To collect and analyse the facts is a task for a government department (possibly the Department of Economic Affairs); but discussion and interpretation of the facts might better be undertaken by a permanent commission – independent and advisory – to which any issue could be referred. To such a commission the government and the nation would look for commentaries and reports that would be a firm foundation for public opinion.

What then are the reasons against this modest step? Four are commonly given:

1. Our population growth-rate is so small that we have no population problem in this country.

2. If there is an excess it will correct itself.

3. Foretelling the future is highly fallacious.

4. Action would in any case be useless because birth-rates pay no attention to government policy.

'NO PROBLEM IN BRITAIN'

By the standards of San Domingo or Ghana, our natural increase of 0·7 per cent per annum sounds small. Even so, the end of each three years finds us with well over a million more people to accommodate in our small island. For their sake we are building what could become an almost continuous conurbation, obliterating what was perhaps the loveliest countryside on earth. Our agriculture is at present losing rather more than 100,000 acres a year, 50,000 for urban development.

Now that buildings are higher, we may be able to stop this outward expansion of our cities, and still find room in them for another twenty million by the end of the century. Indeed with new techniques we may be able to give everybody an elegant flat. But at the threshold of the age of automation can we be confident about finding even another fifteen million regular employment? And how are they going to spend their leisure? Is there reason to suppose that human beings could tolerate life in these cities indefinitely? In our existing cities environment is improving but behaviour is not. Are we sure that mere crowding is not pathogenic – damaging – to Man? It was Henry Ford, oddly enough, who once said that the ultimate solution will be the abolition of the city.

In asking these questions about the future, I also ask a question about the past. Why has this country for a dozen years made so little real progress in some of the things that matter most – in schools, in hospitals, and houses? Various answers are possible, but undoubtedly in Britain as in developing countries improvement has been partly defeated by numbers: at the end of the day we find ourselves providing, instead of something new and better, much the same thing, but for more people. Forty-three years ago Maynard Keynes asked a key question when he said: 'Is not a country over-populated when its standards are lower than they would be if its numbers were less?'

Whether you care about the size of classes or the state of hospitals, the preservation of rare plants or the parking of cars, the clearing of slums or the advance of crime, among the factors to be considered is the growth of population. If we act on the time-honoured principle: 'Don't look now and perhaps it'll go away', what is still a *problem* with possible solutions will inevitably become a situation leaving no room for choice. Once people are born, their necessities – houses, schools, transport – will always take precedence over such luxuries as the preservation of fauna and flora, of old buildings, or of beautiful views. So if anyone wants to save Westminster Hall or Kew Gardens, or any other space-occupying treasure, the time to worry about it is now – not in 1980 or 1990 or 2050. For when its removal comes to be proposed there will probably be no defensible alternative.

'EXCESS IS SELF-CORRECTING'

The second argument for doing nothing is that over-population corrects itself. And, in the last resort, it must certainly do so.

Whatever mathematicians may say about the multiplication of man, the world can never have more inhabitants than its food can keep alive; and even the economic slump of the 1930s greatly reduced the birth rate in industrial countries.

Those who believe that some sort of biological thermostat ensures that population is always adjusted to circumstances will be heartened to see that, after a long baby boom, the birth rate shows signs of turning downwards. But the present fall could be explained by mothers merely postponing the birth of their children, and it may not affect the number they eventually have. The size of families has risen with postwar affluence, and different estimates suggest that couples marrying now will on average have somewhere between 2·4 and 2·7 children in their completed families. There might be from a quarter to half a child more than is needed to keep the population at its present size. And these innocent-sounding fractions soon add up to enormous numbers.

Whatever the tendency of population ultimately to regulate themselves, experience certainly does not suggest that the number of inhabitants of any country is always the number that would suit that country best. People like having children, and consequently they have as many as they can manage – and very often more. Their baby hunger is suppressed by starvation, or in sophisticated societies by lack of money or by doubts about the child's future; but nature's advice to them is always to breed first and take the consequences later. This may be good advice to all other animals; but now that man has a degree of foresight, such irresponsibility is precisely what he should avoid.

'PREDICTION IS INACCURATE'

The word 'foresight' brings me to the third objection to having a population policy – namely, that it could, at best, be based on guesses. As the *Economist* says 'recent history is littered with serious and repeated underestimates of population growth, contributing to the failure to plan proper resources for housing, education and other areas of social development'. True enough. But much of today's forecasting of the future is hardly guesswork at all. For instance, unless there is a war or calamitous epidemic, we cannot now avoid having in 1985 nearly nine million people aged twenty to twenty-nine – the same nine million who between 1975 and 1984 will be putting so big a load on higher education. If we go on to calculate how many children these nine million will themselves have, we move of course into uncertainty; but demographers are now accustomed to producing alternative estimates based on alternative assumptions. If we were to appoint a permanent commission concerned with population, this would always have before it both the basic facts and the alternative predictions.

Admittedly to use our minds is dangerous, for they are fallible. But not to use them can be more dangerous still.

'A POLICY WOULD BE USELESS'

The fourth excuse advanced for inaction is that birth rates pay no attention to what authority wants. When revolutionary France sought to increase its population, no good came of taxing bachelors or even of proposals to guillotine those who did not marry. Governments cannot raise or lower the birth rate as they raise or lower the bank rate. Even now we do not really know why the British birth rate began to rise in 1955, and in affluent societies the fashion for larger or smaller families may have little more basis than the fashion for longer or shorter skirts. To the expert therefore action may seem premature: he may feel that, until we have found out why birth rates go up and down we can do no more than watch them do it. But, with all respect, the real world cannot accept the academic thesis that one has to know everything before doing anything.

In this country we probably still have hundreds of thousands of unintended pregnancies each year – a ridiculous and inexcusable anachronism in a civilized country and scientific age. Here, as anywhere else, a government wishing to lessen population increase could reasonably do so by helping all its citizens to avoid having babies they do not want. After this it could, if need be, go on to the harder – but not impossible – task of persuading them not to want so many.

A FIFTH OBJECTION

Those are four objections to our working out a rational population policy for this country; and they are all weak. A stronger, if unacknowledged objection is that we already have a population policy.

Nor is the existing policy wholly irrational; for in 1949 the Royal Commission recommended that birth should be encouraged. But the tax allowances for children and other fiscal measures then introduced for the purpose would hardly have persisted to these very different days unless 11 Downing Street and the Treasury and their friends and relations, had all known in their hearts that more children are always a good thing.

This belief is deep seated. In the past survival of the race really did depend on most women having babies over and over again; and we are not yet reconciled to the new situation in which survival depends on most women not having babies over and over again. In resisting a scientific approach to population the Government all too faithfully represents a society whose pressures still favour abundant procreation – a society in which Mr Wilfred Pickles' audience loudly applaud the mother of ten; in which women's magazines incessantly present motherhood as the normal girl's only possible goal; and in which the childless (particularly the intentionally childless) are made to feel guilty, if not peculiar.

Moreover in this, as in other countries, to preach anything less than expansion is difficult for political leaders. Though ancient Greece showed how civilization can thrive in small cities, history has generally equated power with numbers; and, to the bystander, God has seemed to be on the side of the big battalions.

But perhaps the greatest obstacle to rational action is the assumption by so many that the birth rate, high or low, is outside the power of man to modify. Because they think it the 'great unalterable', people are prepared to alter everything else to fit it. They are as helpless as the tailor who can do nothing for his customer's obesity except enlarge his clothes.

The real reason why we are doing so little to stop our population from getting bigger and bigger is that we are still blindly following the instinct that bids all animals breed up to their limit. But man's further evolution, unlike that of animals, no longer depends on natural selection – on the survival of a few from an enormous number. Insofar as it is social and cultural our evolution stands or falls by its promotion of quality; and we are going backwards when we sacrifice the quality of human life to its mere abundance.

Even for our own little country this is conspicuously true. The doctrine that bigger is better is certainly inappropriate for us; and the time has more than come when we should stop supposing that there is virtue in numbers and should devote ourselves to cultivating other virtues, of the mind and heart, by which we could contribute far more to the world's advance. This cannot be done if we go on drifting helplessly: we must decide in which direction we want to go and do our best to go there.

The other day Sir Joseph Hutchinson told the British Association that he thought this island should aim at a population of forty million; and if we had a permanent commission concerned with population, it might likewise propose an optimum. But far more probably it would merely recommend a slowing of our present growth rate – a slowing which would bring economic relief here, as in other countries, by reducing the ratio of dependants to workers, thus raising our productivity. This is only one possibility – though one that economists should surely be studying. What is certain is that a permanent commission, looking at our situation objectively from year to year, would produce a policy more rational than the one now holding the field – a collection of assumptions made by people living, biologically, in the past.

When we say to the newer nations that they must collect the facts, must face them, and must shape their future accordingly, we are right; but we invite the reply: 'Is this what you do in your country?' As Professor Stycos says – and this is true of much besides population control – the greatest service the

United States and Britain could now do to other nations would be to set their own houses in order.

NOAH'S NEW FLOOD

Thus we come back to the world situation – so complex yet so simple. Contrary to what many people suppose, man is a fertile animal, capable of multiplying rapidly. In the past half-century he has escaped from the high mortality that formerly kept his numbers down, and he is replenishing the earth at a rate previously unprecedented. The first result of this excessive breeding is that he remains poor; and the last result must be that, if he does not control himself, the old and horrible triad of war, pestilence, and famine will return to control him.

But these things are not inevitable: we can prevent them if we are prompt. Noah's new flood is advancing; but the remedy this time is not to build an ark for the few. It is to show the many how, if only they can refrain from becoming too many, they can live prosperously in the land the Lord has given them.

We now have knowledge and resources that fifty years ago we lacked. Not to use them is deliberately to choose unreason.

2
Family Limitation in the Past

E. A. WRIGLEY

In the modern world birth control has become an accepted practice; but this acceptance is only recent. We may think that our ancestors knew nothing of family limitation and never thought of the subject. But had they done nothing, their natural fertility would have been unimpaired and every couple might be expected to have ten to twenty children.

It is becoming clear from recent historical research, that family size was limited in a variety of ways, centuries before 'modern' methods of birth control were known.

Although the public battle in this country over the use of chemical or mechanical methods of contraception is only about a hundred years old, social or individual control over fertility is not a recent phenomenon. It is a social feature of great antiquity, found in societies at all levels of material culture from the most primitive Australian aboriginal tribes to advanced industrial society today. Only very rarely has fertility (the number of children born) approached fecundity (the childbearing potential) in large groups.

PRIMITIVE FORMS OF FAMILY LIMITATION

Family limitation in the past has taken many forms. In some cases its nature shows that it was a deliberate act. The Tikopia, for example, practised *coitus interruptus*. In some African societies the birth of twins was regarded as a great misfortune and either one or both of the children were killed. In many societies abortions were procured both outside marriage and within it. In other cases fertility was kept well below the maximum attainable by social customs whose effect upon fertility levels was less direct. Marriage customs have often been of great importance in this connection, especially those which determine the behaviour of women. If, for example, the mean age at marriage of women is as high as thirty then more than half the total childbearing potential of the women of the community is gone before entry into marriage and, unless there is a large number of illegitimate births, this is a very effective means of limiting the reproductive capacity of the community. Similarly, a ban upon the remarriage of widows, though of less importance, will also reduce the number of years which the women of the community spend at risk of pregnancy. Other social institutions or customs serve indirectly to restrict fertility: some types of polygyny, taboos on intercourse for long periods after the birth of a child, and the prolonged suckling of children at the breast (often extending for two, three or four years) reduce significantly the chance of a new conception.

DELIBERATE CONTROL

In some cases the reasons given for acting in ways which restricted family size make sense to ears attuned to modern debates about family limitation. Some Australian aboriginals, for example, were keenly aware of the problems posed for the tribe as a whole if it contained mothers each with several young children. The speed of movement of the group is not greatly affected if each mother has only one child too young to keep pace with his elders, since she can carry him. But if there are two children too young to move quickly themselves the mother's difficulties might cause problems for the tribe as a whole. Again, the Tikopia recognized that, living on a small island, land was in short supply and large families led to quarrels about the produce of the land which might well provoke serious violence to the detriment of the whole community.

UNCONSCIOUS FORMS OF CONTROL

More frequently, however, even when the form of family limitation practised involved deliberate acts, the immediate purposes of the individuals concerned bear little resemblance to those which move people in industrial societies today. When pairs of twins, or children who had the misfortune to cut teeth in the upper part of the jaw before those in the lower, were put to death for example, this was usually done because the children were regarded as monstrous or unlucky. *A fortiori* if the connection between a social custom and lowered fertility was indirect, there would commonly be no conscious linkage in the mind of the agent between his or her behaviour and the lower level of fertility which resulted from it. Taboos upon sexual intercourse either after the birth of a child or at other prescribed periods were observed for religious reasons. The remarriage of a widow in India was thought utterly improper but the effect of such a ban upon the fertility of the community played no part in determining its propriety.

FERTILITY PATTERNS IN PRE-INDUSTRIAL SOCIETIES

In pre-industrial western Europe, as in other pre-industrial societies, fertility was almost invariably considerably less than the reproductive capacity of the population. In the vast majority of pre-industrial societies very few women remained unmarried after their twentieth birthday. Marriage at or close to puberty was normal for all except deformed or defective women, and most men also married young, though they were commonly allowed greater latitude. In the main those practices which limited family size were aspects of behaviour within marriage.

In pre-industrial Europe, on the other hand, it was by delaying entry into marriage until long after women had reached full sexual maturity (and by strong sanctions against illegitimate offspring) that the limitation of family size was achieved. By the mid-sixteenth century certainly, and perhaps much earlier (the absence of suitable records makes this much harder to judge) in parts of western Europe, the average age of women at marriage was the middle or late twenties. In the late seventeenth century in some areas the figure was close to thirty. The control of fertility levels by restricting the number of years spent in marriage rather than by practices within marriage is a most important difference between western European and other pre-industrial societies. If, for example, changes in age at marriage are sensitive to prevailing economic conditions, adjustments between population and resources are comparatively easy to achieve. In Ireland in the eighteenth and early nineteenth centuries marriage was often contracted in the late teens or early twenties: but after the ghastly experiences of the famine years society very quickly threw up a radically different pattern of behaviour; marriage for both men and women was much longer delayed and many remained single throughout their lives. Where this pattern exists marital fertility rates may well be very high and yet the general fertility rates remain quite modest.

REGULATION OF FERTILITY BY AGE AT MARRIAGE

Once a society has adopted a type of fertility regulation which depends upon age at marriage and proportions marrying rather than upon practices within marriage, an interesting range of institutional arrangements is immediately possible. For example the rule of land holding for one married man can be enforced by social sanctions; this rule obliges a man to delay marriage until the death of his father or the opportunity of marrying a widow who held land in her own right, and may mean that only one among several brothers can ever marry – this will also have repercussions on the age of women at marriage and on their chances of marrying at all.

FAMILY SIZE AND COMMUNITY ATTITUDES

Widespread practices which reduce family size do not necessarily reflect a conscious appreciation of the advantages of a lowered fertility. Indeed with rather rare exceptions (usually in small hunting groups or in societies confined to a tiny island) conscious attitudes are much more likely to be favourable to high fertility. Men or women with many children are more likely to be honoured than despised or derided. Yet it remains true that in many societies family limitation in one of its many forms kept family sizes comparatively low. The most promising solution to this apparent paradox lies in the development of the idea that a pre-industrial society as a whole is best served by restrained fertility, and that societal practices which produce this result are likely to be favoured by what might be called societal selection. It is now more than forty years since Carr-Saunders made a first full statement of this idea, assembling information from a formidable range of sources to show how societies regulated their population in ways which kept numbers well below the maximum levels attainable if fertility had been higher.

In many mammal, bird, fish and insect populations a selectional advantage is conferred on types of group behaviour which restrict the inflow of new individuals into the population to a level which enables those already in existence to maintain themselves in good health through access to an adequate food supply. In some animal communities, as for example with territory nesting birds, the mechanism involved bears a striking resemblance to that which has appeared on occasion in pre-industrial peasant societies. It is thus probable, and in line with much that is known of animal as well as human communities, that the limitation of family size, often to levels far below what is physiologically attainable, is the normal situation, and that the reservoir of additional fecundity is seldom tapped because to do so would prove harmful to the welfare of the community as a whole.

RESEARCH BY PARISH REGISTER

Until comparatively recently knowledge of the fertility and mortality characteristics of pre-industrial European society was very limited. Crude totals of baptisms and burials could be obtained for many areas and in some cases population counts having some at least of the features of a modern census were also available. At best these permitted only a very rough and ready measurement of fertility and mortality, usually subject to substantial margins of error. Within the last decade, however, by the development of the method known as family reconstitution, French historical demographers have made it possible to measure fertility and mortality much more delicately and accurately wherever good parish registers are available. Recently this technique has been used on English parish registers. These are in the main less suitable than the French, but it is in some cases possible to analyse the demographic history of an English parish from the mid-sixteenth century onwards, whereas in France it is rarely possible to do so before the last third of the seventeenth century.

BRIDES AT THIRTY

So far only one English parish has been studied fully in this way – Colyton in the Axe valley in south-east Devon. The results are very interesting and suggest that there is still much to be learnt about the range of method employed in communities in pre-industrial Europe to restrict family size. But two points of particular interest have emerged. Age at first marriage of women was always rather high and fluctuated considerably. During the sixteenth and early seventeenth centuries the average age at marriage of women was about twenty-seven. Then for a period of more than two generations from about 1650 to about 1720 the average age rose to thirty. Thereafter it fell, slowly at first but later with increasing rapidity, until by the early decades of the nineteenth century (the period studied ended in 1837) the average age was only about twenty-three, and a quarter of the brides at first marriage were teenagers. As might be expected these changes alone had a great influence on family size since they radically changed the proportion of fertile life which the average woman spent in marriage. The flexibility of this social mechanism for restricting family size is perhaps surprising, though its presence and importance is not, since it was so widely prevalent in pre-industrial Europe.

BIRTH CONTROL IN SEVENTEENTH-CENTURY COLYTON

Much more surprising, however, is the discovery that during much the same period the age at marriage was high enough to suggest that fertility within marriage was also being restricted. During this period age-specific fertility rates among women already long married were far lower than among women of the same age who had recently married. This is out of keeping with the normal pattern. Both in the earlier and later periods in Colyton and in the several parishes in France on which family reconstitution studies have been carried out, fertility among married women was always a function simply of age and not to any significant degree of length of marriage or size of family. There are also other tell-tale signs of limitation of fertility within marriage (for example a pronounced increase in the average interval between penultimate and last births in completed families). The methods employed to secure this reduction of fertility within marriage are not known with certainty, though, by analogy with the changes which took place in France at the end of the eighteenth century, the most likely principal method was *coitus interruptus*.

It would be premature to treat the results of the work done on the Colyton parish register as more than an indication that there is much more to be learnt about the historical demography of England in the pre-industrial period. Only a great deal more work can clear up the many uncertainties and obscurities which remain. This and other demographic work done on pre-industrial societies will in time make much clearer the relationship between the demographic structure of a community and its economic and sociological functioning. In due course it may throw much light upon the interrelationships between the family, the most omnipresent of all social institutions, and other aspects of social and economic life.

DISCREET MULTIPLICATION

Meanwhile historical demography is strengthening the impression gained from the study of contemporary or near-contemporary pre-industrial societies – that many societies, at all stages of material culture, have thrown up institutional and other mechanisms which serve to restrict the size of families in order to insulate themselves from the ill effects of excessive fertility. When Malthus exhorted those contemplating matrimony to delay until they felt confident that they could support the likely issue to the marriage he was furthering much the same end as those who urged the importance of birth control upon the Edwardian working man. The former advocated the 'traditional' European solution of delay in marriage; the latter the 'novel' method of controlling fertility within marriage. Yet both are related to a common theme, echoed repeatedly in societies in all periods and places, that the injunction to increase, be fruitful, multiply and replenish the earth has often been obeyed with discretion.

3
The History of Family Planning in Britain

JEAN MEDAWAR

Family planning has now come to be accepted as part of normal life in Britain. The subject is openly discussed in public, in the press and in schools, and opposition is negligible. But it was not always so. Only a few years ago hostility was intense and where there was not a conspiracy of silence by press and radio there was furious opposition from the churches and others. To a great extent this remarkable change in public attitude and practice is due to the Family Planning Association and is reflected in its great success. It is the largest medical organization outside the National Health Service.

THE NEW IDEA

Until the twentieth century birth control was largely a problem for individual parents and not for society as a whole. Whenever the relation between intercourse and pregnancy was understood – and until recently there were people who believed that the west wind was a fertilizing agent – men and women have tried to avoid, or to ensure, pregnancy. The methods they used were mostly unpleasant as well as ineffective; but when the birth of a child is either passionately desired or feared, there is little women will not do, from swallowing live tadpoles to risking health and life.

For society in general, however, birth control was not a problem, because the size of the population was kept down by a high death rate – family size was the result of a cruel sum in which parents added children and death subtracted them; but even uncontrolled fertility barely achieved more than the survival of the population; in the United Kingdom in 1700 it was only six million, or three quarters of the size of Greater London today. Belief in the value of fertility was generally unquestioned in this country until death rates began to be reduced by the great social reforms of the second half of the nineteenth century and has persisted long after ceasing to be necessary. This is understandable: we cannot easily forget an idea which our ancestors had generally to accept for some 200,000 years, nor easily replace it with another – birth control – which is its complete antithesis.

DEATH CONTROL

Between 1801 and 1831 the population of this country increased by 5½ million – not because more babies were being born, but because fewer were dying. The reduction of the death rate was due to gradual improvements in public health; the improvements could have been faster if the ideas underlying them, like all new ideas, had not been strongly resisted. When London's first modern sewer was planned in 1858, *The Times* wrote 'we prefer to take our chance with cholera and the rest than be bullied into health. England wants to be clean, but not be cleaned by Chadwick.' When the National Health (Family Planning) Bill was proposed in 1967, *The Times* again protested against the new idea that birth control should be available to all who needed it, irrespective of marital status. It preferred the risk of an unwanted baby to that of appearing to condone sexual relations outside marriage.

PIONEERS

Many men and women have helped in the struggle to win acceptance for the idea of birth control. In this struggle two of society's oldest ideas had to be challenged and changed: first that fruitfulness was divinely ordained and parental control of the number of children in a family was therefore a form of impiety; second that intercourse, which gave pleasure, should be atoned for by the pains of childbirth.

The History of Family Planning in Britain

The Rev. Joseph Townsend[1] (1739–1816) made the first serious attempt to describe a method of controlling fertility. Like his friend Jeremy Bentham, whom he first met in 1781, he was compassionately concerned with the misery of the poor and in 1786 had written *A Dissertation on the Poor Laws*. When Bentham published his *Situation and Relief of the Poor* in 1797 he used information given to him by Townsend to describe how a vaginal sponge might be used as a contraceptive; but because the idea of separating intercourse and reproduction was then so revolutionary, Bentham concealed the idea in an obscure passage.[2]

The Rev. Thomas Malthus was also concerned for the lot of the poor. He was a kindly man but although he saw the danger that a rapidly growing population might outstrip its food supplies, he could never accept the idea of separating intercourse from reproduction. He recommended only late marriage and continence to solve the hazards he described in 1798 in his *Essay on the Principle of Population*. In the 1817 edition he wrote that he would 'always particularly reprobate any artificial and unnatural modes of checking population, both on account of their immorality and their tendency to remove a necessary stimulus to industry'.

Francis Place and Richard Carlisle were bolder, perhaps because each had suffered a childhood of poverty and hardship. When Place finally succeeded in opening a tailor's shop in Charing Cross he had made up his mind to become rich enough to retire at forty-five and devote his life to social reform. The leaflets which he printed in 1822 were written to help working people understand the many advantages of regulating their family size by 'such precautionary means as would, without being injurious to health and destructive of female delicacy,

---

1. Peter Fryer, *The Birth Controllers*, Secker & Warburg, 1965
2. Norman Himes, *Medical History of Contraception*, Gamut Press, New York, 1936: 'Rates are encroaching things. You ... are, I think, for Limiting them ... but how? Not by a prohibiting act ... not by a Dead Letter, but by a Living Body: a body which, to Stay The Plague, would ... throw itself into the Gap: yet not ... be swallowed up in it.' Norman Himes interprets Dead Letter as Condom, Living Body as sponge, Plague as too many unwanted children, and Gap as vagina.

prevent conception'. Place's handbills, posted outside northern factories, were torn down and condemned as 'diabolical', but he was undeterred. His letters to Richard Carlisle, then in prison for publishing Paine's banned book *The Age of Reason*, gradually convinced Carlisle that he was wrong in believing that 'if the means to prevent conception were publically taught' they might 'encourage immorality by making it easier to conceal illicit relations'. Two years later Place was trying, unsuccessfully, to deter the by then wholly convinced Carlisle from publishing the first treatise on birth control, called *What is Love, or Everywoman's Book*. This booklet, which contained sensible advice, went into four editions and sold 10,000 copies in two years.

QUIET INFILTRATION

In England agitation for birth control dwindled after 1830 into what Norman Himes called 'quiet infiltration' or 'limited percolation downwards of contraceptive knowledge'. The quiet was disturbed in 1868 when Bertrand Russell's father, Viscount Amberley, dubbed a 'Vice Count' by the popular press, lost a by-election in Plymouth, merely because he had mildly supported Charles Bradlaugh during a meeting of the London Dialectical Society at which his own tutor, James Laurie, had read a paper on the need for birth control.

In America the new idea had also begun to ferment. In 1831 Robert Dale Owen (whose favourite author was Jeremy Bentham and who had read Carlisle's *Everywoman's Book*) summarized the social and economic case for birth control in a booklet under the title *Moral Physiology*. Owen calculated that by 1874 50,000 to 60,000 copies had been sold in England and America. Then in 1832 Dr Charles Knowlton of Massachusetts published *The Fruits of Philosophy*, a pamphlet he had written to lend to his patients. It was published in Britain for over forty-three years without interference until a bookseller was sentenced under the Obscene Publications Act to two years hard labour for publishing an illustrated edition.

Charles Bradlaugh, the freethinker, decided to challenge the verdict. As a freethinker Bradlaugh sometimes had literally to fight for the right to think freely. He was elected to Parliament after twelve years of campaigning; once there he claimed the right to affirm and not swear allegiance to the Queen; winning this right took a further six years and several tussles with policemen trying to prevent him from entering the House. As a boy he stayed with Richard Carlisle's widow and must have read *Everywoman's Book*. In 1860 as part of his freethinking he founded the Malthusian League to spread information about the need for birth control. He and Mrs Annie Besant, a fellow member of the National Secular Society, republished an enlarged edition of Knowlton's book, wrote a preface to it and sold it openly, after telling the police when and where they could be found; 500 copies were sold in the first twenty minutes after opening the shop. He and Mrs Besant were duly imprisoned and tried, as they had expected. Mrs Besant conducted her own defence, and the trial had an enormous effect on public opinion.

By now several influences had had time to work on it: the death rates had been falling since the beginning of the century, Factory Acts forbade the employment of children under ten, people were moving from the country to the town and an economic crisis was developing. As women began to see the chance of a life beyond reproduction, they demanded and got more than a polite education. Ruskin wrote that education 'does not merely mean that one knows more but that one behaves differently' – and educated women now indeed began to behave differently and to consider their rights as human beings.

'NOT GUILTY BUT DON'T DO IT AGAIN'

In the climate produced by these changes, the arrest and trial of Charles Bradlaugh and Annie Besant sparked off violent controversy. They were in fact acquitted on a technicality; the verdict, given after an hour and a half of discussion so loud that it could be heard outside the jury room, was: 'We are unanimously of the opinion that the book in question is calculated to deprave public morals, but at the same time we entirely exonerate the defendants from any corrupt motives in publishing it.' Mrs Besant translated this into plainer English: 'Not guilty, but don't do it again.' The trial gave the birth-control movement a great push forward and helped public opinion to crystallize to the point of admitting that limitation was both desirable and necessary.

Bradlaugh's Malthusian League was revived and continued to fight against poverty and to spread knowledge of the need for birth control. Its chairman, Dr C. V. Drysdale, chaired the first international medical congress on birth control in London in 1881, attended by thirty to forty brave medical practitioners. Four years later the General Medical Council struck Dr Henry Albutt off the register for having published *The Wife's Handbook*, a decent, popular treatise on pre-natal and baby care which included a chapter on 'how to prevent conception when advised by the doctor'. Dr Albutt commented that in condemning him his judges had been 'out of touch with the real wants of the suffering' and were 'a tribunal of aristocratic physicians whose legislation clogs the wheels of progress and prevents medical men from being the friends of the poor'.[3] By 1926 half a million copies of his booklet had been sold.

At the time of the Bradlaugh–Besant trial, the birth rate in England was thirty-five per thousand. From then on it began to fall, first in the richest districts – and went on falling until it reached 14·9 in 1933.

The principles and benefits of hygiene were recognized by the intelligentsia long before they were made available for the masses. It became clear that cholera made no distinction between rich and poor (it carried off Prince Albert in 1861 when he was only forty-two), and that the high death rates were affecting the supply and quality of labour needed for defence and industrial expansion. But in spite of opposition from doctors and bishops (the Lambeth Conference of bishops in 1908 demanded prohibition of all 'Neo-Malthusian appliances') more and more parents used their commonsense – and birth control – and their families benefitted accordingly. By the

3. H. A. Albutt, *Artificial Checks*, London, 1909, 14th ed., p. 6.

1880s there was widespread adoption of family-planning methods.[4] Even the demographer Lotka warned in 1946 that the declining birth rate 'contained the threat of rapid descent towards extinction' but his fears were never realized.

By 1921 forty years dogged work by the Malthusian League had laid ground for the next big advance. Marie Stopes advanced over this ground at top speed. She was intelligent, emotional and highly educated and was determined to save others from the misery and frustration she had experienced in her own sexually unhappy marriage. Her book *Married Love* sold 2,000 copies in a fortnight and shed light into many dark corners. She founded the Constructive Birth Control Society and in March 1921 opened the first birth-control clinic in England. The Malthusian League opened the second in Walworth in November of the same year, and a new period began in which organized societies provided practical birth control instead of literature pleading for a recognition of its importance.

ORGANIZED SOCIETIES

Five birth-control societies were formed during the next few years. They were organized by energetic, intelligent women and were supported by distinguished physicians. Lord Adrian, Dr C. P. Blacker, Lord Brain, Dr John Baker, Lord Dawson of Penn, Sir Julian Huxley, and Lord Florey were among those who helped the birth-control movement. Lord Dawson, while physician to George V, spoke in favour of birth control at the Church congress of 1921 in Birmingham. What he said then reflected what he had thought for more than thirty years. As a medical student he had written to Dr Drysdale that teaching the need for birth control depended 'more on medical men than upon any other class in the community'. Faced with the bishops so many years later he spoke very plainly and condemned the idea of family planning by abstention as 'an invertebrate, joyless thing – not worth the having'. He told them that birth control *had* to be accepted and appealed to

4. Royal Commission on Population, 1949.

them to approach the question in the light of modern needs, without the burden of traditions which had outgrown their usefulness. The *Sunday Express* attacked him at length and demanded that he be removed from his court position, but the *Spectator* called his speech 'wise, bold and humane in the highest sense of that word'. Lord Dawson was not dismissed and by 1930 the bishops at the Lambeth Conference voted 193 to 67 in favour of a resolution on birth control 'where there is a morally sound reason for avoiding complete abstinence'.

By 1924 the societies were not strong enough to stop the Roman Catholic Minister of Health from forbidding municipal Medical Officers of Health to pass on birth-control information to their patients; and two years later Mr Ernest Thurtle's bill, intended to allow local authorities to give birth-control advice to women who wanted it, was thrown out by the Commons. The Lords wiped out his defeat in April 1926 by passing Lord Buckmaster's motion proposing that the ban should be withdrawn – but though this made them the first legislative body in the world to vote in favour of birth control the result was not a practical victory.

It was then still possible for a clergyman to write to an Oxford city councillor and birth-control pioneer, Mrs William Collier, in the following terms:

practice of birth control is contrary to the Christian religion, the shipwreck of home life [*sic.*] – and reduces the intercourse between man and wife intended for the production of children into mere self-indulgence. It is an outrageous thing that people who ought to know better use their money and influence to introduce vice to people whose poverty has so far protected them from it. I am more shocked by the opening of this clinic than I should be by that of a brothel: because nobody even pretends that there is anything good or uplifting about a brothel. ... I shall refuse holy communion to anyone whom I know has made use of the clinic.

A year of great advance for the birth-control movement was 1930. In April family planners and leaders of women's organizations met representatives from thirty-five local authorities and agreed to send a resolution to the new Minister of Health asking him to 'recognize the desirability of making available medical information on methods of birth control to married people who need it'. The Minister, Mr Arthur Greenwood, acted within four months: he issued a memorandum allowing authorities to give contraceptive advice in cases where further pregnancy would be 'detrimental to health' – the so-called 'medical grounds'.

Nobody then knew that this was to be the last word of the Government on birth control until Edwin Brooks' bill became law in June 1967, but it produced great hopes and activity.

The five existing birth-control societies decided to strengthen their position by combining under a chairman of recognized standing and organizing ability. They chose Lady Denman; she was the wife of a former Governor-General of Australia until the war and was the first chairman of the Women's Institutes; these she had helped to develop from a tiny start into an organization representing a quarter of a million country women. Lady Denman had from its start in 1921 supported Dr and Mrs Drysdale's birth-control clinic in Walworth and she had the experience, imagination and concern for justice to become all that the movement could have wanted.

The five birth-control societies met in July in her drawing-room in London and amalgamated to form the National Birth Control Council[5] with Lord Horder as president and Lady Denman as chairman. Mrs Margaret Pyke, the first secretary of the new Council, listed the impressive names of the first executive in her Galton lecture of 1963 and added 'the office and staff were not so grand. They consisted of one room and one staff – myself,' Lady Denman gave the money to start the National Birth Control Council and remained its chairman until her death in 1954.

START OF THE PATTERN

The newly formed Council decided that their first task was to persuade the local authorities to implement the Minister's memorandum, but even with encouragement most of them

5. 'Council' was changed to 'Association' in 1931, and to Family Planning Association in 1938.

were either timid or hostile. Finally in 1932 the Medical Officer of Health of Plymouth, Dr Nankivell, offered Mrs Pyke the loan of one of his maternity and child-welfare premises; a local branch was formed, Lady Astor gave £100, the Ministry made no objection, and the pattern of the future development of the Association was set.

In 1938 the National Birth Control Association changed its name to the Family Planning Association, (FPA) partly because of general fears that birth control was the main cause of the falling birth rate and partly in order to emphasize that its aim was positive; children by choice and not by chance.

By 1935 there were forty-seven clinics and though the war stopped development, a skeleton structure was maintained and in 1943 the annual branch conference and meeting was restarted. A service to help infertile couples began the next year and the Association was asked to give evidence to the Royal Commission on Population which reported in 1949. Two paragraphs from this report show how far the idea of birth control had become personally and socially accepted. They first advised that 'public policy should assume and seek to encourage the spread of voluntary parenthood' and second that 'the giving of advice on contraception to married persons who want it should be accepted as a duty of the National Health Service and the existing restrictions on the giving of such advice should be removed'. Unfortunately this report, like many before it, was not implemented and the Family Planning Association remained outside the framework of the National Health Service.

The clinics run by the Association still continued to expand and the central office moved from rooms lent by the Eugenics Society to a house in Sloane Street in 1948. A pregnancy diagnosis service was then added to the other services already provided.

TWENTY-FIFTH ANNIVERSARY

In 1954 Mrs Margaret Pyke succeeded her friend Lady Denman as chairman of the Family Planning Association. The twenty-fifth anniversary of the founding of the National Birth Control

Council was in 1955 and to mark the occasion the Minister of Health, Mr Iain Macleod, officially visited the North Kensington clinic and the central office in Sloane Street. For the first time the work of the Association was officially praised and acknowledged; *The Times* carried a report of the occasion and Mrs Pyke spoke on BBC television.

In 1958, three years after the Minister's visit, the Anglican bishops changed their outlook on birth control and on the relation between intercourse and reproduction. Their report from the Lambeth Conference decided that it was 'utterly wrong to urge that, unless children are desired, sexual intercourse is of the nature of sin'. They added that birth control responsibly used was 'a duty laid by God on the consciences of parents everywhere'. Professor Gordon Dunstan discusses these changes in chapter 8.

THE LAST DECADE

By 1958 the battle for the idea of birth control as a human right and social need was almost won; but contraception and the subtleties of human sexual needs were still not routinely taught in medical schools. The FPA remained the main source of information and advice. It now had to administer and support, without any financial help from the Government, the services offered in its 500 clinics, increasing at the rate of two a week. It trained 300 doctors and 400 nurses a year, both at home and overseas, providing the training they could not otherwise get, raised £250,000 for family-planning work all over the world and reorganized itself from an association of clinics into a national body with uniform standards of practice and nationally agreed policies.

When Margaret Pyke died in 1966, £60,000 was raised in order to set up a model training centre for the study of family planning, within the FPA's new premises, opposite the Middlesex Hospital in London. Here home and overseas doctors, nurses, and social workers of all kinds are trained in all aspects of family-planning work, and cooperate with London teaching hospitals.

NATIONAL HEALTH (FAMILY PLANNING) BILL

In February 1966 the Minister of Health, Mr Kenneth Robinson, sent a circular to all local authorities, not just their health committees, reminding them of the reasons why it was important to provide family-planning services in their areas, as the 1930 memorandum had for so long allowed them to do. He asked them to provide these services as part of other community services, and in full cooperation with the FPA, the great majority of whose clinics were run in their maternal and child-welfare centres.

With this sort of directive all that prevented family-planning advice from being available to all who needed it was the clause in the 1930 memorandum, limiting the help to those for whom 'a further pregnancy might be detrimental to health'; this, the lawyers advised, could only be changed by an act of Parliament.

EDWIN BROOKS'S BILL

The Act owes its birth to a Private Member's Bill, presented by a new member, Mr Edwin Brooks, who had seen the results of poverty and unwanted children in his Merseyside constituency of Bebington. His bill became the National Health (Family Planning) Act on 28 June 1967. Like the 1930 memorandum it made no distinction between the married and the unmarried – it merely added 'social' to the existing 'medical' grounds. In the debate which preceded the passing of the Act through Parliament, only one member doubted that the bill was necessary – because, he said 'engaged couples already receive a great deal of literature through their letter boxes, as soon as they announce their engagement'. Parliamentary manners prevented this objection from getting more than incredulous attention and the bill became law without a dissident vote, after thirty-seven years of campaigning by many of those listening to the debate in the public galleries of the House.

SUMMER 1968

A year after the bill became law, the Family Planning Association completed a census of the number of local health authorities who had done as the Ministry asked. Of the 204, a quarter were offering the full family-planning service which the Act empowered them to give. Of these forty-nine, thirty-eight had asked the Family Planning Association to continue to act as their agent, 117 were offering a partial service and thirty-eight had done nothing at all.

The half-hearted response was not because councillors have not accepted the idea of birth control, but because they feel it is a luxury which they cannot and almost should not provide for all who need it. Yet there is mountainous evidence that planned families are cheaper in terms even of money, let alone misery, than are unwanted children.

It took over 150 years for the idea of birth control to become a matter of common sense. The longer the delay now between acceptance of the idea and the provision of means to carry it out, the greater the human and avoidable cost. Yet the sins of the fathers need not be visited on the children, even for one generation, if the compassion commonly reserved for cure could now be devoted to intelligent prevention.

4
The Key of the Door

EDWIN BROOKS

The conspiracy of silence which used to enfold the subject of birth control applied even to Parliament. A few lone MPs asked questions, but the Government took no notice. In 1955 the then Minister of Health, Iain Macleod, paid an official visit to the Family Planning Association and suddenly the well of publicity was tapped.

Although the Government still took no action, a private member, Edwin Brooks, introduced his Family Planning Bill into the Commons in 1967 enabling local authorities to give birth control advice to women, even when there was no medical reason against childbearing, and even if the woman was unmarried. So dramatically had the situation changed in the previous decade that the bill became law without an opposing vote.

Before I became a professional politician I was a professional geographer. And nothing in politics – with all its tumult and passion – is nearly as alarming as the reverberations, both in the natural environment and in social relations and institutions, which are being set off by the population explosion.

As a dockside councillor for many years on the Merseyside, I knew about the strains put upon women who had been made prematurely old and tired by the treadmill of uncomprehending motherhood. I had seen too many unwanted, unloved, rejected children to want to see the ignorance and foolishness of the parents visited upon the next generation. It was, in other words, time to lift family-planning services out of the twilight where superstition jostles hypocrisy; to cease hiding ties with the FPA, a brave voluntary and charitable organization, which for years had been left to carry the heat and burden of calumny and misrepresentation; and, most of all, to give people through the National Health Service the knowledge and opportunity to behave like responsible and loving human beings, in their personal and family lives.

When I first announced my decision to introduce a family-planning measure, I suppose I was – like most people familiar with the work of the FPA – thinking in terms of helping the traditional clinics to develop further. But if this is all that matters, then the Act would have done little more than legitimize an already encouraging situation. It was two articles which widened my horizons and gave me the head of steam which drove the Family Planning Bill onto the statute book.[1] These articles highlighted the need to provide domiciliary services: the facts needed no verbal varnish – they told simply and statistically and in cost-benefit terms what was possible throughout all the urban slums and ghettoes of Britain.

This was the background against which I decided, within weeks of becoming a somewhat startled MP, to introduce a Bill which would at last remove the legislative barriers which had hindered local health authorities from providing family-planning advice and help on other than narrowly medical grounds. Can this small and modest Act grapple with the deep-seated problems of a sexually confused society? The legislation simply unlocks a door; we can now pass through and beyond that door as far as determination, stamina and enthusiasm will take us. I put these qualities even before money, because even money will be found only to the extent that the public can be convinced of the need for an extended, comprehensive service.

Many people have spoken to me as if this is a purely permissive Act, to be ignored or implemented just as each local authority sees fit. Perhaps, with the analogy about the unlocked door, I have encouraged the idea that if an authority refuses to turn the handle or maybe claims that the hinges are too rusty (and there will be many squeaking protests) then nothing will happen except that a few more unwanted children will be born to grow up as best they may in its unen-

[1] One was by Dr Mary Peberdy: 'Fertility Control for Problem Families'; the other was by Dr Dorothy Morgan: 'Acceptance by Problem Parents in Southampton of a Domiciliary Birth Control Service'.

lightened streets. This is an illusion, for the Minister of Health was prudently given potentially limitless reserve powers to intervene. I have no reason to anticipate that he will be anxious to use these powers nor, as an old local government man whose love-hate relationship with Whitehall was always a bit short on love, have I any personal wish to see him do so.

The important implication of giving the Minister such powers nevertheless needs stressing. It will mean that henceforth the Minister will be exposed to Parliamentary pressures, to questions, to adjournment debates; and he will have to defend his reasons for not intervening in those areas whose members are voicing criticism of a poor penny-farthing of a state-run family-planning service. No one, from the Minister to the chairman of the local health committee, will from now on be able to shelter behind legal barricades. The Act permits help to be given to the unmarried. Then let the authorities who do nothing bear the responsibility of publicly defending their inaction and their illegitimacy rates.

The Act permits the establishment of a domiciliary service – to my mind the most important single requirement of all. Authorities which cannot be bothered to bring help to those most in need – and most incapable of showing the initiative to go voluntarily to the family-planning clinic – will have a lot to answer for; and they will need to give those answers to a public which is well aware of the strains imposed upon our welfare and health services by the so-called problem families.

THE LOST YEARS

Although nothing now can restore the lost years, there are signs of a new awareness by local as well as national government of the need to define priority areas for special help. As the Seebohm Committee described them:

> localities which have a profusion of pressing social problems, offer only a dismal and squalid physical environment, are inadequately served by social services and are considered to justify special attention and a generous allocation of resources.

One might also add, although Seebohm – characteristically enough – ignores family-planning services, that such priority areas, which like all ghettoes serve as dumps for the socially inadequate and despised members of the community, will also be marked by disproportionately high birth rates.

There may be exceptions to this generalization in areas, say, where there is a large number of immigrant single males, but I am sure it is usually valid. Perhaps one key to this is given by Dr Morgan in her article on Southampton: 'The mothers too are often being reminded of their inadequacies, so it is hardly surprising that they frequently participate in an act at which they feel adequate.' My general argument then is this. Up till now family planning has been basically to do with the emancipation of the enlightened, with the freedom of the educated woman. It has not been easy, but at least the battle's result was inevitable once that formidable historical force, the enlightened middle-class lady, joined the fray on behalf of herself and her sisters of the suffragette vintage. That battle has now been largely won, and the occupation army is well entrenched in 1,000 FPA clinics throughout the country.

From this stage we are passing to another, in some ways more difficult battle, a sort of guerilla engagement in which the objective is the emancipation of the less enlightened women – and their families – from ignorance and fear.

This will be a difficult task, expensive in time, and most certainly requiring a substantial effort in terms of training schemes for health visitors and other supporting services. It will need a profound revaluation of the role of the hospitals, and we shall have to ensure effective liaison between the welfare clinics and the local authority's health and – perhaps in the future – its new social-service departments.

I am conscious that we are only scratching the surface in many fields, as for example in developing family-planning services among immigrant communities and in the training we give to both medical students and visiting doctors from underdeveloped countries. But I think that the law is now on the side of the angels – on the side of the Medical Officer of Health who is prepared to be an innovator – the sort of person who is prepared to stick out his neck. By itself such a law will not guarantee success, but if in ten years' time there is still no adequate domiciliary family-planning service in this country, then the act will have foundered on the rock of indifference and been beached in the shallows of prejudice. Now that Britain has, as it were, a family-planning act under its belt, I hope it will stomach no delay in providing a worthy service throughout the country.

5
Planning Today

Although the ideal contraceptive has not yet been discovered, there are a variety of fairly simple methods which give different degrees of protection. Many people still prefer them to the pill or oral form of birth control, described in section (ii).

(I) CONVENTIONAL METHODS

NORMAN MORRIS

The ideal contraceptive has yet to be discovered. Meanwhile we have a variety of methods which together provide contraception suitable for each individual. After considering the various contraceptives available I will review their relative merits and disadvantages in relation to one another and to oral contraception. This form of birth control is described in detail by Dr Peter Bishop in Section (ii) of this chapter.

Rhythm Method

The rhythm method or 'safe period' is widely used, particularly by Roman Catholics as, apart from continual abstinence, this is the only method of birth control officially permitted by the Pope. The method is based on the assumption that ovulation occurs between sixteen and twelve days before the start of menstruation. It is assumed that the ovum can be fertilized during twenty-four hours and that the spermatozoa can fertilize the ovum for about forty-eight hours. Sperms can actually live in the genital tract for seven to ten days – but whether they retain the ability to fertilize an ovum is doubtful. Calculations for establishing the fertile days are made by subtracting eighteen from the shortest cycle length to give the first day of the fertile phase, and subtracting eleven from the longest cycle length to give the last day of the fertile phase, during which time intercourse should be avoided. For a twenty-eight-day cycle this would give twenty-eight minus eighteen, i.e. ten, as the first day and twenty-eight minus eleven, i.e. seventeen, as the last day of the fertile phase. In fact the Catholic Marriage Advisory Council recommends subtraction of nineteen from the shortest cycle and ten from the longest cycle. This allows even fewer days for intercourse. The time of ovulation can also be worked out by a daily recording of the temperature, taken each morning before rising. There is a distinct rise in temperature at the time of ovulation which usually persists until just before the next menstruation (figure 1). Just before ovula-

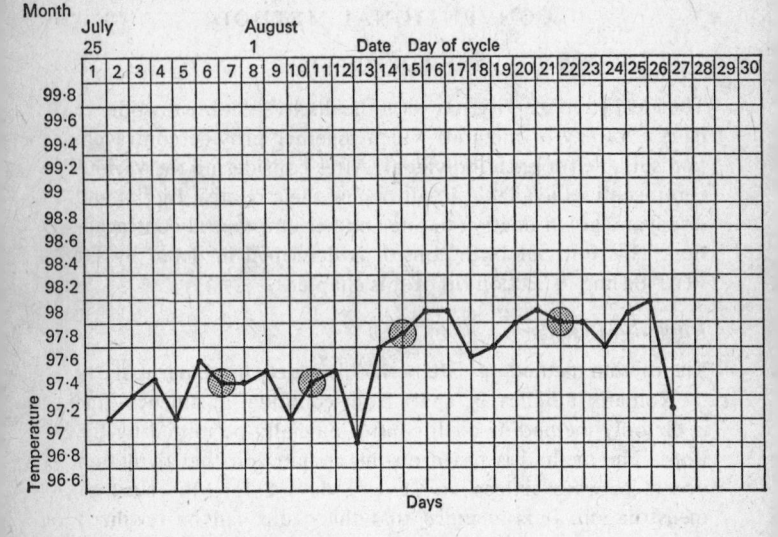

Figure 1. Showing rise in temperature on fourteenth day associated with ovulation

tion the temperature may actually dip down before rising to the higher level – this is referred to as a 'biphasic' swing. Intercourse should not take place until at least three days after ovulation has been detected.

This method provides some protection against conception

but on the whole it is unreliable, probably because sperms may fertilize the ovum even though they have been in the genital tract for some days and because ovulation can occur twice in a single cycle.

Coitus Interruptus

Withdrawal of the penis from the vagina before ejaculation is still a common method of birth control, used by nearly a quarter of the couples who use birth control at all. It is sometimes called 'being careful' although nearly a quarter of the women whose partners practise it become pregnant, because some sperms can be discharged in advance of the ejaculation. Some men also have difficulty in controlling ejaculation, and this can then be a source of anxiety to both partners. It also appears that when this method is used very few women manage to achieve an orgasm. This failure in turn has been claimed, perhaps incorrectly, to lead to dysfunction of the ovaries. Failure to experience an orgasm can sometimes lead to sexual frustration, and this may show itself in various forms of tension and anxiety, which may in turn lead to various psychomotor disorders. It is important that people should understand how unreliable and even potentially dangerous this method can be.

METHODS NOT REQUIRING MEDICAL SUPERVISION

The Condom

The condom, sheath or french letter is a thin rubber sheath, made in various thicknesses, to be worn over the penis. Some have a teat at the end to hold the ejaculate. Most are used once only and are then discarded, but the thicker varieties can be used more often. All french letters and particularly the thicker types interfere slightly with male sensation, and if no lubricant is used, intercourse can be painful or unpleasant. When used with a spermicidal lubricant the risk of pregnancy is reduced if the sheath should rupture or has any small holes. Some women are allergic to one of the ingredients in the rubber of the sheath, but this is usually overcome by changing to another make.

The condom is often used in the early days of marriage when it may be impossible for the woman to use a cap and she does not want to use oral contraceptives. It is probable that the condom is still the most widely used contraceptive.

Chemical Spermicides

Spermicidal preparations have to be inserted shortly before coitus and are available in the form of foaming tablets, jellies, creams, gels, pessaries and aerosol foams. These differ mainly in the mode of insertion, the lubricating qualities, the actual spermicide used and the type of base and perfume. Their efficiency is increased if they are used with a condom or cap, but very often they are used alone. The available spermicidal preparations have been tested for efficiency, acceptability and clinical harmlessness, and Delfen and Emko foams have scored the highest points. Some couples use spermicides because they are simple to use and need little forethought. They are most commonly used as a temporary measure and also with intra-uterine devices for additional protection.

METHODS REQUIRING MEDICAL SUPERVISION

Cap and Chemical

There are several types of cap and the correct size and type has to be chosen for each individual by a doctor who can teach the patient how to insert it with the right amount of spermicidal cream. The cap is inserted routinely each evening and removed next morning unless the last intercourse was less than six hours earlier. Check visits are essential for the continued success of this method.

Types of Cap

1. The *Diaphragm* (dutch cap) may have a coil or watch-spring type of rim, and is the most commonly used type. The vaginal muscles must be firm to keep the cap in place (figures 2 and 3).

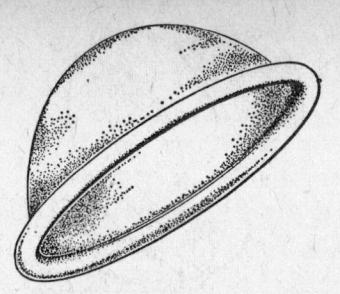

Figure 2. The diaphragm (dutch cap)

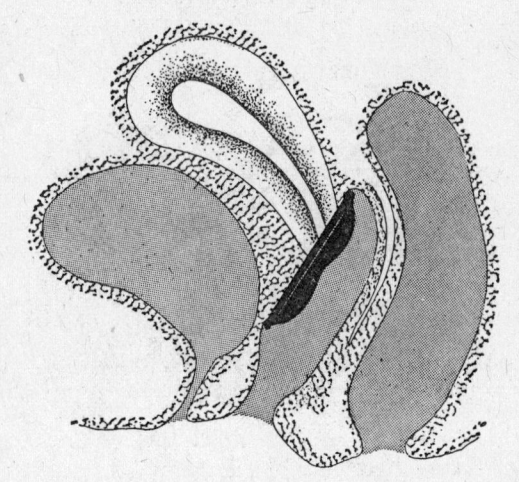

Figure 3. Diaphragm in position

2. *Cervical caps* are used where the cervix is long, healthy and parallel-sided, and can be reached by the patient herself. In Germany and Israel plastic cervical caps are fitted each month at the conclusion of the period and are removed during the periods (figures 4 and 5).

3. *Vault caps* made of rubber or plastic are occasionally used where the cervix is short, healthy and accessible.

4. The *Vimule*, which is a combination of a cervical and a vault cap, is rarely used these days (figure 6).

Figure 4. Cervical cap

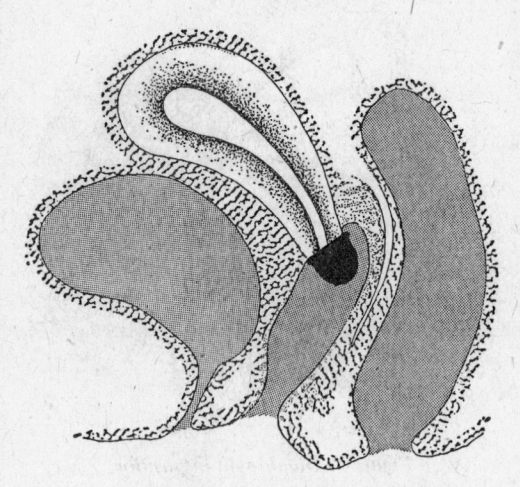

Figure 5. Cervical cap in position

The cap-and-spermicide method is liked by women who want to be responsible for their own birth-control methods. It is effective and does not diminish the husband's sexual feelings. The disadvantages are that it must be carefully fitted by a doctor, and must be inserted before intercourse It is most useful when other methods are feared or advised against and it is still widely used, acceptable and non-controversial.

Conventional Methods

It cannot be used if the patient is sensitive to the rubber or the spermicide. This may be caused by an undiagnosed vaginitis and may be overcome by changing to another make. Physical defects such as fixed hips or deformed hands, make it difficult

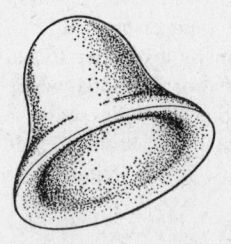

Figure 6. The Vimule

to fit a cap. In cases of repeated urinary tract infections the diaphragm may be preventing complete emptying of the bladder. Some cases of cap failure may be caused by ballooning of the vagina during coitus, but if the diaphragm is used conscientiously it is on the whole a good method of contraception.

HOME-MADE METHODS

Occasionally it may be necessary to make a simple contraceptive at home. The following measures are temporarily useful:

Barriers

1. *Vaginal pads* can be made from clean soft cloth cut into 6 inch squares. The cloth need not be new but should be well washed. A strong soft thread is tied or stitched to the centre to hold the pad together.
2. *Plugs* can be made from clean silk or cotton waste rolled into a rounded plug about the size of a hen's egg. Here again a strong thread should be attached for removal.
3. *Sponges* may be made from sea sponge, foam rubber, latex or plastic material to which a thread should also be attached. These methods are even safer when used with spermicidal creams or gels.

Spermicides

1. One part of vinegar or lemon juice should be mixed with 20 parts of warm boiled water.

2. Any cooking oil or fat such as butter and margarine may be smeared over the plug or sponge.

3. A soap solution of a quarter to half inch cube of pure soap in a quart of warm boiled water makes an effective spermicide, but strong carbolic soaps and detergents injure the vagina and must never be used. Salt solution is also not recommended because it can irritate the vagina.

INTRA-UTERINE CONTRACEPTIVE DEVICES

Intra-uterine devices (IUDs) of one kind or another have been used for hundreds of years to prevent conception. The modern devices are related to the old form of metal stem pessary, collar button and wishbone, which were placed in the cervical canal; only a small portion of the device entered the uterine cavity – sufficient to anchor it in position and to block the external os of the cervix. Over forty years ago Grafenburg concluded that such cervical devices provided a pathway for ascending bacterial infection and therefore began to use a device that lay wholly within the uterus. At first he made them from silk worm gut rings entwined with fine silver wire which were easy to identify either by sounding or by X-ray examination. Later in 1928 he substituted rings made entirely of silver or gold wire. This method largely fell into disrepute because of reports of a high incidence of pelvic infection, menorrhagia (heavy bleeding), extrusion and pregnancies. In 1959, however, Oppenheimer reported good results from using four strands of twisted silk worm gut as an IUD. At about the same time others reported on the use of metal and plastic intra-uterine devices, and the results met worldwide interest. Modern devices are made mainly of plastic and the four most commonly used are (a) Lippes loop, (b) Margulies spiral, (c) Birnberg bow and (d) the Saf-T-Coil.

The great advantage of the IUD is that after its insertion the patient can almost forget about it except for an occasional check-up at the contraceptive clinic. This advantage, however, is offset by a series of disadvantages.

An anaesthetic may be required in order to insert it painlessly and occasionally uterine collapse may follow this procedure. *Perforation of the uterus* occurs rarely (three to four per thousand). Six to fourteen per cent of women feel pain in the abdomen and lower back during the first few months after insertion but this gradually gets less. *Heavy bleeding* (menorrhagia) and *intermenstrual bleeding* (metrorrhagia) are also experienced by up to fifty per cent of women; this too gets less in subsequent months but may persist in four to seven per cent of cases.

Pelvic infection may also occur and require treatment with antibiotics. At the moment there is considerable disagreement about the incidence of pelvic infection, many authorities claiming that it is relatively uncommon (one or two per cent). In very poor communities the figures are naturally higher than in districts with a high standard of housing and living. In my department at Charing Cross Hospital we consider that a mild degree of infection may occur in three to twenty per cent of cases, and our results suggest that the Lippes loop is associated with a higher incidence than other devices. The device drops out in two to fifteen per cent of cases. Finally, pregnancies still occur and in this respect the IUD is not an absolutely effective contraceptive. The incidence of pregnancy shows a considerable variation and differing results are reported from various centres. Sometimes the rate may be as high as two and a half to five per cent.

In spite of the drawbacks outlined above, the IUD is now in widespread use in Britain, in the USA and in most of the main centres of family planning all over the world.

In my view the risk of pelvic infection is a serious objection to using this method in women who are anxious to have children later on. For this reason I consider that it should never be inserted into a woman who has no living children. I also feel that the possible risk of infection should be discussed with any woman who expresses a wish for this kind of contraception.

TABLE I

Method, author(s)	Year of publication	Locality of study	No. of couples	Aggregate months of use	Accidental pregnancies	Failure rate
Condom						
Tietze and Gamble	1944	North Carolina	387	7,788	72	11·1
Tietze et al.	1961	Puerto Rico	494	7,963	188	28·3
Coitus interruptus						
Westoff et al.	1961	U.S.A.	—	1,287	18	16·8
Rhythm ('safe' period)						
Tietze et al.	1951	Boston	409	7,267	87	14·4
Spermicides						
Aerosol foam						
Paniagua et al.	1961	Puerto Rico	142	1,723	42	29·3
Foam tablets						
Koya and Koya	1960	Japan	82	1,809	18	11·9
Dingle and Tietze	1963	Cleveland	240	1,749	32	22·0
Tietze et al.	1961	Puerto Rico	166	1,565	50	38·3
Finkelstein	1958	Baltimore	147	1,514	54	42·8
Jelly (cream) alone						
Margulies et al.	1962	San Francisco	259	3,250	21	7·8
Finkelstein et al.	1954	Baltimore	291	4,253	39	11·0
Finkelstein et al.	1952	Baltimore	371	5,173	83	19·3
Frank	1962	Chicago	684	6,594	127	23·1
Dingle and Tietze	1963	Cleveland	170	1,789	35	23·5
Finkelstein and Goldberg	1959	Baltimore	366	4,381	87	23·8
Tietze et al.	1961	Puerto Rico	462	4,987	150	36·1
Beebe	1942	West Virginia	1,108	11,252	354	37·8

Spermicides—contd.
Suppositories

Madsen et al.	1952	Denmark	183	2,649	7·7
Tietze et al.	1961	Puerto Rico	207	1,846	42·3

Diaphragm and jelly (cream)

Stix	1939	Cincinnati	1,579	33,830	8·8
Beebe and Overton	1942	Nashville	380	4,336	8·9
Stix and Notestein	1940	New York City	867	8,902	9·2
Stix	1941	South Carolina	709	8,219	12·7
Dingle and Tietze	1963	Cleveland	189	2,012	14·3
Tietze and Alleyne	1959	Barbados	541	6,035	17·3
Beebe and Belaval	1942	Puerto Rico	188	1,796	28·7
Tietze et al.	1961	Puerto Rico	272	4,355	33·6

Intra-uterine contraceptives

Hall and Stone	1962	New York City	184	8,134	0·9
N.C.M.H. (Spiral 5)	1964	United States and Puerto Rico	2,580	17,191	0·9
N.C.M.H. (Loop 2)	1964	United States and Puerto Rico	1,580	9,891	1·1
Zipper and Sanhoeza	1962	Chile	628	6,745	1·6
Jackson	1962	Great Britain	190	10,711	2·0
Ishihama	1959	Japan	350	2,867	2·5
Oppenheimer	1959	Israel	329	9,516	2·5
Peng	1962	Taiwan	521	5,507	3·7

The risk of heavy menstrual bleeding could intensify a pre-existing anaemia and this may prove a major objection in areas where malnutrition and consequent anaemia are very common.

(From these comments it is probably clear that I have a slight personal prejudice against the widespread and indiscriminate use of IUDs. For this reason I may have over-emphasized their disadvantages.)

GENERAL CONCLUSIONS

As I mentioned at the beginning of this chapter the perfect contraceptive does not exist. Meanwhile we have to make the best use of those methods that are available, according to needs and attitudes of the patient. The effectiveness of different methods is illustrated in table 1.

From this analysis it can be seen that the most effective methods are the intra-uterine device and the diaphragm. The latter method has the great advantage that *as far as we know* it does not produce any serious complications in either partner. This is a major argument in its favour. But it may yet be shown that certain constituents in the rubber are carcinogenic under certain circumstances – as far as I know this possibility has not yet been fully investigated, but until it has this complication cannot be completely excluded.

Table 1 also demonstrates very clearly the very wide difference in results that have been reported from different centres. This emphasizes how difficult it is to draw firm conclusions from the findings of one centre and how difficult it is to obtain reliable results from studies in this field.

(II) ORAL CONTRACEPTIVES

P. M. F. BISHOP

HISTORICAL INTRODUCTION

The two fundamental ingredients of the oral contraceptive preparations are the ovarian hormones oestradiol and progesterone, now represented by their synthetic analogues. Thirty-five years ago artificial menstrual cycles were reproduced in women whose ovaries had been removed by administration of extracts of these natural hormones and from that time onwards experience was gradually gained of the effects and side effects of the therapeutic administration of these hormones and their synthetic analogues. It is important to emphasize this fact as there is a tendency at the present time to suggest that experience of the components of the oral contraceptives dates back only to the pioneer work of Pincus and his colleagues in 1954. Those of us who were groping in the unexplored wilderness of what has now become respectably established as gynaecological endocrinology must have committed many therapeutic indiscretions within the limits of the feeble activity of the compounds then available. Perhaps therefore we were mercifully spared from doing much harm.

Let it also be remembered that thirty years ago there appeared on the scene a really potent oral oestrogen, stilboestrol, and this in its turn was inexpertly, indiscriminately, and inordinately used therapeutically until one came to refer to patients as being 'soused in stilboestrol'. No obviously sinister complication, such as increase in the incidence of breast cancer, warned us to be extraordinarily cautious in our therapeutic ministrations. At about the same time a partially synthetic oestrogen, ethinyl oestradiol, became available and gradually supplanted stilboestrol because it was less liable to produce such undesirable side effects as nausea and vomiting.

Progress in the production of potent progestogens was much slower. For many years the natural hormone progesterone was administered by injection and was so transient in its effect that it had to be given daily or at least on alternate days. There was an oral substitute, ethisterone, but it was thought not to produce full progestogenic activity. The most outstanding event in the history of the development of oral contraceptives was the synthesis in 1954 from a steroid compound extracted from a plant, the Mexican yam, of a series of really potent and orally active progestogens.

Armed with effective and easily applied oral oestrogens and progestogens the way was open not only to administer them more efficiently in the treatment of menstrual disorders but to contemplate other implications.

BEGINNINGS OF HORMONAL BIRTH CONTROL

For many years the problem of the management of infertility had been, and still is, insoluble in about fifty per cent of the couples seeking advice. All the available investigations prove negative. Undoubtedly there are some couples who are subfertile as opposed to infertile, and one always hopes that by chance and in due course conception will take place.

It was argued therefore that if only the pituitary and ovaries could be given a temporary rest they might respond with a 'rebound' increase in efficiency. It was hoped that such a temporary response could be ensured by means of a combination of oestrogen and progestogen to suppress the release of pituitary hormones that normally stimulate the ovaries and thus inactivate the hormonal production of the ovaries. The oestrogen–progestogen combination was administered for twenty days in each cycle, leaving seven days' interval between successive courses. Three courses were administered and some workers claimed that conception occurred within four or five months after discontinuing the treatment in about fifteen per cent of cases. It is doubtful whether this rebound effect was achieved.

However, from this supposition Pincus and his colleagues developed the idea of an oral contraceptive and in retrospect it seems amazing that the earlier pioneers had not thought of it. After all they had been using stilboestrol since 1940 to prevent dysmenorrhoea (incapacitatingly painful periods), which was believed to occur only in cycles in which ovulation had taken place.

Oestrogen alone inhibits ovulation in the great majority of cycles, but is not totally effective and after some months may give rise to excessive and prolonged menstrual bleeding. But if combined with the newly discovered and powerful oral progestogens it was found to provide perfect contraceptive protection and to result in artificial periods which closely simulate a normal period in duration and amount of loss.

In the early days of the combined oestrogen–progestogen pill the ovulation-inhibiting property of oestrogen was neglected and emphasis laid on the need for adding oral progestogens to the oestrogens throughout the period of administration. In due course people recalled that oestrogen alone could inhibit ovulation and the 'sequential' regime was introduced in which oestrogen alone was given for a sufficient number of days to prevent ovulation occurring as it usually does on the fourteenth day of the natural cycle. Progestogen was later added in order to ensure that the subsequent 'period' simulated a normal one and was not excessive and prolonged.

And so oestrogens and progestogens, which had been employed since 1933 and in really potent doses since 1938, were launched in 1954 as oral contraceptives to be used by normal healthy women to prevent them from becoming pregnant.

THE NEED FOR CAUTION

In the therapeutic correction of a diseased condition one may be justified in taking the risk of undesirable side effects or even serious complications; but to apply drugs to a healthy person to deal with a social rather than a therapeutic condition introduces a serious ethical problem. It is essential to be as certain as possible that the drugs cannot harm the patient, let alone cause her death. In this particular example one must compare as carefully as possible the risk to the patient during a natural pregnancy, with the risk she undergoes in preventing an unwanted pregnancy by taking oral contraceptives. This involves a much more stringent assessment of the facts than was provided by the pioneers of oestrogen and progestogen *therapy* as they applied it in their carefree and ignorant fashion from the 1930s onwards (though as one of these pioneers I am apt to discount some of the more sinister bogeys such as the possible carcinogenic properties of these hormones).

MECHANISM OF OVULATION, FERTILIZATION AND IMPLANTATION

Ovulation is the rupture of a mature egg-case or follicle with the release of its ovum. This follicle begins as a minute structure lying in the rind or cortex of the ovary where it was originally placed in the early stages of embryonic life. Millions of these primordial follicles may occupy the cortex and their number may be added to during intra-uterine life. No more are formed after birth and indeed their number is inexorably diminished by the process of atresia (degeneration and shrinkage) up to the time of puberty. From then on until the menopause a crop of these follicles matures during each menstrual cycle. One or very occasionally two or even three (and these may give rise to twins or triplets) ruptures and releases its ovum into the Fallopian tube, where it may be fertilized by a sperm. The rest of the mature follicles of that cycle undergo atresia, and indeed at the menopause there are no follicles left that are capable of becoming functionally mature and able to be fertilized. Furthermore, even if ovulation is prevented for many cycles by oral contraceptives, this will not delay the age at which this final atresia and consequent menopause takes place.

The released ovum continues its journey down the tube and enters the uterine cavity. If it has not been fertilized it passes out of the uterus and is lost. If it has been fertilized its single cell undergoes myotic division into two cells, then four, eight, sixteen, and so on; the resulting multicellular 'blastocyst' enters the uterine cavity.

Under the influence of the two ovarian hormones the endometrium that lines the womb first proliferates by mytotic division of its cells so that it increases in thickness and then becomes 'secretory'. Proliferation is a characteristic of oestrogen, the hormone that dominates the cycle before ovulation takes place. Just before ovulation, and more characteristically after the formation of the corpus luteum,[1] progesterone converts the endometrium into its secretory phase at the height of which, on about the twenty-first day of the menstrual cycle, it is in the ideal condition for embedding the ovum.

INHIBITION OF OVULATION

Pincus and his colleagues aimed to achieve an infallible method of inhibiting ovulation. This involves the suppression of the production and release of the gonad-stimulating ('gonadotrophic') hormones of the pituitary by the oestrogen and progestogen content of the pill.

Early in the menstrual cycle (figure 1) the pituitary, probably under the influence of the gonadotrophin-releasing factor (GRF) of the hypothalamus, releases follicle-stimulating hormone (FSH). The hypothalamus lying at the base of the brain consists of a number of nuclei that control many of the automatic but essential processes of the body, such as the regulation of temperature and appetite. FSH stimulates a number of primordial follicles of the ovary to enlarge and mature. GRF also regulates the release of another gonadotrophic hormone, the luteinizing hormone (LH), and it is under this hypothalamic influence that a trickle of LH is maintained throughout the cycle, though at certain phases, such as just before ovulation, GRF stimulates the release of much greater quantities of LH (the mid-cycle LH peak). In the presence of the LH trickle the maturing follicles are filled with fluid, the liquor folliculi, which contains oestrogen. As the many maturing follicles enlarge more and more oestrogen is secreted and gets into the blood stream. Not only does it ensure the proliferation of the endometrium but it suppresses the GRF that releases FSH and may at the same time stimulate

[1]. The small body which develops from the ruptured egg follicle.

the GRF to release more LH. At a certain stage a ratio of FSH to LH is reached that enables one of the mature follicles to rupture and shed its eggs. This is ovulation. The ruptured follicle is immediately invaded by yellow cells and becomes a solid structure, the yellow body or corpus luteum. Predominantly this secretes progesterone, though oestrogen continues to be secreted. There is now evidence that progesterone is also secreted by the cells immediately surrounding the maturing follicles even before ovulation takes place and the corpus luteum is formed. This progesterone may be responsible for stimulating the GRF to produce the mid-cycle peak of LH. Once the corpus luteum is formed, however, the combined influence of the relatively large amounts of oestrogen and progesterone that it is producing suppresses the further release of more than the trickle of LH and another gonadotrophin, the luteotrophic hormone (Lt. H), ensures the maintenance of the corpus luteum for the rest of the cycle. Thus small quantities of endogenous oestrogen and progesterone may stimulate the release of FSH and LH respectively but larger quantities suppress it. The combined administration of oestrogen and progestogen will therefore suppress FSH and

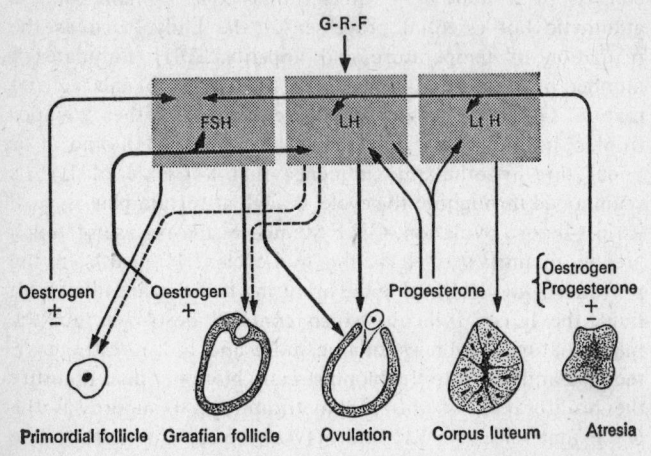

Figure 1. Diagram of the menstrual cycle

especially the mid-cycle peak of LH and so inhibit ovulation. This is the mechanism of inhibition of ovulation by means of the combined pill. In fact oestrogen given alone can inhibit ovulation, probably by preventing FSH from reaching a high enough concentration to achieve the critical FSH ratio necessary to induce ovulation.

The above account must be regarded as provisional because there are still difficulties in estimating the blood and urinary levels of FSH and of effecting an absolute separation of FSH and LH. Furthermore there seems to be considerable variation in the circulation and excretion of the daily quantities of these hormones, not only as expressed in the reports received from different laboratories but also from cycle to cycle in the same patient investigated in the same laboratory.

CERVICAL MUCUS

Not only is the endometrium controlled by the ovarian hormones oestradiol and progesterone but so is the cervical mucus. This is the fluid secreted by the glands situated in the cervical canal (the neck of the womb). Early in the menstrual cycle the fluid is scanty and tacky but devoid of cells. As the time of ovulation approaches and the blood level of oestrogen increases the fluid becomes copious and clear and renders the sperms even more active and progressively motile than they are in their own seminal fluid. As soon as ovulation has taken place, however, the cervical mucus under the influence of progesterone becomes thick and cellular and hostile to the passage of sperms. In fact even a very small dose of progestogen will cause the mucus to act as a barrier to the progress of sperms into the uterine cavity, though it may not have caused the mucus to thicken and become cellular.

We are now ready to consider the use of synthetic oestrogens and progestogens as oral contraceptives. The oestrogen suppresses the release of FSH and ovulation is inhibited. Furthermore some of the synthetic progestogens employed distort the structure of the endometrium to such an extent that even if ovulation did take place and the ovum were fertilized it would be impossible for the resulting blastocyst to be embedded. Finally sperms could not reach the ovum, even supposing ovulation did by chance occur – provided progestogen was being administered at the time – because of the hostility of the cervical mucus.

OTHER FACTORS CONCERNED IN THE CONTRACEPTIVE PROCESS

It is possible that after prolonged administration hormonal contraceptives may alter ovarian responsiveness to gonadotrophic stimulation or that they may interfere with the biochemical synthesis and breakdown of the hormones being manufactured by the ovary itself. They may alter the rate of transport of the ovum down the Fallopian tube so that it arrives in the uterus at an inappropriate time for embedding. Finally it may be that sperms need to be 'capacitated' before they can fertilize an ovum and that administration of progestogen may prevent this process.

ADMINISTRATIVE REGIMES

There are at least four methods of administering oral contraceptives. The first two involve the administration of both oestrogen and progestogen. Some of the 'combined' preparations and all the sequential preparations contain doses of oestrogen greater than 0·05 mg. and were on the market for some time before the Committee on Safety of Drugs – the Scowen Committee – issued a warning in December 1969 that there was a significantly greater tendency for thrombo-embolic incidents to develop if this dose was exceeded. So from this date only preparations containing 0·05 mg. of oestrogen have been used in this country and all the sequential preparations have been abandoned as they all contained oestrogen in higher doses.

The third method, low-dosage continuous progestogen, has also been abandoned because experimental dogs treated for several years with chlormadinone acetate (the progestogen employed in this low-dosage method) developed benign breast tumours.

At the present moment therefore the choice of oral contraceptives is very limited but it has been decided to describe the situation as it was before the Scowen Committee's warning and the decision to withdraw the chlormadinone preparations, as it gives a more complete picture of the alternatives that were available until recently.

The Combined Method

Oestrogen, in the form of ethinyloestradiol or mestranol, in doses of 0·05 mg. (to 0·15 mg.) is given in combination with a progestogen in doses of 1 to 5 mg. from the fifth to the twenty-fifth day after the commencement of the previous menstrual bleeding. This course is followed by a withdrawal bleeding two to four days later and the next course starts five days after the commencement of this bleeding. If the withdrawal bleeding does not occur within seven days of the end of the course another course is commenced.

This method is totally effective provided that the woman remembers to take the tablets. If one or two consecutive tablets are missed, especially within the first twelve days of a cycle, it is probable that protection has been lost. If tablets are missed it is likely that a withdrawal bleeding will occur about three or four days after the last tablet was taken. This should be regarded as the first day of a new cycle, and one should not attempt to complete the twenty-one-day administration but start the next course on the fifth day of the new cycle.

The Sequential Method

The oestrogen is given from day five to day twenty-five to inhibit ovulation and the progestogen is added for the last five or more days to ensure that the endometrium is shed cleanly with normal blood loss and within five days as in a normal period. This method seems to be very slightly less reliable (98·7 per cent) than the combined method. This slightly smaller degree of reliability may be due to the fact that one is relying on only one of the three modes of contraceptive action –

namely inhibition of ovulation. Oestrogen does not primarily prevent nidation of the ovum, should ovulation by chance occur, and it actually encourages the passage of sperms through the cervical mucus.

Low-Dosage Continuous Progestogen Administration

The endogenous progesterone produced by the ovary after ovulation dramatically changes the physical consistency of the cervical mucus. Within twenty-four to forty-eight hours the clear and copious cervical fluid, which is even more amicable to the sperms than their own seminal fluid, assumes the consistency of chewing gum and is difficult to aspirate from the cervical canal. On microscopic examination it is found to be cellular and to immobilize sperms. This effect on the cervical mucus is produced by the administration of the combined tablet.

It has been shown that progestogen given continuously in very low daily doses, 0·5 mg. or even less, is extremely effective in preventing sperms from progressing through the cervical canal even though these small doses may not produce any obvious change in the physical appearance of the cervical mucus. The only side-effect of this type of treatment is that it upsets the rhythm of the menstrual cycle in the early days of its administration, though the rhythm eventually settles down to a twenty-five to thirty-five-day cycle. If the irregularity becomes annoying 0·02 to 0·04 mg. of ethinyloestradiol or mestranol, or 2·5 to 5 mg. Premarin, given for seven to ten days every twenty-eight days for three to six months, in addition to the continuous progestogen, produces regular withdrawal bleeds and at the end of this time the menstrual cycle is found to have returned to its normal rhythm.

It has many theoretical advantages. It does not interfere with the normal activity of the pituitary. It certainly cannot be accused of causing cancer and it is unlikely to induce thromboembolic phenomena, which seem to be due to the presence of oestrogens and not progestogens. Whether this method is totally effective has not yet been established. It probably isn't quite, though very nearly.

The 'Morning-After Pill'

Fertilization of the ovum, immediately following ovulation, leads to the formation of the blastocyst, which may eventually become embedded in the endometrium. This blastocyst is almost certainly blighted by administration of oestrogen and will consequently fail to become embedded. At the moment it seems likely that large doses such as 50 mg. stilboestrol or even as much as 5 mg. of ethinyloestradiol should be used for at least five and possibly ten days. Furthermore there is at the moment no guarantee of total effectiveness. If therefore a blighted blastocyst were to become implanted it might possibly lead to the birth of an infant with congenital anomalies. The 'morning-after pill' is certainly not a serious competitor of the conventional combined oral contraceptive or the sequential method, or indeed of the continuous low-dosage oral progestogen. It can be regarded only as an emergency method of attempting to kill the product of an unfortunate conception.

Long-term 'Injectables' and Subcutaneous Capsules

This subject is not strictly within the terms of reference of a chapter on oral contraceptives, but it is an important recent development.

Since 1938 pellets consisting of the fused crystals of a steroid hormone have been implanted subcutaneously or intramuscularly, in order to produce a continuous, concentrated, and prolonged effect. This method has been modified for contraceptive purposes so that the hormone is contained in a plastic capsule, which is implanted subcutaneously. The hormone is continuously and very slowly absorbed and it is suggested that by this means permanent contraception could be assured throughout the woman's reproductive life. This is an attractive idea but it is not yet substantiated.

At the present long-term treatment with progestogen has been shown to have two possible disadvantages. It may cause heavy and irregular bleeding, and ovulation may not reappear for many months after the activity of the hormone is presumed to have ceased. This method of treatment would be suitable therefore only for women who never want to have any more children.

SIDE-EFFECTS

Side-effects may appear during the first cycle after starting an oral-contraceptive course and may be repeated during the second and third but then tend to disappear. They are not of serious significance but may be sufficiently annoying or confusing to make the woman abandon oral contraception. Many of the effects are subjective and their appearance may to some extent depend on the temperament of the user or indeed of her medical adviser who may 'have his suspicions' about the pill. Some of them are similar to effects the pregnant woman experiences and for the same reason – that they are due to oestrogen and progesterone. To enumerate them gives the impression that they are very commonly experienced, which they are not, and that each woman may expect to experience all or most of them, whereas if she complains of any it is likely to be only one or two. When you take any 'medicine' you expect it to have some 'effect' and to feel different in some way. The pill has been submitted to so much criticism that most women expect and are prepared to put up with some vague side-effects, such as tiredness, irritability, nervousness, dizziness, cramps, or insomnia. Nausea, vomiting, headaches, and blurred vision may also come into this category or there may be a more rational explanation for them. *Nausea* and *vomiting* have long been recognized as characteristic side-effects of synthetic oestrogens such as stilboestrol and ethinyloestradiol and are indeed common complaints in pregnancy. *Headaches* of a migrainous type have been recognized and timed as occurring a day or two after progestogen is discontinued and have in some cases been associated with an abnormal appearance of the blood vessels of the endometrium. It is therefore thought that progestogen withdrawal may activate latent migraine associated with some vascular mechanism under hormonal control. *Transient blurring of vision* is not an uncommon complaint in women being treated with hormones and may be due to localized fluid retention in some area of the retina.

More specific or objective complaints are the following:

1. *Break-through bleeding and spotting.* The former consists of bleeding similar to a normal period and occurring while the tablets are being administered. This is confusing, to say the least, but the woman should stop taking the tablets and start again five days later – in other words regard this as a period. Spotting may be even more confusing and if it occurs in successive cycles it is well to change to another preparation. Break-through bleeding and spotting are often the reason why a woman abandons oral contraceptives. Their occurrence, however, like any other side-effect, is uncommon.

2. *Gain in weight* is naturally very much resented when it occurs. It is thought to be due to a combination of three causes – increased appetite in a more contented woman freed from the fear of an unwanted pregnancy, retention of fluid in the tissues, which is a characteristic property of sex hormones and especially oestrogen, and the 'anabolic' effect of the progestogen, especially if it is a compound chemically related to male hormone, which tends to conserve protein and lay it down as muscle. The tendency to put on weight gradually disappears after six months or so, but it may cause women who are not highly motivated to abandon oral contraception. The lower the dose of oestrogen in the compound the less likely it is to occur and progestogens that are not chemically related to male hormone are to be preferred in these cases.

3. *Excessive vaginal discharge* due to the oestrogen sometimes occurs and some women find it abhorrent.

4. *Erosion of the cervix* is a condition of which the woman herself is seldom aware and is usually found only on routine internal examination. It is of no sinister significance.

5. *Difficulty in breast feeding* was relatively common in the early days of high-dose hormone combinations such as Enovid and might be of serious significance in countries where infants are dependent on mother's milk for adequate nutrition. This is no longer a serious problem especially on low dosage regimes.

6. *Chloasma* is a brown pigmentation of the skin, especially

of the face, such as not infrequently occurs in pregnancy. It is found particularly in countries in which there are many hours of sunlight such as Mexico and Puerto Rico, but affects undernourished women especially: rich Mexicans living in Texas are less prone to chloasma. Treatment with vitamin B is sometimes effective.

Apart from adverse side-effects there are many beneficial effects of oral contraceptive administration. The most striking is the contentment and self-confidence which replaces the anxiety and fear in the woman who dreads having an unwanted baby. Furthermore her periods are now absolutely regular, she has less tendency to period pains and premenstrual tension, and if she suffered from a greasy or spotty skin this tends to clear up. There is no reliable evidence concerning the increase or loss of libido, but many contented users of oral contraceptives now enjoy carefree intercourse.

COMPLICATIONS

Much more serious than the side-effects are the possible complications of oral contraceptive treatment. The three most important are the dangers of developing thrombo-embolic disorders, cancer of the breast or uterus, and liver damage. In addition to these, various metabolic disorders are being carefully examined in women using oral contraceptives.

Thrombo-embolic episodes

It has now been clearly shown that women using oral contraceptives are more liable to develop clots in various blood vessels than those who do not use this form of contraception. Nevertheless they are less likely to develop clots than normal pregnant women, and in any case the number of oral contraceptive users who develop these complications is very small indeed.

The thrombo-embolic lesions are (a) *deep vein thromboses* chiefly in the leg; (b) *pulmonary embolism*, which may result from a clot formed in one of these deep veins being dislodged and carried in the circulation to become impacted in one of the vessels of the lung, thereby denying a blood supply to the area – possibly a considerable area – of the lung which this vessel supplies; (c) *coronary thrombosis*, in which one of the narrow vessels that carry the blood to various portions of the heart muscle becomes blocked by a clot so that an extensive amount of the heart musculature is deprived of its blood supply; and (d) *cerebral thrombosis*, in which one of the arteries supplying the brain becomes occluded.

Here are the facts as we now have them. The Scowen Committee (the Committee on Safety of Drugs) has shown that the risk of death from *pulmonary embolism* for women on the pill is 2·35 per 100,000, that is to say 0·002 per cent. For women between the ages of twenty and thirty-four, however, the risk is 1·3 per 100,000 but for women over thirty-four it is nearly three times as much – 3·4 per 100,000. If there are no predisposing causes, such as a history of previous clotting of veins in the leg, the mortality from pulmonary embolism is four times as great as would be expected, though if there are predisposing causes it is not statistically significant. However, the overall increase in death rate from pulmonary embolism is statistically significant.

The increased death rate from *coronary thrombosis* in pill-users with not more than two children is statistically significant among those with no predisposing causes. Among those with predisposing causes the number of deaths was actually less than statistically expected.

Death from *cerebral thrombosis* was between three and four times more likely than would have been expected in the group in which there were no predisposing causes.

These studies did not suggest that any particular oestrogen–progestogen combination was more liable to produce these thrombo-embolic episodes.

These observations resulting from the data analysed by Inman and Vessey on behalf of the Committee on Safety of Drugs were published in April 1968 (*British Medical Journal*, vol. 2, no. 193) and they did not prompt this Committee to recommend that the administration of oral contraceptives should be banned, though it did insist that they should be supplied only on a doctor's prescription.

Concurrently a study was undertaken on behalf of the Medical Research Council by Vessey and Doll (*British Medical Journal*, 1968, vol. 2, no. 199) on women admitted to hospital for deep vein thrombosis and pulmonary embolism. They found that one in 2,000 women using oral contraceptives was admitted to hospital each year compared with one in 20,000 women who were not using oral contraceptives. They found no link, as far as hospital admissions were concerned, between oral-contraceptive users and the incidence of coronary thrombosis, and that only very occasionally were oral contraceptives associated with cerebral thrombosis.

The evidence at present available suggests that it is the oestrogen component that is responsible for the thrombo-embolic phenomena, and this is relevant in connection with the development of continuous low-dosage progestogen administration.

Thrombo-embolic incidents are the complications that cause most concern in relation to the administration of oral contraceptives. In terms of hundreds of thousands of women there is statistical evidence that oral contraceptives are more likely to induce these conditions and even in some cases to cause death. To some it may seem logical – even mandatory – to argue that any drug that is being given for purely social as opposed to therapeutic purposes and that may kill three women in every 100,000 each year should be banned. Obviously every promiscuously minded teenager should take serious note of these statistics. But what of the woman who has three or four children, possibly as the result of less certain forms of contraception than oral contraceptives can guarantee? She may possibly think that the total effectiveness of oral contraceptives is worth the minute risk involved. The risk of death in childbirth is four times greater – and the risk of death in a road accident is twice as great, and from heavy cigarette smoking much greater still. It is a matter for the individual woman and her doctor to decide.

Risk of Cancer

Oestrogens are powerful proliferative agents (stimulators of growth) especially of the endometrium, vaginal lining and breast tissue. Anything that stimulates tissue growth might logically be considered likely to stimulate 'new growth' or neoplasia, and neoplasms are often cancerous.

The females of certain strains of mice are especially likely to develop breast cancer spontaneously. Sterilize these mice early in life and they do not develop cancer. Treat the males with oestrogen and they, like the females, are susceptible to the development of breast cancer.

Bitches and doe rabbits may develop breast cancer if their livers have been damaged by pregnancy toxaemia so that they can no longer convert 'free' oestrogens to a less potent form. These animals, however, never develop cancer of the breast if they are treated with oestrogens. On the other hand, rats never develop breast cancer spontaneously but do following administration of oestrogen. Rhesus monkeys develop breast cancer – or for that matter endometrial or cervical cancer – either spontaneously or following exogenous administration.

Species differ, so what about the human female? It has been stated by various workers including the present author that a late menopause or an ovarian tumour continuously secreting large amounts of oestrogen may encourage the development of cancer of the breast or endometrium; that 'chronic cystic mastitis' (but not premenstrual tenderness and swelling of the breast) or an endometrium constantly under the influence of endogenous oestrogen, unopposed by progesterone because ovulation is not taking place, may also give rise to breast or uterine cancer, and that cervical cancer is more common in women who have had many children. These assertions, however, have been vigorously denied and not without good evidence. Nevertheless, let us presume that endogenous oestrogen may be a factor in causing breast and uterine cancer. If so it is an easy process of presumption to argue from mouse to man, and from the endogenous carcinogenic tendencies, to the assertion that administration of oestrogen is dangerous because it might induce breast or uterine cancer.

But does it? Stilboestrol, a very potent oestrogen, has been available for therapeutic use for thirty years. Retrospective follow-up studies have been conducted and published on at least 2,000 patients. This included a series of forty-three patients of whom three developed cervical cancer and these cases were reported only because this was a most unusual finding and it is now agreed that cervical cancer results more from inadequate hygiene and poor social conditions than from hormonal influences. There were four cases of cancer of the endometrium and two cases of cancer of the breast. Furthermore reference to exhaustive abstracts of the world literature revealed how remarkably few papers there were reporting cases of cancer following oestrogen administration.

However, one must not lose sight of the fact that prolonged exposure, such as for a period of ten years, may be necessary for chemical carcinogens to take effect in the human species and that the development of breast cancer in woman has a long latent period. Large-scale, long-term studies are now in progress on women who have been taking oral contraceptives for a prolonged period. While we are awaiting the result of these studies it would seem prudent not to administer oral contraceptives to women in whom cancer of the breast has been diagnosed.

As for progestogen, there is now a substantial body of evidence that shows that this hormone actually retards and reverses the malignant progress of breast and endometrial cancer.

Liver Damage

Liver function can be measured by a number of tests and liver damage has been reported to occur in women on oral contraceptives by doctors in Scandinavia and Chile, where liver dysfunction is far more common than in the United Kingdom and the United States, where little or no evidence of liver dysfunction has been found in oral-contraceptive users.

The disorder is more often due to stasis of the flow of bile and may give rise to jaundice, rather than to actual damage of the liver cells themselves. It seems to be caused by the progestogen rather than the oestrogen component of the pill.

Women who suffer from recurrent jaundice of unknown origin in pregnancy tend to develop jaundice when using oral contraceptives and oral contraceptives should not be used by such women or by women with hereditary defects in the excretory function (bile elimination) of the liver.

Metabolic Disorders

Oestrogen increases the ability of the proteins that circulate in the blood, especially globulin, to bind hormones to them. Thus the concentration of *protein-bound iodine* (PBI) increases to levels often found in patients with over-active thyroids, and the amount of cortisone, measured as *plasma cortisol*, is also significantly raised as it is in some patients with the clinical picture of adrenal gland overactivity – Cushing's syndrome. The salt-and-water-retaining hormone, *aldosterone*, also appears to be increased because it is more easily bound to protein, and this may be an additional cause for the tendency to put on weight as the result of fluid retention. These metabolic changes are not of serious significance and do not indicate excessive activity of the thyroid and adrenal glands.

What may be of some significance is the effect of oral contraceptives on *carbohydrate metabolism*. Glucose-tolerance tests and other tests designed to test the response to sugar indicate that women taking oral contraceptives are more sensitive than is normal and come to resemble the potentially diabetic group, which these laboratory tests tend to identify – individuals who may eventually become diabetic. There is, however, no evidence at present that oral contraceptives have induced real diabetes and the results so far obtained resemble the pattern of individuals who will eventually suffer from 'steroid' diabetes and this may merely reflect on the ability of oestrogen to facilitate the binding of cortisol – a steroid – to plasma protein. Nevertheless these and other metabolic deviations from the normal must be borne in mind and studied intensively.

CONCLUSIONS

It is usually ethically justifiable to administer female sex hormones to relieve menstrual disorders and similar conditions, despite the extremely remote risk of serious and unforeseen complications. But in giving these hormones to normal healthy women to prevent them from becoming pregnant it is important to be satisfied that the risk of complications, or even death, is far less than they would be exposed to during an unwanted pregnancy. So far as our present knowledge and observations go we can be satisfied that this is the case. Nevertheless the administration of oral contraceptives is not without risk, and on very rare occasions serious risk, not only to health but to life.

For this reason alone it should be a matter of serious reflection whether a teenage girl should use oral contraceptives in order that she may be promiscuous. On the other hand oral contraceptives may avoid the tragedy of an unwanted pregnancy and possibly a subsequently induced abortion. Possibly continuous administration of low-dosage progestogens may prove to be the most suitable form of oral contraceptive in a nulliparous woman. It may also be appropriate as a 'spacer', so that a couple may be able to leave the desired interval between one pregnancy and the next. Conventional twenty-day courses of the combined pill are still the classical and well-tried method. They give complete protection and may therefore be preferred. Long-acting progestogens, given by injection or implantation, are at present not free from undesirable complications such as bouts of heavy bleeding and uncertainty as to when ovulation will return after the treatment is discontinued and should probably be reserved for women who never wish to have another child.

A WHO report on oral contraceptives (WHO Technical Report Series No. 386) estimated that one half of fertile women in the United Kingdom used oral contraceptives for at least one cycle in 1966, and there is no doubt that the figure has increased in the subsequent years.

The conventional combined compound of oestrogen and progestogen is completely effective provided the tablets are conscientiously taken according to instructions. Other methods discussed in this chapter may be slightly less reliable, but are nevertheless considerably more reliable than any other form of contraceptive. Oral contraceptives are therefore the ideal method for individual couples to whom it is personally important to avoid conception and who are therefore prepared to ensure that the tablets are taken conscientiously according to the instructions. Furthermore oral contraceptives are aesthetically preferable to methods that require application immediately before intercourse. For less motivated people some method that does not require intelligent cooperation, such as an IUD, is probably preferable and this has been found effective in halting or reversing the alarming tendency to over-population. Certain side-effects may be encountered that are mild enough to be tolerable and are usually transient. In a few cases, however, they are sufficiently severe to make the woman abandon this form of contraception.

Finally, there are serious and sometimes even fatal complications, of which the most important are thrombo-embolic manifestations, which though they occur extremely rarely make it necessary to insist that oral contraceptives should be obtained only on a doctor's prescription.

(III) VOLUNTARY STERILIZATION

L. N. JACKSON

Until 1966 it was widely believed that it was illegal for a man to be sterilized except when medically necessary. The Simon Population Trust then obtained legal advice which defined the circumstances under which it was possible to use this simple operation as a form of birth control. There are now more than two hundred surgeons to whom the Trust refers those who ask its help, and the follow-up of the first thousand couples has been prepared.

THE PRESENT POSITION

Since the Simon Population Trust launched its sterilization project in May 1966 a large measure of success has been achieved. Many thousands of inquiries about sterilization have been made and more continue to pour in daily. The project is concerned almost exclusively with male sterilization because most men are willing to undergo this quick, simple operation which requires little or no hospitalization rather than subject their wives to a major abdominal procedure. In the rare cases where the couple opt for female sterilization we are able to help the wife.

THE FIRST 2,000

The precise number of men who have been sterilized through the agency of the Trust is not accurately known because we are not always informed if and when an applicant's search for sterilization has met with success. To our certain knowledge, however, up to the end of August 1968 more than 2,350 men had been vasectomized.

WHO APPLIES FOR STERILIZATION?

Many of the inquiries we receive come from couples ranging in age from thirty to forty, with two or more children. Almost as many come from couples aged between twenty and thirty who have three or more children. All these have definitely decided that their families are complete. The majority of them have found other contraceptive methods unreliable (resulting in unwanted pregnancies) or otherwise unsatisfactory.

Applicants fall into four groups:

1. Those who, having read our literature, decide for themselves, or are advised by us, to take no further action.

2. Those who, acting on our advice, consult their family doctors. Many doctors doubtless refer such applicants to surgeons without further reference to us.

3. Those whose family doctors, while prepared to refer them, do not know the names of surgeons interested in this field. To such doctors, on request and on receipt from the applicants of their names and addresses, we send the names of the appropriate surgeons with whom the Trust has established contact. We also send consent forms and information. Surgeons' names

are sent to family doctors only, never to applicants and never to anybody else. What happens to applicants in this group (as in group 2) is not always known to us but it is probable that most of these men are sterilized. Although we do not press for information we are always glad to hear how they have fared.

4. Lastly come those who have, to our certain knowledge, undergone the operation. Nearly all of these have consented to cooperate in a follow-up inquiry which is well under way. Not one of these has complained of any diminution of potency or of any adverse effect on sexual life. Indeed with the fear of pregnancy removed, marital relations have often improved.

A report on the first 1,000 completed questionnaires has been published.

DOCTORS AND SURGEONS

We are in correspondence with a steadily increasing number of family doctors. Few have raised religious or other objections. Some doctors still quite mistakenly believe that sterilization is illegal and a surprising number are still unaware that there are a large number of surgeons doing this work.

Starting with only two or three, the surgeons helping the Trust now number over 200 and more join us every week. Sterilization is now being performed all over the British Isles. Some of these surgeons perform vasectomies solely through the mediation of the Trust. Most use the Trust's form of consent and many ask for copies of the Trust's leaflet explaining the operation in simple terms, which they give to their patients. The operation is not usually performed under the NHS. The cost depends on the circumstances and on the surgeon.

PROCEDURE

In the light of experience a satisfactory method of procedure has been evolved. An applicant for sterilization is asked first to furnish us with particulars about himself: his age, his wife's age, the number of children in the family, and any relevant medical history. This screening of applicants serves a twofold purpose; it prevents disappointments and also avoids a waste of doctors' and surgeons' time. Only such applicants as appear to have a reasonable case are advised to go further and discuss the matter with their doctors.

SPERM COUNTS

An important fact has been learnt. A man does not become sterile immediately after vasectomy. Indeed the length of time after which it is 'safe' to have sexual intercourse without contraception varies from man to man. Until two consecutive postoperative sperm counts have proved negative, sterility cannot be counted upon. The first of these counts should not be done until twelve weeks after the operation.

SAFEGUARDS

The safeguards laid down by the Medical Defence Union are scrupulously observed. No initiative is taken without first securing the cooperation and consent of the applicant's family doctor. It cannot be too strongly emphasized that, provided that a consent form signed by both spouses is obtained beforehand, the operation is perfectly legal.

This project is clearly gathering momentum. Press publicity has been widespread and favourable.

Editor's note: Since this article was written in October 1967 vasectomy has become widely accepted as a contraceptive method. It is now available on the National Health Service under certain circumstances and the Family Planning Association has opened several vasectomy clinics in different parts of the country. The Simon Population Trust has now wound up its Voluntary Sterilization Project, since its aim – to promote general public knowledge of vasectomy – has been achieved.

6
Problems and Solutions

If all couples, married and unmarried, always practised birth control there would be no unwanted pregnancies and therefore no need for abortion. In spite of the wide availability of methods of birth control and of knowledge about them, unwanted pregnancies are becoming more common, rather than less.ABortion is bad from all points of view, the mother, the doctor, society – but not as bad, often, as the alternative.

One way to prevent the birth of unwanted babies to already overburdened mothers is to take birth-control service to the women in their own homes. This may seem an expensive approach, but it is cheaper than caring for children in local authority hostels – and more humane.

For some couples the problem is not how to control fertility but how to produce it. Modern techniques can achieve remarkable results – sometimes they are almost too successful. But when the man is incurably sterile and his wife is fertile artificial insemination may provide the best solution. When this was first introduced there was an outcry; it was opposed on moral, social, political and even genetic grounds. Experience has shown that these fears were exaggerated.

(I) ARTIFICIAL INSEMINATION

A PHYSICIAN

A couple may not be able to have children because the man is sterile. In this case they may use AID (Artificial Insemination by a Donor), when a doctor injects the sperm of another man into the wife's womb. AID is probably used in only a few cases, but it raises important theoretical and practical questions. There are two kinds of artificial insemination, AIH, where the husband's semen is used and AID, where semen from another man is used. The insemination is artificial since the semen is injected into the woman by herself or, more often, by a doctor. The procedure is only slightly uncomfortable and can be performed simply and quickly.

AIH is used when for some reason a man, although producing normal semen, is unable to fertilize his wife, although she too is fertile. This may happen if the man has an abnormal opening through which the semen escapes before reaching the woman. But more often the difficulty is psychological; there is some impediment which prevents the man from performing the act of intercourse normally. In these cases the semen can be collected and injected into the wife.

AID may be employed when the husband is sterile and the wife is fertile. There are other and much rarer situations in which AID may be used, for example where there is rhesus blood group incompatibility between husband and wife which makes further successful pregnancy unlikely. AID could be used in other situations but it is very doubtful whether it ever is. It has been mentioned, for example, that AID might be used for improving the stock by using donors of outstanding qualities. This is of only theoretical interest. What woman would rather conceive a baby by AID than by natural means, however outstanding the donor?

HOW FREQUENT IS AID?

About nine per cent of all married couples are involuntarily sterile. In about one tenth of these cases the man produces no spermatozoa. Thus in perhaps one per cent of all marriages the man is totally sterile and the woman is fertile. These are the couples who might resort to AID. Since there are about 375,000 marriages a year there are about 4,000 in which AID might lead to children being born to couples who would otherwise be childless. It is impossible to give any sort of accurate estimate of the present frequency of AID but a guess that it is used in one or two hundred cases a year may be reasonable – that is AID is used in about $2\frac{1}{2}$ to 5 per cent of the marriages in which it might help. Even if AID were generally available probably not more than about one half of the suitable couples would prefer it to adoption or permanent childlessness. If this is a correct estimate it follows that AID is never likely to be employed more than about ten times as frequently as it is at present, perhaps 2,000 times a year.

AID is not always successful. The semen used is normal, but some men are more fertile than others and the fertility of one man varies slightly from time to time. The fertility of the wife too may be low. For these and for other reasons artificial insemination is often unsuccessful. In nearly every successful case several inseminations are needed before pregnancy results. Insemination may be repeated several times in one menstrual cycle or it may be performed once a cycle; in either case, because of the difficulty of predicting the time of ovulation, it may be several months before fertilization results.

SELECTION OF A DONOR

The selection of the donor is made by the doctor. There are of course no rules for selecting donors, but every doctor who practises AID, one may be sure, selects a donor whose family and medical history is free, as far as can be judged, from any disorder likely to affect the child. The doctor cannot be certain that no undesirable qualities will be transmitted, but the same applies to all normal matings. The fear that the donor might suffer from a venereal disease was expressed by one medical authority. There *is* a risk, as with natural insemination. But it is most unlikely that syphilis would be transmitted by artificial insemination, far less likely indeed than by natural intercourse. Furthermore the doctor can make fairly sure that the donor does not suffer from the disease by a simple blood test. Since donors are probably selected from people who run a less-than-average risk of contracting syphilis it is probable that the chance of a baby born by AID developing congenital syphilis is less than it is for a baby born of a natural insemination.

The doctor's other reported criticism of the selection of donors, that they might have negroid ancestry (assuming this to be undesirable), also applies to natural matings. One might think that a doctor would have less compunction in asking a prospective donor about his ancestry than a girl would have in asking her fiancé. Normal matings are dictated in the main by affection of the partners. On purely genetic grounds this is not necessarily the best method. It is difficult to think that a doctor who carefully chooses a donor of semen cannot avoid a carrier of disease or other unwanted traits at least as well as a love-sick maid can.

The donor produces the semen for insemination by masturbation. The semen is collected into a plastic container and is used within three or four hours.

AID IS NOT ADULTERY

There has been much legal interest in AID. It started when a Scottish judge, Lord Wheatley, decided that insemination of a wife by a donor did not constitute adultery. There is nothing new in this. Commonsense (and even the law!) prescribes that sexual intercourse must take place before there can be adultery. The English courts had already decided that artificial insemination is no bar to nullity, i.e. that it does not constitute consummation. It surely follows that AID could not be adultery. Lord Denning's view, expressed in a House of Lords debate in February 1958 that AID is adultery, was not supported by two other eminent lawyers, Lord Merriman, President of the Probate, Divorce and Admiralty Division, and the then Lord Chancellor.

It happens that in the Scottish case the wife's AID was alleged to have been performed without the knowledge or consent of the husband. Whether this will be held to constitute grounds for divorce, for example under the heading of cruelty, has yet to be decided. Unfortunately this will have to wait for another law suit. In this case, as the wife refused to substantiate her statement that AID had been performed, her defence was excluded.

After Lord Wheatley's judgment the then Archbishop of Canterbury, Dr Geoffrey Fisher, made a pronouncement in which he said 'early consideration should be given to the framing of legislation to make the practice [of AID] a criminal offence'.

Artificial Insemination

After this AID became a burning issue and was debated on all sides with a forthrightness which would have been unthinkable a few years ago. The discussion has on the whole been sober and sensible. In striking contrast to the treatment by some of the press of the Wolfenden proposals on homosexuality there were few emotional outbursts.

Although the general tone of the discussion has been moderate it has revealed ignorance[1] and confusion in many people's minds. There are legal, genetical and ethical considerations as well as the medical.

LEGAL CONSEQUENCES OF AID

One of the main concerns of the critics of AID has been the legal consequences of the act. But the critics have often revealed an ignorance of AID which has led to muddle. By the rejection of AID as adultery the main legal question is decided. Other questions concern the registration of birth, legitimacy and inheritance.

The Difficulty of Proving a False Registration of Birth

Many commentators have written as if the doctor who performs the AID is committing some crime in relation to the registration of the birth. This is unlikely to be so since it is the mother and 'father' who register the birth, not the obstetrician, still less the doctor who has performed the AID (who are unlikely to be the same person, a point often overlooked). It is difficult to see that the doctor practising the AID is breaking the law. The person who registers the birth falsely is doing so. However, it might not be easy to prove that a man registering the birth of a child to his wife knew for certain that the child was not his. It might be impossible to prove in court that a man was at the time of his wife's conception totally sterile. The fact

---

1. Lord Blackford, who moved the motion in the House of Lords that AID without the husband's consent 'is tantamount to adultery' and that 'all children so conceived are illegitimate' put this critical and important motion down 'knowing nothing about artificial insemination'.

that at a later examination, to which he might submit, he was found to be sterile would be far from the same as proving that he was sterile at the appropriate time. It might be possible, by elaborate blood-grouping tests, to prove that the child could not have been begotten by the 'father' but this would require his cooperation in submitting himself and the child to a blood test which he might, without seriously damaging his case, refuse to do.[2]

It seems doubtful to me, with no specialist knowledge of the law, whether a prosecution for false registration of birth would succeed, assuming that it was initiated at all which is unlikely. The only circumstance in which one could foresee such a prosecution is after the much more important questions of divorce or inheritance had been raised. If it had been established in a divorce case that the child was not the offspring of the 'father' or if this had been established by a disinherited relative, then one could imagine that a Director of Public Prosecutions might realize that an offence must have been committed in the birth registration.

AID Without the Husband's Consent

If AID had been performed without the husband's consent it might be relevant in a divorce case. AID (or AIH) might also be relevant in a nullity suit where non-consummation was claimed in spite of the birth of a child. It is difficult to see how else AID could be brought into divorce proceedings.

If this interpretation is correct we are left with only two circumstances in which AID could be proved in the divorce courts, one where there is non-consummation of a marriage (so that this situation ceases to exist immediately the marriage is consummated) and the other where AID is performed without the husband's consent, when it might – we still do not know – be held to constitute cruelty. In the Scottish case the AID was alleged to have taken place in America where standards and practice may be different from here. It is extremely

---

2. That he would not be ordered to submit to a test is shown by the decision of Lord Wheatley, in another case, which was upheld by the Court of Session in Edinburgh in 1958.

unlikely that any doctor in this country who performs AID does so without the explicit approval of both partners.[3] Assuming this to be so, most of the legal complications of AID disappear.

It might be that the ethical behaviour of British doctors is not to be relied upon in this matter and that legislation will need to be introduced either to prohibit AID without the consent of the husband (but that might not be enough deterrence) or to make it grounds for divorce. Everyone would agree that AID without the husband's approval is an outrage. Should it ever occur in this country and be proved in the courts one would imagine that the General Medical Council would inquire into the doctor's conduct.

Legitimacy

The law assumes that every child born in wedlock is legitimate. This assumption can only be rebutted by 'strong, distinct, satisfactory and conclusive evidence'. Thus the question of legitimacy could hardly be raised except as a consequence of some other legal action in which AID was proved.

C. H. Rolph in an article in the *New Statesman* asked what would happen if a 'father' disowned a child born to his wife by AID or withdrew his consent. These questions have not of course been decided by the courts but one would suppose that a man could no more disown a child born to his wife by AID, to which he had consented, than if the child had been conceived in the natural way, and that his consent to AID, once having been given, could not be withdrawn. If adultery is condoned by a man resuming sexual relations with his wife it would be illogical to allow a man to reject obligations incurred by AID, which he condoned, indeed approved. If a decision on this point is needed it should be made in the courts, not in the legislature as Mr Rolph suggested.

Inheritance

The difficulty of inheritance in relation to AID may be more

3. It is interesting that, according to one authority, the husband asks for AID more often than the wife.

apparent than real. If AID were proved a child might be disinherited but this does not raise any new legal problems. It should simply be a case of proving AID.

Those whom this distresses will want to change the law. But the change could only be to acknowledge AID children as equal to natural-born children. Unless AID is made illegal[4] no other change is possible, since under the law as it stands children proved to have been born by AID would (presumably) not be entitled to inherit titles, etc. from their 'fathers'.

It is difficult to believe that the possibility of AID being made illegal is a serious one, because of the difficulty of enforcing the law (much greater than in the case of criminal abortion) and, more important, because it would be confusing sin with crime to forbid AID.

It might be argued that it should be compulsory for all cases of AID to be registered or made public (and registration of any kind would be made public if relatives were to be able to assure themselves that they were not being cheated of inheritances). It is doubtful whether making registration compulsory would alter the situation, except to substitute two offences for one, for cases would not be registered, whatever the law required. A doctor, one feels confident, would refuse to register an AID birth, whether the register was public or in some way private, in the same way as doctors at present do not notify cases of attempted suicide. Legally they should and by not doing so a doctor becomes an accessory after the fact. Nevertheless doctors scarcely ever do notify the police of attempted suicide and, as far as I know, no doctor has been prosecuted for this omission.

In the case of AID there is another difficulty. It would be possible for the doctor to plead that he did not know that conception had in fact occurred. He might admit to having performed AID but, as we have seen, this is far from the same thing as being sure that conception has resulted. The doctor might say that the patient did not tell him that she had become pregnant (the fact that she did not return for another

4. Suppose AID were illegal but nevertheless performed, would the child not exist legally?

appointment would not mean anything; she might have become discouraged and decided to give up trying for a baby). Even if the patient did tell the doctor that she had become pregnant she might not have told him of the date or place of birth, which indeed might be a long way from the doctor's home town. If registration were compulsory the onus to register would have to be on the mother, and it is hardly likely that she would carry it out. If she were not minded to ignore the law she might even travel to another country for the confinement and return to this country afterwards.

If it is the intention to make it compulsory to register the act of insemination, as distinct from the birth of an AID conceived child, the proposal would run into the refusal (so one presumes) of any doctor to disclose, let alone register, what he does to a patient. It seems that registration would be impractical, even if desirable.

The legal position can be summarized: the only problem which may, if the courts do not decide the issue first, need the attention of Parliament is that of AID without the husband's consent which, as the Royal Commission on Marriage and Divorce recommended, should be grounds for divorce. The law relating to the registration of births is at present being broken when the husband's name is recorded as the father, but it is difficult to see that any legal change can remedy this deception. To make AID registrable would be impractical.

GENETICS

If a child is born after AID the identity of his real father is not known. It is possible that when the child grows up he might marry his half-sister without anyone at all knowing that this was the case.

The Improbability of Incest

It is not possible to predict accurately the chances of a child born by AID subsequently marrying his half-sister because the number of children born by AID is not known. Let us assume (1) that 150 AID children are born each year, (2) that each donor is responsible for two conceptions in one year (both of these assumptions are guesses). Each year about 750,000 people are married in Great Britain. Thus in any one year the chance that an AID conceived person might marry his or her half-sister or half-brother is

$$\frac{750,000}{150 \times 2} = 2,500 : 1 \text{ against}$$

If AID had been practised on the present estimated scale since the time of William the Conqueror it is unlikely that a case of semi-incest would yet have occurred. Or if it were practised throughout the world on the same scale, one case would occur about every fifty years.

Hitherto, the much greater possibility that an adopted or illegitimate child might unknowingly marry his half-sister does not seem to have disturbed the ecclesiastical or legal authorities.

If AID were to increase so that marriages between half siblings might occur more often perhaps an unhealthy inbreeding might result? Genetic harm might result from this form of inter-marriage (although it can hardly have been said to have done so from the intense inter-marrying between the Darwins and the Wedgwoods).

A Comparison with Cousin Marriages

The danger is perhaps not so great as might appear at first sight. Compare the genetical situation in a marriage between half-siblings (one of them, we are assuming, having been conceived by AID) with that in a marriage between first cousins which is, of course, legal. As can be seen from figures 1 and 2 the genetical situation is similar in the two cases; in each, two of the four grandparents are common to the man and woman who are getting married. If, say, the fathers of the couple (figure 1) were not merely brothers but identical twins the genetical situation would be exactly the same as that which would apply in the case of the AID child marrying his half-sister (figure 2).

To complete this paradox one may cite the instance of first cousins marrying whose fathers were brothers and whose

Artificial Insemination

mothers were sisters (figure 3). This would represent even greater in-breeding than in the AID situation, as the couple would have all four grandparents in common. And if the fathers and mothers were identical twins the in-breeding would be even greater – but still legal.

These comparisons of genetical effects can be seen in proportion when one recalls that two per cent of all marriages are between first cousins. Thus there are 7,500 first-cousin marriages a year in this country, compared to an estimate of one AID half-sibling marriage every 2,500 years.

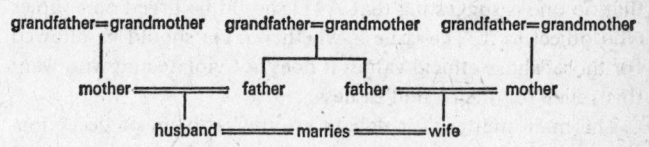

Figure 1. First-cousin marriage. Two of the four grandparents are the same for husband and wife

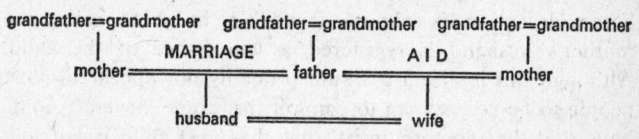

Figure 2. Marriage between a man and his AID half-sister, two of the four grandparents are the same for husband and wife

Figure 3. First-cousin marriage where both parents of the couple are brothers and sisters. All the grandparents of the couple are the same. This represents greater in-breeding than in the AID situation (figure 2). Furthermore the marriage would still be legal if the fathers and the mothers were identical twins, which would be genetically the equivalent to marriage between a full brother and sister

ETHICAL CONSIDERATIONS

The ethical problems raised by AID will vary according to the individual's own religious and philosophical beliefs. Some Christians may feel that AID violates the unity of marriage and they will condemn it. Others, equally devout, may decide that it is not offensive to their view of marriage to make a barren union fertile in this way.

These are personal views and there seems to me to be little point in publicly debating them. We need only to remember that no one is suggesting that AID should be urged on couples who object to it. The issue is whether AID should be allowed for those whose ethical values it does not violate and who want this relief for their childlessness.

The main matters for debate are the problem of deception, the motives of the donor and the principles of the doctor.

Deception

Some deception is almost inevitable in AID since the mother's husband is registered as the father of the child. Although this is illegal it would probably not appear to most people to be very wrong to commit this crime. Several people have said that doctors 'insist' that the AID child is not told the truth. Even if this is so it does not have much meaning. Whether or not the child is told is no special concern of the doctor who performed the AID; it is a decision for the couple. They may be influenced by the doctor's advice but the doctor has no power to enforce his view.

It is probable that most couples would prefer to keep the facts of AID from the child. Whether this is a good thing is a matter for the individual conscience but it is difficult to see what is gained by telling the child.

Motives of the Donor

Comments on the motives of the semen donors have been critical. The donor is reproached with being irresponsible in allowing a child to be conceived for which he will take no responsibility. His morals are thought to be so low that he is unworthy to become a father. In the words of the director of the fertility clinic of a London teaching hospital (quoted by *The Times*) 'the mere fact of a man becoming a donor suggested there was something wrong with him'. This is the argument which I find hardest to understand. The donor is not fathering a child which he knows will not be cared for (as the casual fornicator is). He knows that the child will be born to a couple who want it and will care for it. The couple have, one would have thought, shown an unusually strong desire to have a child by seeking AID at all. It is scarcely a procedure which a couple would resort to, or a doctor practise, if they did not want a child.

Possibly the objection to the donor is that the semen is produced by masturbation. Yet recent inquiry has shown that masturbation is almost universal amongst boys and young men at one time or another. To condemn the donor for masturbation is to condemn almost all men and many women.

I find it difficult not to think that the donor is acting from generous motives. His part in the affair is unlikely to give him particular pleasure, unless it be the knowledge that he is helping other people. And if this gives him pleasure, he is hardly immoral.

Suppose one were to concede that a man is immoral in agreeing to be a semen donor, would even that matter? Morals are not carried in the semen. Indeed it might be argued that AID children are the only ones an immoral man ought to have; he should not have children of his own whom he *will* know and meet and therefore corrupt!

It has been said that donors are paid. I have no information on this except the remark ascribed to one doctor that he paid his donors nothing. The figures, such as £50, which have been quoted probably apply only to America. It would surprise me if many donors in this country receive more than token payment and it would surprise me even more if C. H. Rolph's statement that 'there is a living in this' were true.

A letter in the *Manchester Guardian* from 'a wife and mother' described how a marriage had been saved by the appearance of a child conceived by AID. One would hesitate to endorse AID as a means of saving a marriage, any more than one would commend the having of a child by normal means for this purpose. It is unfair to the child, however conceived, if the marriage does break up. A child should not be conceived by AID if the marriage does not promise well, any more than a fertile couple should start a child if they are unhappy together.

THE ROLE OF THE DOCTOR

The choice of a donor, the maintenance of anonymity and the selection and rejection of couples throw a big responsibility on the doctor who practises AID; so does the decision to perform, let us say, a Caesarean section on a pregnant woman, and the operation itself, place a big responsibility on the obstetric surgeon. The purpose of a doctor's training is to fit him to take responsibility. The doctor performing AID has a delicate and difficult task. He undertakes a big, but not overpowering, responsibility.

CONCLUSION

Much has been said by many public men and women about the sins, crimes and difficulties of AID. Less has been heard of the happiness which it can bring to a childless couple. As so often, objections and difficulties are more vehemently championed than advantages and benefits.

It is true that we are ignorant of the actual results of AID, of whether the children are accepted and the families are happy. But there must by now be several doctors who have had enough experience to answer these questions. If they had found AID unsuccessful they would presumably have discontinued it, yet apparently the practice is growing. If this is so AID must be bringing happiness to couples who would otherwise have been childless, and it is difficult to see that anyone is being harmed in the process. It is well to remember this before talking of sin and crime.

(II) SUBFERTILITY

P. M. F. BISHOP

Conception takes place when an ovum, shed into the Fallopian tube, is fertilized there by the spermatazoon. The ovum is not shed from its follicle in the ovary unless the follicle is first stimulated by a hormone (called FSH or follicle-stimulating hormone) produced by the pituitary gland. The pituitary, in turn, must also be stimulated by the hypothalamus at the base of the brain, to secrete a constant trickle of another hormone called LH or luteinizing hormone. This trickle causes the stimulated follicle to secrete oestrogen which inhibits the output of FSH and stimulates the release of LH.

The normal ovarian cycle is thus controlled by a delicate balance between a number of hormones and failure to conceive may be caused by a deficiency or imbalance at one or several points. Biological tests can determine whether a woman is failing to conceive because the pituitary is not secreting enough FSH, or because the hypothalamus is stimulating an insufficient supply of LH, or because of primary ovarian failure.

Between 1938 and 1958 gynaecologists tried to induce ovulation in infertile women by treatment with various extracts containing FSH or FSH-like substances; the results were largely disappointing and it was accepted that long-standing amenorrhoea or failure to produce ova could not be cured. In 1958, however, a team of Swedish doctors induced ovulation and conception in amenorrhoeic women by injecting extracts of human pituitary glands, followed by an extract containing a substance very similar to LH. Since then similar treatment has been developed at Yale and in Britain. Although there is still no general agreement on the regimen to be followed, it seems certain that the FSH only prepares the ovarian follicle for ovulation and the actual ovulation is induced by subsequent injections of LH. The size and frequency of of the dose of FSH needed varies between one individual and another and can only be calculated by daily assays, carried out by skilled workers in specially equipped and necessarily expensive laboratories.

Even under such conditions the margin between an ineffective and an excessive dose is so small that more than one follicle may be stimulated and more than one ovum fertilized. Twins or even triplets may bring joy to a previously childless couple, but quads or quins that do not survive may add tragedy to the previous deprivation.

Conception is, however, only the first step in achieving a full-term baby. The patient's ovary may not secrete enough progestogen to allow the ovum to embed and to maintain the pregnancy; in order to check that the pregnancy is proceeding as it should the patient must be able to supply daily collections of urine or have vaginal smears taken.

Ovulation may also be induced if a synthetic compound called clomiphene is given by mouth. The exact mode of action is not known, but the results are so far promising and the treatment is relatively easy to manage.

To summarize the position, it is safe to say that there is now treatment and good chance of success for some of those women who have hitherto not conceived because of failure to ovulate; but even if conception is successfully achieved, it is necessary to continue careful, expert and exacting supervision throughout most or all of the pregnancy.

(III) ABORTION

Before the Abortion Act was passed in July 1967 a doctor could terminate a pregnancy only if satisfied by psychiatric advice that the health of a potential mother was in grave danger of breaking down. In these circumstances many of those who could not afford the fees charged by private nursing homes for a convenient dilation and curettage turned to the amateur abortionists.

Once the Abortion Act was passed, abortion became legal if the pregnancy may seriously affect the physical or mental health of the patient, or of existing children, or where a child is likely to be born deformed. In the two months following the act nearly as many hospital abortions were performed as in the whole of 1964.

In July 1967 a woman (C. H.) in prison for having procured an abortion wrote down the story of her married life. The editors have checked the authenticity of the story and have made only minor changes of spelling.

Mrs Moya Woodside, a psychiatric social worker, interviewed forty-four women who had been sent to Holloway prison when abortion was still illegal; many had had nursing experience; most saw nothing wrong in using a douche as a delayed contraceptive or regulatory measure. 'It's only because doctors and hospitals won't help that they come to people like me' was the general feeling.

(a) Abortion without Birth Control
MADELEINE SIMMS

Over the world as a whole abortion has long been recognized to be the most commonly used form of birth prevention. It is in only a handful of advanced western countries, where sophisticated methods of birth control are available, that abortion is no longer the dominant form of family limitation. Even Britain with its comparatively long history of scientific birth control has still a long way to go before it can regard its own abortion problem as satisfactorily solved. Each year over 80,000 women end up in the emergency wards of National Health Service Hospitals suffering from the after-effects of abortion. Many of them are there as a result of complications after natural miscarriage, but many are there as a consequence of resorting in desperation to the unskilled abortionist. In the big city hospitals the proportion of such patients is high, as is the cost to the community of restoring them to health. It is estimated that for each patient who has to seek hospital treatment for the after-effects of amateur attempts at abortion, at least three others have also resorted to illegal operations but been lucky and needed no after-care. These figures are a direct reflection of the prevailing ignorance of modern methods of birth control that still exists in our society.

The Abortion Act of 1967 may be seen as an attempt to persuade women to abandon their traditional reliance on the back-street operator and to come forward and discuss their problems with their doctors. The act makes abortion legal not only where the patient's mental or physical health is at stake, but also where the child is likely to be born deformed, and where the health of the existing children of the family may be seriously affected by the mother's further pregnancy. For the first time too doctors may take into account the woman's 'actual or reasonably foreseeable environment' when arriving at their decision.

Before the Abortion Act private abortions did not have to be officially notified, so it is not known how many took place. In the first two years after the act, 100,000 legal abortions were performed, three fifths of them in NHS hospitals and the remainder in private nursing homes approved by the Department of Health. A reduction in abortion deaths and abortion emergencies in some areas suggests that the number of criminal abortions may now be declining. The first signs are therefore that the more liberal law is transferring increasing numbers of abortion cases from the back-streets to the hospitals.

(b) *Reflections of an Abortionist*

C. H.

EARLY LIFE

Going back to when I was just a girl, we lived in what was then the slums of Reading, in a three-roomed house; one room for meals and two to sleep. My mother had eleven children, nine are still living, six girls and three boys. All we could get in the bedroom was a full size bed, so we had to sleep top and bottom. When I think back, I think of what a life my mother had. She worked hard all her life to help keep us all, but in those days people were so ignorant, they all had big families. Although there was little money to live on we were kept clean and tidy; we were never taught anything about sex even in my younger days; what we know today, we had to learn as we went along, to talk about such things in the home in front of us children was like a crime in those days, so we knew nothing. We were taught right from wrong, and never to use bad language, and, believe me, living where we did we heard plenty of that – but it was drummed into us never to repeat what we heard.

A NEW HOUSE

I lived there until I was thirteen years old, then we were given a new house. I shall never forget going to bed the first night in that new house and waking up, and seeing such a white ceiling; I thought I was looking at the sky. Funny how you think back in life.

My mother died at the age of sixty-eight, worn out with hard work and all of us children, such a sweet gentle mother as anyone could wish to have; never all my life have I heard one bad word or talk about anyone. What wouldn't I give to have her with us today, and see all the comforts of home life we are able to have today. (I'm sure lots of people who may read this will think the same.) At the age of eighteen I was engaged to be married but as ignorant as ever, like I've said.

ENGAGED AND IGNORANT

We were never taught about sex, but it was always drummed into all of us children never do any harm to anyone. If you can't do anyone a good turn, don't do them a bad one – that's one thing I've lived up to. I've always tried to help people in any way I could. I'm soft-hearted, I hate to see anyone in need of help; I wish at times I wasn't like this, but people can't help the way they're born. I was nearly nineteen years old when I got married. My husband was in the regular army, my allowance was twenty-eight shillings per week. I was living with one of my sisters then, as he only came home week-ends; I kept at work to have a bit of money ready for such time as I got a house. My first child was expected; this I wanted very much. I was working in a laundry ironing all day, it was sevenpence halfpenny per hour in those days, and it was piece work, and we had to work to earn any sort of wages then, but I was expecting a baby, I wanted everything nice for it, so I didn't mind hard work.

STILLBIRTH

My first child was born on the first of August 1935, it was stillborn, I was three days in labour and it was a breech birth. All this took place at my sister's home, we never had the antenatal care and attention they have today, just a midwife and someone to help look after you; my husband was given leave to do that, but he didn't want to be with me; he was at the pub while all this was going on. My mother was with me, so she was sent to fetch him as I was having such a bad time, but all he done was send a small brandy up to see if that could help, and the smell of it made me sick. However, I got over it, and started back to work again. It wasn't long before I was expecting again; this one was due the following year, September 5th 1936, so I got my first council house. I can remember how proud of it I was. I'd managed to buy what was needed downstairs, but the bedroom furniture had to be HP so my allowance being twenty-eight shillings that was ten shillings and eightpence rent and ten shillings HP, so I had to keep at work as long as I could to be able to live. I done everything in that house myself, even to laying of floors, my husband was hopeless in regards to doing anything about the house or garden, which made it very hard for me. I can remember the time I had to mend punctures in my bike which I used to get to and from work, when he couldn't or didn't want to do it. Now with this child I'm expecting I kept under my doctor all the way. I didn't want to go all through that again for nothing, and I must say I was dreading the thought of going through it, after the first. But when it did arrive, I was surprised, it was all over in two hours. It was a ten-pound baby girl.

THE FIRST BABY

I can picture her now as I write this. Today she is married and has three children, and has never caused me any worry at any time; I'm proud of her and her children. Anyhow when she was only a few weeks old I had to put her on the bottle and go out to work again. A neighbour of mine looked after her at seven shillings and sixpence a week. My husband was coming out of the army by this time, but I remember thinking at the time, what sort of job is he going to get, as I knew by now he wasn't one for any real hard work – all he had done was nursing. So he got a job at first aid treatment in our local factory, but that didn't last long, he left me and the baby to go up to his home to get work and by this time I was expecting another child, and worried to death how was I going to keep them, with him so unreliable and me not being able to keep at work. He was away for five weeks and I never had a penny piece from him. He did write to say he had his keep to pay. I suppose it didn't matter to him how I and the baby was. I can remember the times I rode three and a half miles to work and back again with nothing to eat all day, yet I wouldn't let people see I was in that state. What money I earned I had to pay out; I hardly had anything left to buy any food, not even a penny for the gas. I suppose I could have got help, but my pride wouldn't let me beg.

MOVING HOUSE

However, I got a letter telling me he had somewhere for us to live, so 'pack up and come'. A van picked my home up, and I had to travel from the south to the Midlands in the back of the van with my baby and seven months gone with my next, as I had no money to do otherwise; on the way they stopped at a café, I had nothing so didn't make any attempt to move, but they brought me a tea and a cake also the baby some hot milk, I felt so grateful I was choked. We got to this house at about seven in the evening, so I've been travelling all day long.

The two men unload my furniture in the two rooms he'd got me; my husband was not there to help us in, and by the time he got in, I've got the most of it put straight but believe me it broke my heart to think of the house I had to give up, and he had brought me to this; he couldn't have cared less. I thought at the time if only one could put the clock back, I think I would have thought twice of doing what I had. All he thought about was pubs, and the old lady who owned the house made it clear she wasn't having her front door open after ten at night, so many a time I've had to go and get him out of pubs to keep the peace.

THE SECOND BABY

On February 4th 1938 I had my next child. I was up and out of bed the next day of having my baby, so as to get my room clean and tidy ready for the nurse, and even when he came in lunch times he expected me to have some food ready for him. When I look back on my life, what a fool some of us women are. This was the beginning of my marriage breaking up, I could not go on like it. However, he gets fed up with work so in seven months he goes back into the army again, so I'm left on my own; I ran around looking for a better place than the two rooms I was in and get a little four-roomed house at eight and six a week. Now I soon got to work and made it look nice and I also had a little garden at the back for the two babies. But this wasn't to be for long; he sent for me to join him again.

IN AND OUT OF THE ARMY

I left most of my home with his people as I could not afford to bring it all the way south again so that was good-bye to all I had worked hard for. I just packed all I could in the pram and travelled by train – this time to Aldershot. There I kept house for a man and small son, doing cooking, etc., so we lived rent free. This wasn't for long. My husband was sent abroad, so I packed again and went back where I started from, with my sister; by this time I think I had been through it enough, but I was thinking while he's away there'll be no more children to worry about.

So I start work again. At times I was at work from seven-thirty in the morning till nine at night. We had our breaks in between, and I didn't mind. Work never worried me no matter how hard it was. It was to keep me and my children so why should I worry; I kept them fed well and dressed them nice, that I was proud of. Now I'm just going to get back on my feet again, and he was away so you can guess how I felt when I discovered I was left expecting another child.

UNWANTED PREGNANCY

I was at the end of my tether. I still knew nothing, but I took everything but the chemist shop to try and get rid of it as I didn't want it or my husband. I had turned right against him. He was supposed to think such a lot of me. I thought then, what a way of showing it. He must have known, as I hardly ever wrote. Some men don't care what us women are going through as long as they haven't got the worry, and when they're abroad they enjoy themselves. I've been there myself and seen it happen so I know what I'm talking about. Still, I'm broad-minded, what the eye don't see the heart don't grieve for; but let them hear the wife has been doing the same. . . . But by now I'm fed up with everything so I start going out to get away from it all.

GETTING AWAY FROM IT ALL

This is where I get introduced to what now is my second husband. I didn't think so at the time, as I was married with two small children and another on the way. He was a single man, two years older than myself, so to me that was too much for any man to take on. But even when he found out I was in hospital with my third child, he couldn't do enough for me. I'd never had that treatment from my husband. I remember when this happened I thought whatever did I marry my husband for; it wasn't for true love. I'd never felt the way I did for him like I do for my second.

SECOND FAMILY

So we make up our minds we were going to make a go of it. What a difference, he was everything the other one wasn't; hard working, able to put his hands to everything, always willing to do anything in the house, help bath the babies, take them for walks. I just couldn't believe it, as he was a single man, and he had never had to do this sort of thing in his life. But although we were what some people call living in sin we were so happy. The only dread I had was children. I fell very quickly and I had three more by him; so now I was thirty-two years old and had seven children.

FAMILY OF SEVEN CHILDREN

I made up my mind that I wasn't going to have any more. At this time I had heard about abortion, so when I became pregnant again, I went and had an illegal operation. Why all the fuss about this, I do not know; it was nothing. I'd go through it over and over again, sooner than have any more children which I could not afford. It's all right for people with money; it's always been a law for the rich and a law for the poor. We all know this is going on all over the world, people with money just hop on a plane and go and have this done where it is legal and nothing is ever heard of it; but can any working-class woman do this? No, because they haven't the money – she's lucky to be able to hop on a bus let alone a plane. I know how desperate women get, I've been through it all myself. And believe me, the person who helped me was like an angel sent from heaven. It cost me nothing because I had nothing, but if I had, I could never have paid enough I was so grateful; I still am to this day. I knew it was against the law to do this. I also knew that the person who was helping me was taking a risk, but if I had been dying no one would have got anything from me. I took that risk, so it's up to me. It's my life, I can do what I like with it. I don't think there's a law about that.

BIRTH CONTROL OR ABORTION?

Well once I had this done, I could do it myself; had it not been so I could have finished up with another seven. Don't think that because I didn't want any more children I hated them. No one could love them like I do. I've got eight grandchildren and I've all of them round me. I brought my eldest grandchild up from fourteen months old till she was eight, and I've had another four living here with me. I could never hurt a child. When I see some poor little children, I can tell at a glance if it's from a large family. My heart aches for them; it never ought to be, though I don't think a marriage is a marriage without children; I also don't think one child is fair as it's inclined to be so lonely, but as things are today, two are plenty to keep in any working-class family. If they keep having children, what chance or hope of getting on have they got?

THE START OF TROUBLE

Now I'll tell you how all my trouble started; I helped a friend, and that one told another. Being soft-hearted, I took pity on her too as she was single and the one responsible didn't want to marry her. I explained what she would have to do, she tried, but just couldn't do it. So like a friend I helped her and everything was OK, then she told a friend of hers how easy it all seemed and that led to me again; it cost them nothing, as they were like me, had a family to keep and had to go to work to help.

In 1946 I went to Germany, so there, meeting new friends, and all women together, all married of course, it was just a matter of conversation, that I knew I wouldn't have any more to my family, and mine the biggest in our quarters. I was soon to be of help again. Again everything was OK with no trouble – that was always on my mind. When I helped anyone, I hardly slept thinking about what could happen; but the next morning, my first thing was to call in to see whoever it was, and what a relief to see them up and about full of the joys of spring to think they were OK again. They couldn't thank me enough. It didn't matter who it was in any of our married quarters, if anyone was hurt or wanted help, it was always me they would come to, so I made lots of good friends over there.

BACK TO ENGLAND

In 1951 we returned to England again, at first in Hull – I went to work, then to Woolwich – I was working in the Woolwich Arsenal then, and from there back to my home town again – I went to live with my brother and his wife. It was only a three-bedroom house, so you can guess what a house full it was. My two eldest went to their grandmother, which left me with the four youngest, so I went out to work again. Now I was helping my sister-in-law out; she had three, and had lost two, so she didn't want any more, and she never had no more; her children are grown up and all out at work now, but she has always said that she has only me to thank for that.

That's how it went on, one telling another, and believe me its frightening at times the amount of people that get to know. You have people coming from London, and you know what a lot of this goes on up there; but I think it must have been that it cost money and I was doing it to help and not for gain; but looking back at what I've been through, it isn't worth it. For doing what I call a good turn I got nine months in prison.

HOLLOWAY PRISON

When I went to Holloway – what a grim looking place – I was told by my escort on the way there never to let the women know what I was in for as I would be pestered by them. But not to worry, the publicity and name and address in the papers was an advert on its own; she also said, 'the six months you're in here you will learn more than you have done in a lifetime'. How right she was. For anyone who would want to listen to such talk, it is an ideal place for corruption, and some of the language you hear, it sounds awful coming from women, but I wasn't there long.

I went to an open prison, much cleaner and more open; it is just boredom that gets you down, same old thing to do day in and day out. I think the ones you have left behind suffer more. I worked in the laundry all day ironing; we got two shillings and elevenpence a week, but if you get on and cause no trouble you keep getting threepence or sixpence rise, so I soon was on more pay. I've never smoked in my life, so that never worried me, so I did six months.

'IT SPREADS LIKE A DISEASE'

I came home and went back to work again; now if I was a woman who wanted easy living and easy money, I would never have to go to work. Since I've been home I can't keep count of the number of women that have tried to get in touch with me for help, I don't know them, but through the papers and for just helping out once, word spreads like some disease. So why don't this law do something and do it quick, then people like myself would never be bothered. I'm happy to go to work, I got a good job, so why do I want to worry about other people. and their troubles? At first I felt so ashamed of being in prison, I never went out much, but I made up my mind to get a job and forget; this I did. I had a good job and good money, but it wasn't long before I was being asked for help again, by people I never knew, but they soon got to know about me and where I worked, and even waited outside the works for me to go home.

MORE TROUBLE

I made a promise I'd never go through that again, but I've lost count of the number of people that stopped me to see if I would help them. Now I've said, I never wanted to do this, but I got asked by my close friend to help a friend of hers out. I said to her at the time she asked, did she realize what would happen to me if I was caught doing this again? She was so certain nothing would be said; this was a married woman, having an affair with another man; they didn't want anyone to find out about it. So, soft-hearted again, I said alright just this once. I heard from my friend everything was alright – never gave it another thought. Then six months after, I got five police at my home – would I go with them for questioning. I just couldn't think what it was all about. My husband was more shocked than I; he was certain that it was a mistake. And when I told him what I had done he just could not believe it. 'You must want your head seen to,' he told me. I thought it would have been the end for him, but he stood by me, and all my children were a great comfort to me.

THE FUTURE

I've been given a chance this time with three years probation; so I've left home now and am working away, doing season work. In October I shall return and by then hope to get things sorted out; whether to stop or move to start afresh. It will only be my husband and I, and I couldn't go through any more of that worry. I know I've made lots of friends, and all I've got out of this is the joy of seeing people happy and free from worry, but it's caused me plenty – my life nearly. All I want now is peace of mind and no more worry, and my advice to anyone else is never get mixed up in this, it's not worth it.

(c) *Attitudes of Women Abortionists*

MOYA WOODSIDE

From time immemorial women have tried to control their own fertility and avoid the conception or birth of unwanted children. Abortifacient practices, ranging from magic to drugs, starvation and physical violence, existed in all primitive societies; throughout the centuries, almost every known poison and every conceivable type of instrument has been employed. Women whose own attempts failed sought help from others believed to be skilled, undeterred in their desperation by risks to health and life, or by the heavy punishment attendant on discovery. No one knows how many millions of pregnancies have thus been terminated; the number of illegal abortions which come to light is but a fraction of the total incidence. Hospitals and general practitioners see some but not all of the women who require treatment after the interference with pregnancy; police and coroners see those who die; the great majority who suffer no immediate ill-effects never come to the notice of the authorities. In the past, abortion attracted severe and savage penalties. The act of George III, 1803, made abortion a felony, punishable by death if the woman were 'quick with child'.

'Abortion' is an emotive word, arousing deep feelings and strongly-held opinions even among those whose profession – law, medicine, psychiatry, social work – brings them into responsible contact with the problem. It is understandable that the sordid and often tragic evidence heard in those cases which reach the courts and the coroner should provoke detestation for the offence and its practitioners. But the extent of clandestine abortion among women, particularly working-class women, is such as to suggest that legal and moral sanctions are not effectively accepted on this social level. Here lies a field, still unexplored, for sociological inquiry. The opportunity was therefore taken of interviewing a series of convicted women abortionists in prison, and asking them to tell their stories. What they said, and the police report on each case, provided the material for this present study.

WHAT CAME INTO THE NET

The investigation started at Holloway Prison in October 1959 and was completed in April 1962 when 44 women had been interviewed.

As the investigation proceeded it became clear that abortion was an offence of older married women. The sample contained no single women: everyone was or had been married (25 married, 11 widowed, 5 separated, 3 divorced). All but 3 had children, 13 had grandchildren (1 had 10, another 17), one had great-grandchildren. Only 3 were aged between 25 and 29, 10 between 30 and 39, 9 were between 40 and 49, 5 between 50 and 59, and the greatest number, 14, were between 60 and 69. Even threescore and ten did not halt the activity: 2 women were over 70 and 1 was over 80. It was unexpected to find grandmothers making such a large contribution to crime.

Less than half were in paid employment at the time of their coming to prison. Twenty-three were housewives at home (this included the pensioners and elderly women partly supported by their children). Ten were doing domestic work of one kind or another (5 as cleaners), 2 worked in factories and 2 were assistant nurses in hospital. The other miscellaneous occupations listed were all of a semi-skilled nature, e.g. saleswoman, dressmaker.

Sixty-five per cent of the women came into the Registrar General social class 3; this marked excess is interesting, because it does not accord with a previous survey of Holloway's prison population where almost fifty per cent were in social class 3.

Eighteen of the women had been born in London, 15 elsewhere in England. Wales and Scotland contributed 3 and 2 respectively. Five were foreign born, including 2 from Cyprus; 1 was born in India of British parents. Thirty-three, or three quarters, gave their religious persuasion as Church of England; 5 were Roman Catholic (2 foreign born), 3 Nonconformist, 1 each of Greek Orthodox and Moslem. One who was listed as 'no religion' said she was 'studying to be a Jehovah's Witness'. At the time of their arrest 26 were living in London and the suburbs, 8 in the Home Counties and 10 elsewhere in England.

On admission to Holloway after conviction, 19 of the women took part in the routine group psychological test (Raven's Standard Progressive Matrices, 1956 version).

The grading classed 10 as 'average', 8 as 'very dull', 5 as 'dull', 4 as 'superior' and 2 as 'very superior'.

It was considered that the large proportion in the 'very dull' category reflected the blunting and deterioration due to age (2 of these subjects were over 60 and 3 over 65).

COURTS AND SENTENCES

The majority had been tried at the Central Criminal Court (25 cases). Thirteen had been tried at assize courts in the south of England, 6 in the north of England. The distribution of sentences among the sample varied from 2 months to 4 years; the majority were given between 9 and 18 months.

This accords with the general disposition of sentencing for this offence: during the two years 1960 and 1961, 31 of the 41 women sent to prison for abortion had sentences between 6 months and 2 years.

It might have been expected that the nine cases of manslaughter would have incurred the heaviest sentences, but in fact this was not so. Analysis of this subgroup showed that two received 12 months, three 18 months, three 2 years and one 3 years. In a tenth case, although a death had occurred (2 days later in hospital), the charge was still 'procuring miscarriage' and the sentence 9 months. Of the 3 women who received 4-year sentences, 2 had been in prison before for a similar offence (or offences); the third was a foreign-born midwife who was suspected of running an extensive and dangerous abortion practice.

Abortion tends to be a first-time-in-prison offence: 23 or just over half the sample had no previous convictions. They were mainly working- or lower-middle-class women who had never been in trouble before. Of the 21 who had previous convictions, 9 were for abortion; the other 12 recidivists had a miscellaneous and occasionally multiple record of larceny (8 charges), soliciting (4), brothel-keeping (3), drunkenness and false pretences.

METHODS AND CLIENTELE

According to a leading forensic expert, abortionists can be broadly divided into three classes: the medically qualified, the semi-skilled (which includes nurses, chemists and others having medical knowledge), and the unskilled. The sample contained 17 women who admitted some nursing or midwifery experience. Three had been state-enrolled nurses, 2 (both over 65) had been uncertified midwives years ago, 2 from Cyprus said they had worked there as midwives' assistants. Only 1, born and trained in Poland, was a fully qualified midwife. The 9 others spoke of 'helping doctors' or nurses on maternity cases, of first-aid or VAD training or an uncompleted probationary period in hospital. The majority of the sample (27) were in the third or 'unskilled' class.

The operation had been successful in 24 out of the 43 cases (2 women were charged on 1 case). In 5 it was unsuccessful; in 4 no operation took place due to the arrival of the police on the scene. There were 10 deaths. Discovery in non-fatal cases arose from the girl or woman being admitted to hospital (13), or a doctor being called (4). In other cases discovery was attributed to being informed on, anonymous letters, 'spite', gossip and revenge (action sometimes initiated, it was alleged, by women the abortionists had refused to help). An alleged plant by women police officers came in for scornful denunciation in 3 cases (this was felt to be very 'unfair'). These results, weighted by mortality or illness which led to discovery, give a misleading picture of the skill and success of the abortionists in the sample. At interview many revealed extensive previous experience and claimed that none of their clients had ever come to harm.

The method most commonly employed was the Higginson's syringe (35 cases). This accords with the findings of a medico-legal survey reported by Teare. Soap and water were used often with Dettol or other disinfectant added. A catheter was used in 4 cases – all by women who had some nursing experience. Surgical instruments, unspecified, were used in 1 case; in 2 others the syringe had been supplemented respectively by a crochet hook and taking quinine. Steel pills and pennyroyal were said to have been provided by one abortionist. There was no mention of slippery elm or knitting needles, nor of other drugs such as ergot believed to possess abortifacient properties.

Exact information about the age of the abortee was not always obtainable. Quite often the woman did not know herself, or had been misinformed in the attempt to enlist her services, when young girls pretended to be older than they were. Fifteen clients were under 20 (this group included 1 girl of 14, 3 of 15, 2 of 16 and 1 of 17); 10 were between 20 and 30, 6 between 30 and 35. In the remainder (12) the age was not stated or not known. Similar difficulty was encountered over marital status: in 10 cases it could not be ascertained. Twenty-two of the abortees were known to be single, 8 were married and 3 married, separated and cohabiting (the 11 married or cohabiting women all had children already). In 8 cases coloured men had been involved (all the abortionists except one half-caste were white). Length of pregnancy too was often unknown. Except when there had been a hospital or post-mortem report, information was incomplete and sometimes speculative (as will be seen later, deception by abortees was a frequent occurrence). Reliable figures, available in 27 cases, were as follows: 2 months or less, 6; 2½ months, 3; 3 months, 6; 4 months, 9; 4½ months, 2; 5 months, 1. Those whose pregnancy was furthest advanced ran the greatest risks: 8 of the 10 deaths took place among women who were 4 months or longer pregnant.

These then were the bare bones of 43 trials and convictions for criminal abortion. To understand the social background which nourished the offence, and the motives both of those who seek and those who perform the operation, we must turn to the personal stories of the abortionists themselves.

HOW THEY BEGAN

The amount of information obtained at interview varied in relation to the mood and personality of each individual woman. One or two were taciturn and suspicious; three of the foreign-born did not speak enough English to cooperate fully; but the majority, once assured of confidence, poured out their story in uninhibited detail. It was important to see the woman soon after her arrival in prison, while events were still vivid and emotion easy to recall. Those who had already been in prison for a number of months before they were interviewed (as happened at the start of the inquiry) were less interested and might have 'forgotten' what they knew. Police reports gave the facts in each case; they were occasionally supplemented by a personal discussion with the CID officer involved. In some cases it was possible to attend part of the court proceedings.

All the subjects were asked how they learnt what to do, and when they first 'helped' someone else. As the interviews progressed, it was discovered that the Higginson's syringe or enema (employed in 37 of the 43) is a customary possession in working-class homes. Women use it for personal cleanliness, and as a contraceptive measure after intercourse. 'Douching' is also widely practised as a method of inducing miscarriage when pregnancy is feared to have started. This had been resorted to by many of the sample. 'I often use it on myself. My husband wouldn't allow me to use preventives' (age 35). 'Sixty per cent of married women use the Higginson's syringe regular every month, just to be sure they bring the period on' (former SEN, age 37). 'I didn't see no harm in it; I used to syringe myself' (age 38). 'Most women do syringe theirselves if they go a week or a fortnight over, to see if they can bring it on themselves' (age 63). One informant of 65 said she has brought on 5 miscarriages this way. In the old days people didn't know about birth control, and her husband would never take precautions. 'Somebody did it to me once. Then I had the brains to pick it up' (age 45). One or two said that a nursing sister had told them what to do; others said that doctors had described or hinted what might be done.

The news that a woman was successful in aborting herself soon got around to friends and neighbours. Then came requests for help. 'This girl came,' said Mrs A. 'I tried it and all went well.' Some time after, she brought a cousin to be helped. Then friends spread the word around. 'The first one I ever done was a poor woman. She was married, had a big family, about 10 children. I did help a friend. Then the friend told others. My friend Margaret knew I had done it. She brought the girl to see me.' A woman of 61 said tearfully, 'I'll tell you from the beginning. Years ago, I used one (i.e. syringe) on myself.' She'd had six children and lost two. Her husband's brother's wife had 15 children – she was 'frightened' in case her lot would be the same. She aborted herself 'several times' in this way, had no trouble. She had never heard about birth-control clinics – 'not in those days' (this was about 30 years ago). Another informant, who 'did herself first' said her abortion career 'began through my husband'. Some woman he knew, a friend of his, had a child in a mental home, was desperate because of another pregnancy. Mrs B. 'helped her out' but took no money. Then she helped her husband's sisters. Someone else said she taught her daughters when they married what to do.

Those with nursing or midwifery experience were sought after and were often highly skilled. 'They came because they knew I was a nurse.' 'Washing people out is just ordinary nursing routine.' 'I've never had any trouble. I know what to do and how to do it. I'm not one of those "amateurs" [this woman said that doctors sent patients to her because they knew she was skilled and safe]. I've never had anything gone wrong with a person – no trouble whatever,' says Mrs C. age 81 years, who had started maternity nursing 50 years ago. She described her technique in detail, stressing how she was always 'very particular' about hygiene and cleanliness. It was obvious that some of these skilled operators (not all of them with nursing experience) had acquired a good knowledge of anatomy and considerable manual dexterity. Their accounts of the procedure, and the hazards (such as air embolism) to be avoided, could be paralleled in any forensic textbook.

Disasters did happen, nevertheless, but more often befell the inexperienced operators who were unaware of the risks.

WHY DID THEY DO IT?

Except in a few cases financial gain was not the main motive in these women's activities. Had large fees been the rule, it was unlikely that so many would have been living in the poor circumstances described in the police reports, nor was their clientele drawn from those who could afford to patronize 'West End' specialists.

There is no doubt that compassion and feminine solidarity were strongly motivating factors among women who had acquired this skill. They could share the feelings of the suppliant in her plight, or imagine how they would feel if it were their own teenage daughter or granddaughter who was 'in trouble'. Typical comments were: 'I was sorry for her.' 'It was really out of pity. I couldn't have turned that girl away from the door.' 'I did it out of kindness.' 'Friendship – Doreen was desperate.' 'In trouble – that's one word I can't shut my ears to. I took the mother's point of view. The way I look at it is: one mother trying to help another mother's daughter.' 'I let me heart rule me head and I douched her.' This sympathy for other members of their own sex made it difficult to resist importunate pleas, even when they were reluctant to be involved or had decided not to 'help' any more.

WHAT SORT OF WOMEN DID THEY HELP?

Clients fell into three main groups: 'single girls'; married women with families who did not want another child; wives pregnant as a result of an extramarital affair while their husbands were absent abroad. The unmarried girls were often daughters of friends or acquaintances, 'in trouble' by teenage boy friends. Sometimes a married man was responsible for the pregnancy; in eight cases the man was coloured. American servicemen were in the picture more than once; their girls as described (and disapproved of) by the abortionists appeared to be of the 'camp-follower' type. Nurses had been helped; engaged girls who didn't want a rushed wedding; foreign girls *au pair* who feared deportation; girls who dared not tell their parents. Interviewees drew a strong moral line between 'decent girls' (who deserved help) and others who were 'bad'. They were unanimous in their denunciation of the younger generation and the deplorable behaviour of teenagers. 'These youngsters today,' says Mrs I., a sensible nursing assistant with a grown-up daughter of her own, who had 'helped' two girls of 17 and 18, one of them a student at the local technical college, 'they go drinking at a party, egg each other on, have sexual intercourse, think nothing of it.' And, of course, 'once you get engaged, everybody does it'. Mrs I. told how she made the girls bring their boy friends along and 'lectured' them both on their foolishness.

Married women, however, came in for commiseration and sympathy. Many of the older interviewees had known hard times and poverty when they were struggling to rear large unplanned families, perhaps with husbands who gambled and drank. They could understand the panic and dismay which an undesired pregnancy brought.

Married women were also preferred as clients because they were discreet and did not panic. 'I won't help single girls on principle,' says Mrs J., from Lancashire. 'They get you into trouble. They talk. Boast about it (especially when they've had a drink or two). Married women are so grateful – they wouldn't say anything against you.'

The embarrassment of an extramarital pregnancy often brought clients to the abortionist: in these circumstances the help given was regarded as social service. 'I saved several homes during the war,' says a widow aged 63 who had had 6 children herself. They were wives with husbands overseas. 'Those women were grateful.' An informant from a naval station said she had helped married women whose husbands were at sea, who had become pregnant and did not want their marriages broken up. She feels that what she did was for good: 'I've saved so many homes. Prevented divorces.'

Interviewees had plenty to say on the subject of illegitimacy. Although they might disapprove of the character or behaviour of some unmarried girls who got 'into trouble' they felt they were justified in preventing the birth of an unwanted illegitimate child. There were many references to the unhappy fate of children in care. 'All those little babies – brought up in homes. Children nobody wants.' 'Look at all those homes full of unwanted children. No mother's love.' 'All these illegitimate children – it's terrible. Unwanted...' 'Isn't it kinder to terminate a child's life at three weeks, than to bring them into the world to suffer cruelty?' asks one of the younger more intelligent interviewees, herself a mother of four. She referred to recent cases in her own town, where dead infants had been found on a rubbish dump, in the market place, and down a ladies' toilet. 'I don't believe in children with no fathers,' says another. 'The girls were very grateful after.'

At the request of a friend, one abortionist went to visit a girl she had never seen. When she arrived at the house, a man was there who introduced himself as the girl's husband. The abortionist was taken to a room which had a built-in bar in one corner and where the girl awaited her undressed. The man remained while the abortionist syringed the girl out, and left her sitting up on the sofa, all three having had cups of tea.

A 14-year-old girl, one of a family of 7, was pregnant by her father (the father was also charged with sexually assaulting another younger daughter and his two sons of 9 and 7). The girl's mother, herself in advanced pregnancy, asked her mother-in-law if she would try to bring on an abortion for J. The grandmother agreed to 'syringe the girl out' though she'd never done anything of the sort before. Her two attempts were unsuccessful. The girl, who was four months pregnant, was subsequently placed in a mother-and-baby home, and in due course gave birth to what the judge at the trial had termed 'this incestuous bastard'.

WHAT DO THEY FEEL ABOUT SENTENCE, AND THE POLICE?

Interviewees were baffled and annoyed by what seemed to them an inexplicable variation in sentences (these ranged from 2 months to 4 years). After coming to prison they compared notes with others who had arrived before them, and were especially aggrieved if those whose record was blacker received lesser sentences than their own. 'How unfair it is,' exclaims Mrs N., referring to Mrs O., who had been committed on two charges following discovery through one of her clients having to go into hospital. 'She only got two months, I get eighteen – and I've never had any trouble with any of my girls.' Mrs P., who appealed against her sentence of three years and had her appeal dismissed, says she feels 'very bitter'.

HOW DO THEY SEE THEMSELVES?

It is only natural that convicted prisoners should try to present themselves in the best possible light. Guilt may be denied or partially denied; trials deemed unfair because favourable points had not been brought out; mercenary motives played down and other virtues extolled. With experience the interviewer learns to steer a course between cynicism ('they tell you nothing but lies') and acceptant naïvetée, guided by the reported facts and personal assessment of the interviewee. Among this group of 44 women there were a few, perhaps 6 or 8, whose statements were suspect and whose manner was less than frank; the great majority told their story without hesitation and often with tears of relief. These were not hardened offenders from a criminal milieu (23 had no previous convictions) and their committal to prison came as a shock. Many were at pains to emphasize their respectability (in contrast to those with whom they were now forced to associate), or to demonstrate that the offence had not made them a social outcast. 'Since the trouble, I never knew I had so many friends,' says Mrs. S. She had had 'lovely letters', even from people in the local shops.

'I knew it was against the law, but I didn't think it was wrong' – thus in words of one syllable these unlettered women made their own distinction between crime and sin. There was no mistaking the sincerity with which these feelings were held; they found expression over and over again in comment such as the following: 'I'm not ashamed of what I've done, even though it's against the law. It's human nature, and women have to help each other.' 'I know it was wrong and against the law, but in my heart of hearts I don't feel I committed a crime.' 'It'll be a good job when they make it legal.' 'It seems to me tragic that the law isn't changed.' 'I reckon there ought to be a law, so that doctors can help.' 'I definitely think it should be made lawful.' 'It's only because doctors and hospitals won't help that they come to people like me.' 'If a woman feels she doesn't want any more, I don't see any wrong in it.' 'Doctors should do it. Give them the right to do it.' 'Girls should be able to go to a proper clinical place and have their cases heard properly. Then they could be done by a doctor in hospital without anything underhand.'

It was frequently stated that abortion was more easily obtained by those who could afford to pay ('it's one law for the rich and another for the poor'). Interviewees saw this as an added injustice, since their activities had been confined to those who were not in a position to enlist discreet but expensive medical help. 'These lords and ladies – they can go away and have it done privately. But a working-class woman – what can she do?'

(IV) DOMICILIARY FAMILY PLANNING

Families whose need of birth-control services is greatest are often unable to get to a clinic. To help these families several projects have been tried. All aim at making advice and support more easily available and acceptable.

Dr Mary Peberdy in Newcastle,[5] Dr Dorothy Morgan in Southampton[6] and Dr Shelia Dronfield in York[7] have all pioneered

5. M. Peberdy, *Medical Officer*, 16 April 1965.
6. R. Brittain, *Family Planning*, October 1964.
7. S. Dronfield, *ibid.*, October 1967.

'domiciliary' services, which with the cooperation of the local health authority take family planning into the homes of people who need family planning but cannot manage to get to a clinic.

In London the boroughs of Camden and Westminster have, with the support of the Marie Stopes Memorial Fund, a domiciliary service which has 300 families on its books;[8] the borough of Newham has a similar scheme, with a case-load of about 100 families a year, and support from a charity and an anonymous donor. Other projects have been started in a number of boroughs where the local health authority cooperate with the local FPA branch in ferrying services in which patients are collected from their homes and taken to and from clinics.

The City Parochial Fund has made a gift of £9,000 to be spent by the FPA over three years for schemes in the London area, with a view to starting a service and handing it over to the local authority when it is adopted as part of the local health service.[9] The schemes in Southampton and York have already been so adopted, partly on humanitarian grounds and partly because it is cheaper to prevent unwanted births than to support unwanted children.[10] Another service for patients who cannot or do not come to ordinary clinics is provided for women at Holloway Prison and for wives and their husbands at the Intermediate Reception Centre for the homeless at Plumstead in London.

When the FPA, through its own resources, shows the local need and local benefits, the local authorities gradually accept the need and take responsibility for meeting it, using the FPA as their agent.

(a) One Foot in the Door

RENÉE BRITTAIN

From 1958 to 1961 Dr Dorothy Morgan, working in close cooperation with the Southampton Medical Officer of Health, visited problem families living in temporary hostels provided by the welfare authority. Physically handicapped, mentally incapable, socially maladjusted, or simply over-burdened by the difficulties of everyday life, these fecund and distressed families who stood in the greatest need of birth-control advice

8. F. Solano, *ibid.*, July 1967.
9. E. Mitchell, *ibid.*, January 1967.
10. P. S. Florence, *Commonwealth Digest*, December 1964.

simply could not attend a clinic; advice, supplies and support had to be *brought to them*.

By 1961 Dr Morgan had planned a survey, extending over two years, with two slightly different groups of families. She wished to assess the relative success in introducing birth control to both groups and to see if any improvement in their social adjustment would take place if they were relieved of the burdens of uncontrolled childbearing. She also hoped to find a similar number of families in roughly comparable circumstances who would refuse birth control, in order to obtain some statistical comparisons, but it proved impossible to find such families.

Supported by a grant of £1,000 a year from the Marie Stopes Memorial Fund, generous help with supplies from the manufacturers of contraceptives, constant backing of the Southampton Medical Officer of Health, who also made office space and secretarial help available, and the cooperation of the Southampton Borough Council, a consultant gynaecologist, all the GPs in the area, a nursing sister and a number of devoted helpers, the project was planned to last for two years. It opened in June 1961; by June 1963 there was still a little money in hand and with an additional £500 from the Marie Stopes Fund it was possible to continue until March 1964 when the project was financially adopted by the Southampton Borough Council.

THE FAMILIES

Fifty-five problem families were collected, referred by health visitors and other social case-workers. The families, living in hostels or 'problem' housing, presented the full range of difficulties which we have come to associate with the term 'problem families'. The second group of fifty-five 'pre-problem families' were those known to be chronically in minor difficulties who just managed to keep their heads above water until a crisis. This could tip them over into the 'problem' group, to face eviction, the taking of the children into care, or even prison sentences. A further pregnancy resulting perhaps in the mother's illness might prove to be just such a crisis.

How Easy Was It to Get In Touch with these Families?

Referrals came thick and fast since they were well known to the social case-workers in Southampton, but Dr Morgan's first problem was the initial resistance to any hint of officialdom. Since about twenty-five per cent of problem families and seven per cent of pre-problem families had experienced at least one prison sentence in the family and about seventy-five per cent and fifty per cent respectively had received National Assistance, these families might be regarded as hardcore resisters to the slightest suggestion of rehabilitation foisted upon them from above. Indeed many of the early visits were made in vain since the families assumed that their unknown visitor was bound to be unwelcome – a rent or debt collector – and refused to open the door. Dr Morgan overcame this problem by sending postcards in advance and by stopping by to chat with the woman whom she wished to contact, and with her neighbours, but without discussing birth control at all: bit by bit and with tremendous patience she would build up a *rapport* as a result of which the prospective patient in time *asked* for advice; not until then could there be any good chance of the family's adopting contraception. At this point a joint visit to both husband and wife was arranged whenever possible. The men often put up stiff resistance to this interview but it turned out to be a crucial part of the treatment, partly because of the high incidence of marital difficulties among these families, who were often psychologically as well as materially impoverished.

How intelligent were these families? How easy was it going to be to teach them methods of birth control? No intelligence test was suitable but Dr Morgan assessed each separate patient by careful simple questioning, on the way they ran their everyday lives, their backgrounds and their social and economic difficulties.

Roughly five doctor-visits in five weeks were needed before the fitting of the wife could be completed. It was hoped that thereafter about one visit a month for six months, then one visit every three months would give support for the families but in many cases this was not enough. Much of the subsequent visiting was carried out by the nursing sister and by the two men social workers who did most of the work among families which accepted sheaths rather than female contraceptives, but often Dr Morgan had to visit regularly (even as frequently as every week in unbroken succession) in order to maintain the really difficult families. These visits were made to what is politely termed 'sub-standard' housing, in shocking tenement blocks with poor sanitary conveniences, to families at the lowest level of subsistence, some mentally sub-normal, many ill, and all social misfits, whose children were already known to the health visitors, care committees, magistrates, NSPCC, probation officers and other social agencies. The visits were made by busy specialists working only part-time with these 110 families.

The Other Side of the Door

A couple of vignettes may convey what bare figures cannot – the sadness, elation and drama of the actual work.

First, a family which from the standpoint of contraceptive success rates low. Mr and Mrs A. were a charming, blarneying couple of fairly good intelligence. He worked only to avoid prison, which he had already sampled, but otherwise remained on National Assistance. Of their six children the four eldest had been through all forms of care and by 1963 had all been to approved schools; when at home the children were totally neglected but as soon as one was taken into care the parents strove vigorously to have him back home, only to neglect him again on his return. Long discussions about contraception resulted in rejection of sheaths – 'we couldn't possibly let those things come between us'; finally they agreed to use the pill and Dr Morgan encouraged them by weekly visits. But Dr Morgan had to take a holiday, and on returning found that the wife had *not* taken her pills. The seventh child duly arrived and Dr Morgan's weekly visits continue.

In contrast, Mr and Mrs B. also with seven children, were in their forties, not so bright and very unhappy. Mrs B. in particular was extremely irritable and mistreated the children at the slightest provocation. On discussion with both partners, Dr Morgan discovered grave disharmony based on the grounds of Mrs B.'s frigidity. 'How can I stand it?' Mrs B. said. 'Every time I get into bed with him, I'm frightened there's going to be another baby.' She had no faith in sheaths and was not really teachable for a cap, but the oral contraceptive suited her splendidly. Proper sexual intercourse, release of tension, absence of frustration have not transformed Mrs B. into a model wife and mother, but they have produced a relaxed home atmosphere and Mrs B. has not produced any more babies.

RESULTS

Each of the original 110 families plus the thirty which have been added between March and July 1964 has its own miseries, failures and gains. None has so far climbed from its 'problem' position in society to make a real social adjustment, but every one has some degree of achievement. In no case did Dr Morgan fail to provide some form of birth control and to achieve some success in family limitation. This feeling of being able to win against odds has seemingly communicated itself to the Local Authority and has added human weight to the financial arguments in favour of continuing the work; in March 1964 the Southampton Borough Council assumed responsibility for the domiciliary service, employing Dr Morgan, the nursing sister and the two male social workers in part-time posts at a cost of about £900 per annum. They are the first council in Great Britain far-seeing enough to take this vital step in bringing help and treatment to problem families.

Comparative figures for the 55 problem families (PF) and 55 pre-problem families (PPF) over the two year periods June 1959–61 (pre-survey) and June 1961–63 (survey) are as follows:

Births	PF	PPF	Total
1959–61	73	70	143
1961–63	20	12	32
reduction	53	58	111

Naturally it is possible that these families would not have continued to bear children at their previous rates even if there had been no contraceptive service available, but it is unlikely that the reduction would have been as striking.

FINANCIAL COSTS: MONEY AND SERVICES

Ten shillings a week is paid for every child after the first. A reduction of 111 births over two years shows a saving to statutory funds of almost £3,000 in the second year; if an average reduction of about 55 children per annum be assumed, this shows a saving of a further £1,500 per annum in the future. One hundred and eleven fewer births reduces the £16 maternity grant by £1,760 or £880 per annum. Assuming half the 111 births had been home confinements, saving on the £6 allowance is £660 or £330 per annum. The saving for an assumed half of these births is about four to six hours per confinement, two visits daily for three days and one visit daily up to ten days.

The families do not willingly attend ante-natal clinics so that these 111 fewer births have saved approximately one monthly visit by the midwife up to the thirty-second week, and one fortnightly visit till term.

On the eleventh day visiting begins with two visits monthly up to three or four months of age, then visits at six, nine and twelve months, thereafter as necessary up to school entry. Phenstic test visit is made at six months. These are the minimum; in the families forming the survey weekly visits over much longer periods are far more common.

CONCLUSION

Domiciliary visits to the depressed sections of the community who cannot or will not come to a birth-control clinic are an auxiliary part of the service performed by family-planning clinics for the whole population. Enough has been demonstrated in this survey to prove that every local authority, the Ministry of Health and the National Assistance Board could save money by undertaking domiciliary services within the limits of local need. Many needy and inadequate couples are themselves products of broken and needy homes (thirty of the parents in the survey came from broken homes and forty-seven from homes with more than six children). The cost to the country in twenty-five years' time when a percentage of the 1960's babies are themselves needy parents must be borne in mind. Above all, the relief of human suffering and of damage to children cannot be measured merely in terms of money. I hope that Southampton's pioneer move will be matched by other authorities whose problem families can be helped in the same way.

(b) The Domiciliary Service

FRANCES SOLANO

When in 1964 I applied for the job of nurse to the Marie Stopes Domiciliary Birth Control Service, I had not given much thought to what the work would entail, and in fact I did not really know what Domiciliary Birth Control meant. I had not done any home nursing since before the war, and really believed that there was little poverty or real need for the service I was proposing to join.

THREE SCHEMES

This service was one of three projects financed by the Eugenics Society and the Marie Stopes Memorial Foundation. The first started in Newcastle in 1959 under the direction of Dr Mary Peberdy. It was followed in 1961 by the Southampton scheme under Dr Dorothy Morgan. The success of these services and their eventual financial take-over by the respective borough councils encouraged the Committee of The Marie Stopes Memorial Foundation to start this third scheme under its own direction.

The idea was discussed with Dr McGregor, the Senior Medical Officer of Health to the LCC, who readily agreed to support the scheme, suggesting that Division 2 with its densely populated areas, central position and nearness to the Clinic might be the place to start. Dr Oldershaw and Dr Patterson, Medical Officers of Health in the area, were approached, and they were also enthusiastic – in fact during the first year all the families referred were from Dr Patterson's field case conferences.

The service had been in operation for about eighteen months when I joined it. Dr Elizabeth Horder, a GP with FPA training, was the medical officer in charge and had worked single-handed, apart from clerical assistance from the clinic.

THIRTY FAMILIES IN ONE YEAR

During the first year, thirty families were taken into the scheme, but when it was decided that health visitors and social workers could refer patients direct to Dr Horder, the numbers increased to such an extent that it was necessary to employ a nurse to assist her and to do the follow-up visits.

Until this time the whole scheme had been directed from the Marie Stopes Clinic by an already overworked lay staff; with the increasing numbers of patients this was too much for them, so Mrs Peers, a member of the Committee, was appointed Organizing Secretary and took over the clerical work.

As the number of families entering the scheme continued to increase, a second doctor, Dr Fleury, was appointed early in 1965. So far over 300 families had been taken into the scheme.

We all three work part-time; the doctors are paid a set fee per visit plus expenses, and I am paid at a daily rate plus expenses. The nurse usually works one and a half days a week but sometimes it is necessary to work an extra day or so in a month.

NETWORK REFERRALS

The majority of cases are referred by health visitors and social workers; patients themselves sometimes tell us about friends or neighbours who need help. It is surprising, sometimes devastating, to find out how much is known about the scheme. Families are also occasionally referred by GPs and by local authorities and FPA doctors.

The procedure thereafter is always the same: after approval by the MOH all cases are recorded in a case register and case cards for each patient are prepared. These are then sent to the doctor – Dr Horder now sees all the patients living in the Camden area, and Dr Fleury those in Westminster.

This booking-in of patients and making out of case cards is one of the duties of the domiciliary nurse. We have found it most useful for one person to know what cases come in, and when, and which doctor is attending which patient, and the outcome of such visits. As I work as a nurse two days each week in the clinic, this clerical work can be fitted into any spare time I may have.

PROCEDURE

After receiving the case cards the doctor visits the patient as soon as she can. At this visit, the patient (who has been prepared for a visit by the health visitor or social worker) is examined, her medical and obstetric history is taken, and the various methods of contraception are discussed, with partners if possible, and they are encouraged to choose the method most suitable for themselves.

Nowadays the most popular and perhaps the most appropriate method seems to be the IUD, but at this first visit the doctor will give sheaths, chemicals and/or foaming tablets for immediate use.

When the scheme first started, North Kensington FPA Clinic was doing IUD trials and inserted the device free for many of the patients. Because so many patients failed to keep appointments the trials ended, and we therefore decided to put on a special domiciliary IUD session at the Marie Stopes clinic. Dr Malcolm Potts was appointed to take this session.

I make appointments for these patients, and arrange to transport them to and from the clinic. In this way these urgent cases never have to wait more than two weeks and there are very few missed appointments. At least four nurse-visits are needed for each IUD case, one to arrange the appointment and details of transport; another to bring the patient in; a third visit about a week later to see that all is well; and a fourth visit to check the device *in situ* about six weeks later. The patient only returns to the clinic if I feel that a further visit is necessary. She will be checked again about nine months later. If things do go wrong, the health visitor rings me at the clinic and I visit the patient again.

We have now inserted 180 IUDs: ten have been removed for various reasons, and five women have become pregnant.

BINGO AND PILLS

When the doctor, with the patient, decides that the pill will be the more suitable method, she may visit two or three times, or refer the patient straight to the nurse. This usually means that the nurse must make a weekly visit for at least six to eight weeks. It is amazing how muddled some people can become with a packet of pills. The pill packet is always checked at these visits and very often resembles a bingo card with the pills removed at random. Around the third month the patient is encouraged to go to her GP for a prescription for further supplies; this is lodged at the chemist and the pills purchased monthly. Even then the patients forget to buy the pills or have no money with which to buy them. So a record must be kept of starting and finishing dates so that at the eleventh hour a packet of pills can be delivered if necessary.

Not many domiciliary patients choose to use the cap or sheaths, and those who do invariably get fed up after a short while. These people are visited very frequently at first, and even later it is unwise to leave them more than three months because they run out of the chemical or mislay the cap. The highest pregnancy rate seems to come from the people using these methods.

All patients have a smear taken for cancer detection. If for one reason or another the doctor is unable to do this at her visit, the nurse takes the smear. Paddington General Hospital 'read' these for us without charge, and supply the slides, spatulas and boxes.

Pregnancy tests are taken into the clinic and done by the domiciliary nurse, using the Gravindex test – this has proved most reliable and speedy. If a patient does become pregnant the nurse advises the patient to visit an ante-natal clinic. A record is made of the expected date of delivery and a visit made to see if the pregnancy is continuing. Then as soon as possible after delivery we start all over again – visiting, fitting and encouraging.

There are many records to keep – one assumes a lot of responsibility for these people – they are so feckless and so much in need of our care. Is this a worthwhile job? I say *yes* emphatically. It is the best thing I've ever done.

APPALLING LIVING CONDITIONS

People still live in the most appalling conditions. The first family I ever visited lived in a tiny attic room. The husband was on night work and was in bed; three little boys romped around him as he slept; the mother sat on the bed feeding the baby where I joined her – there was nowhere else to sit. In that small room with the gas stove and all the impediments of daily living, the only play space for these children was the bed.

In one house seven rooms are let to separate families. There are thirty-three children and five pregnant mothers using one lavatory and one gas stove. One mother of thirty-four neglects and badly treats her fourteen children and is expecting a fifteenth child.

I know one rooming-house in which the gas stove, sink and lavatory are all in one tiny room – the pedestal is separated from the sink by a piece of cardboard.

FRUSTRATIONS

Of course the work can be frustrating. Most of these people go out to work and even if they don't, the home conditions are such that they spend as little time as possible there and are never in. It is often necessary to visit during the evenings or at week-ends, and one spends hours looking for a patient; but after a while an instinct develops for the places to look, the right time to visit, and the right number of knocks needed to bring the right person to the door.

It is an expensive service, although the patients are now paid for by the boroughs of Camden and Westminster. But the cost is outweighed by the benefits it brings to the families involved and money is saved in other ways – for instance hospital beds, child-care services, and places in schools.

We are only touching the fringe of the problem – but a journey of a thousand miles begins with a single step.

7
Education

Family Planning is not merely a question of technology. Efficient and safe methods of birth control now exist, but unwanted children are still conceived and there is still much ignorance and misery from lack of sex education. Teachers and even doctors may be ignorant – and inhibited. There is a need in all of us for a greater knowledge and understanding of matters relating to sex.

(I) EDUCATING THE EDUCATORS

THEODORE FOX

A community does not work well unless its laws are such as its citizens would freely accept if they worked them out from first principles. By this test the traditional code of sexual conduct is obsolescent; there is an increasing demand for a positive warm morality learnt through education without indoctrination. The best education is to live in a home made successful by parents who enjoy each other and their sexual relationship, in which a belief can develop that some things are right and others wrong in sexual conduct as elsewhere. The first task, whoever the educator, is 'to make youthful sex activities less harmful' and to make responsible parenthood possible and even agreeable.

My subject is the education of educators. Not the instruction of instructors nor the training of trainers; not the indoctrination of indoctrinators; not even the teaching of teachers. Education differs from instruction, training and the rest in that it aims at developing a person's capacity to decide for himself. Though even the best education contains some conditioning and indoctrination, the educator has a higher purpose than to make the new generation share his opinions and repeat his follies. He cannot expect agreement from everybody he teaches; so if we favour education, we must also (within limits) favour tolerance.

I do not suggest that education necessarily makes people happier than indoctrination: to live within a code of rules laid down by authority may be comfortable – so long as one can live within them. And of course every community must have laws governing everyday conduct and must get its citizens to obey them automatically. Even to run a bus service would be impossible if every passenger on every journey felt free to decide from first principles, whether he should pay a fare. But in the long run a community will not work well unless its laws are such as its citizens would freely accept if they did work them out from first principles.

By this test the traditional code of sexual conduct is obsolescent. Always it has been rejected by a substantial minority; but now this minority is becoming a majority – especially among the young. Obviously in so far as the traditional code rests on religion, it does not bind those who do not share the faith. But it is also unacceptable to many Christians because they believe that the organized Churches, in declaring that certain actions are invariably wrong, are misrepresenting the mind of Christ himself. The Churches' code of morals is inhibitory – its text 'Thou shalt not'. The English group who gave us *A Quaker View of Sex* think that instead of concentration on coldly negative codes, Christianity should be concerned with warm positive giving. 'We need,' they say, 'a much deeper morality, one that will enable people to find a constructive way through even the most difficult and unpredictable situations, a way that is not simply one of withdrawal and abnegation.[1]

I shall say more about this change from a negative to a positive morality achieved by education rather than indoctrination. But first let us consider the educators.

PARENTS

Though not a psychiatrist, I readily believe that the person who can do most to prepare a child for a healthy sexual life and a

[1]. Friends Home Service Committee, *Towards a Quaker view of Sex*, 1964.

happy marriage is its mother. And as Dr Sjovall[2] told us in 1965, the training of a good mother begins in her own childhood. But even if she was trained badly as a child, a woman's performance as a mother can still be improved by doctors and nurses and friends and magazines and books. The mistake too often made by those who try to educate her is that like the moralists they devise codes and systems for her to follow, whereas the most important thing is that amid all the artificiality and sophistication of civilized life, the relationship of mother to baby should be natural. I am sure that Sjovall is right in wanting the mother to have what he called a 'basic trust in bodily functions' and to transmit that trust – that acceptance – to her child. Most homes of course contain fathers as well as mothers; and a child's best preparation for marriage is to live in a home made successful by both parents. It is from the customs and attitudes of our early home that most of us derive our conscience.

OTHER EDUCATORS

Sexual education given later in schools and many other places supplements what has been given in the home, and it can do much to make up for deficiencies in the parents. Essentially the function of the schoolteacher and the health educator is to supply at appropriate times all the information a child may need, but also (as representative of the community) to show how the actions of each one of us affect other people – to emphasize responsibility. In giving physiological information to the young much progress has indeed been made. But the facts of life are not all physiological. Most people now agree that, besides knowing how to read and write, every child should know where babies come from and how they begin. But it is just as necessary that children should know about their own development; about the community in which they live and the restraints it requires; about sexual urges and love, passion and friendship; about both the pain and pleasure these can bring;

2. T. Sjovall, *Sex and Human Relations*, Excerpta Medica Foundation, 1965, p. 21.

and above all about the marriage relationship. Though all these things ought to be part of the normal preparation for living today, some of them admittedly cannot always be taught by the ordinary schoolteacher. But they are facts of life that every adolescent is entitled to hear from someone – someone who knows and cares. In England certainly we shall have to give much more time and thought to finding and educating these educators.

I say that the educator must be 'someone who cares'. But does he confine himself to giving the facts? or does he still like the moralists want to persuade? I do not see how he can avoid thinking some things good and others bad. Nor can any of us avoid this. Though in the end the young will build their own world we ought meanwhile to know and declare where we ourselves stand.

COLLAPSE OF MORALITY

First how do we see the present situation? Has there been in Europe a collapse of morals, and is there a new pattern of sexual behaviour? On the face of it, yes: more and more young people do not acknowledge the authority of the Churches, and the English inquiry for the Central Council for Health Education[3] found that by the age of eighteen a third of the boys and a sixth of the girls had had intercourse. On the other hand, promiscuity did not seem to be prominent in teenage behaviour. Moreover at the 1965 FPA Conference Dr Henriques[4] pointed out that some sections of the British community have long gone in for sexual activities before marriage: he explained that 'covert permissiveness' was in fact part of our tradition. All this made him think that what looks like a new pattern of sexual morality is really no more than a widening and deepening of a long-established pattern. It is more conspicuous because defiance of moral authoritarianism has come into the open and is now articulate and loud. Introducing the Health

3. M. Schofield, *Sexual Behaviour of Young People*, Longmans, 1965, p. 247.

4. F. Henriques, *Sex and Human Relations*, London, 1965, p. 40.

Education Council's report on the *Sexual Behaviour of Young People* Sir Herbert Broadley denies that the new generation is bored, undisciplined and sex obsessed; and though Michael Schofield, who writes the report, is disturbed because teenage conformity includes some of the shabbiest features of adult society he seems to see no signs of moral collapse.[5] Professor Ronald Fletcher goes further and says that the majority of young people today are more responsible than they have ever been before.[6] We adults should show ourselves equally responsible. At least we should never lose our heads.

THREE ATTITUDES

We can react to the situation in one of two ways.

Restoration of Discipline

Many people feel that the time has come to stop the rot – to make the unruly young accept the traditional moral code. And of course this appeal for tighter discipline is one of the classical reactions of authority to challenge.

But it is hard to see why such an appeal should be more successful now than in the past. All through the ages a great many people in their sexual behaviour have defied the tremendous powers of Church and State and many have got away with it. No doubt as Schofield says[5] premarital intercourse could still be much reduced by decreasing the opportunities for it – by reintroducing ideas like the chaperonage of girls and the further segregation of the sexes. But how much of our freedom should we be willing to exchange for this kind of morality? Having but lately escaped from one variety of social prison, the young show no great desire to be put in another. Indeed one of their reasons for rejecting advice from their elders is their suspicion that these elders want to control them again. Liberal opinion professes to prefer self-discipline to the kind imposed by authority and hold that when children

5. M. Schofield, *op. cit.*
6. R. Fletcher, *Understanding*, Granada Television, 1966, p. 22.

or adults ask why something is bad, neither their parents nor their Churches ought to answer 'because I say so'.

Further, to many religious people there is something profoundly un-Christian in paying so much attention to criteria that are essentially material and external, in using a code which judges right and wrong according to whether physical intercourse has or has not taken place or whether a marriage ceremony has or has not been performed. Many of those who care most about religion would agree with the Quaker group when it said:[7]

> The Christian standard of chastity should not be measured by a physical act, but should be a standard of human relationship applicable within marriage as well as outside it.... It is not rigid restraint nor refusal to be involved; it is not arid self discipline nor living according to a moral pattern. It is a wholeness of personality, courtesy and charity, sincerity and pureness of heart.

To the proposition that we should restore the fabric of conventional morality I must mention one more objection: namely that it is commonly supported by a system of rewards and punishments that is no longer acceptable. Insofar as the rewards are to be in another world, they may seem too remote (if not too improbable) to have much reality. But the threats of punishment are all too real. Whatever else we do, surely we must fight the idea that God regards venereal disease or an illegitimate child as a proper penalty for boys and girls who stray from the straight and narrow path. These are disasters to be prevented or mitigated – disasters to individuals and to the society of which they, and we, are part. The risks are part of life which must be known and taken into account; but to use them to prop up a code of morality is surely indefensible. As my friend Dr Richard Asher remarked: 'Some people seem to think that the Bible said: "The wages of sin is birth."'

Premarital Intercourse and Marriage

So much then for the first line of approach – the restoration of discipline. The second proposition is altogether different. It is

7. Friends Home Service Committee, *op. cit.*, pp. 51, 54.

that instead of insisting that intercourse before marriage is wicked, the community should withdraw its general ban on this kind of behaviour. Premarital intercourse can be damaging to young people, or it can be beneficial: and personally I believe that we must leave them to decide whether to try the experiment. But on two conditions only. They must have enough knowledge to know and – if possible – understand what they are doing to each other and to themselves. And they must always use effective contraceptives – which at present they very plainly do not.[8]

A new liberalization of policy may now be desirable for two reasons. The first is that with earlier physical maturity more and more of the young are ready for intercourse long before they are ready to look after a home and family. The second is that we have perhaps more need than ever to strengthen and improve marriage; and we certainly shall not do this by encouraging people to marry before they can cope with its duties. Even the least religious of us see marriage as an almost indispensable means of preserving the structure of society, maintaining responsibility for children and affording them security. As the emancipation of women progresses, giving them more often the same interests as their husbands, marriage should increasingly become, in Macmurray's words, a form of friendship. Two friends (he says) decide to combine their resources and capacities in order to create a family. Their marriage makes this friendship more complete and intimate, and in intention perpetual.[9]

But friendship is, Macmurray adds, 'the highest and the hardest of human achievements' and certainly we cannot be sure that it will develop automatically in any two people who happen to fall in love. We need, he believes, education for friendship and especially for what Jeremy Taylor called the Queen of Friendship – marriage.

If intercourse before marriage were accepted there would be less pressure on young people to get married before they are mature enough to settle down. But if we tolerate sexual ex-

8. M. Schofield, *op. cit.*, pp. 105–12.
9. J. Macmurray, *Marriage Guidance*, 1965, vol. 9, no. 379.

Educating the Educators

perience before marriage and perhaps without thought of marriage – if we encourage fun without commitment – are we perhaps promoting what has been called the dangerous trivialization of sex? My own feeling is that we are apt to take the sexual act itself too seriously; for often it is no more than a physiological incident, soon forgotten. On the other hand, we cannot take seriously enough the possible consequences of deep sexual involvement one person with another. And here men and women, as Dr Braestrup[10] has reminded us, are not the same. To my mind the most telling argument against premarital intercourse is that for the girl intercourse is indissolubly associated with the desire for children and a permanent home.[11]

On this view, even when a couple have a dependable contraceptive, they should refrain from intercourse until both of them are fully prepared emotionally, socially and economically for a possible pregnancy. Until thus ready (Still[12] points out) the girl may be disturbed or restless; and a considerate partner would take account of this by refraining from the sexual act. This again, I feel, is something that the two should decide for themselves. Every sexual action ought to be a matter of mutual decision: for the one kind of behaviour whose sinfulness we all accept – even if we all sometimes commit it – is the sin of exploiting another person.

Premarital intercourse does not necessarily tell a couple whether they are suited even physically for marriage: some marriages require years of adaption before they run smoothly and any kind of experimental union lacks the sense of security and therefore the spontaneity and abandon possible in marriage. A better test may be the period of betrothal in countries where intercourse is permitted as soon as the couple have publicly announced their intention to marry.

In some races sex-play among children and adolescents is quite uninhibited but is a matter of indifference to their elders because (for some reason still unknown) it hardly ever leads to

10. A. Braestrup, *Sex and Human Relations*, p. 175.
11. Friends Home Service Committee, *op. cit.*, p. 21.
12. R. J. Still, *Proceedings of the British Student Health Association*, Report of Seventeenth Conference, 1965, p. 157.

pregnancy. As soon as contraception can be relied on to prevent pregnancy in our own young people, perhaps we too should stop worrying so much about what they do, or do not do, before marriage.

Has the time come when we could radically revise all our ideas of sexual relationship in the light of what one may call the Contraceptive Revolution?

THE CONTRACEPTIVE REVOLUTION

My friend Dr Helena Wright (no less a pioneer today than 30 years ago) may say that so far I have barely touched the real problems. In her book *Sex and Society* she points out that the perfection of contraception by allowing the separation of sexual intercourse from reproduction will have profound social consequences. Prostitution and the birth of illegitimate babies will cease of course, but there will be far bigger changes than that. Formerly insistence on female virginity before marriage and prohibition of sexual relations outside marriage were the only means of preserving the integrity of families: the virginity of his wife was a husband's best guarantee that he was the father of her first child; and avoidance of adultery was a necessity if he was to be sure about the rest of the family. But when contraception is perfected these virtues will have lost their value. Before marriage, Dr Wright thinks, sexual relations will be socially approved, provided the couple are self supporting or have the agreement of those who support them.

After marriage we shall have to achieve a new kind of sexual relationship which is free from possessiveness and jealousy. Except when a child is to be conceived, fidelity to one partner will no longer be demanded. Lest her ideas should sound like an invitation to promiscuity, I should add that the first (and most difficult) item in Dr Wright's new code is that 'no new sex relation should cause damage or distress to an existing one'. Whether distress will in fact be caused must presumably be left to the two people concerned: for except for marriage and parenthood all sexual relations in this new world are to be private.

RESPONSIBLE PARENTHOOD

Of the possible attitudes I have outlined few people will want to work for the restoration of discipline. Some people nevertheless may have doubts about any general tolerance of premarital intercourse. Some again though grateful to Dr Wright for pointing to the eventual consequences of contraception may feel that the new type of marriage she foretells is something not for tomorrow but at earliest for the day after.

In educating the educators what should our policy be today? For my part I unhesitatingly accept the view expressed by Michael Schofield in his book – that our immediate task 'is to make youthful sex activities less harmful'. This may be done, he tells us, by increasing the knowledge of the young and their enlightenment on sex; by introducing more and better sex education in the widest sense; and by individual counselling, which will sometimes mean offering contraceptive help to those who need it.[13] (For 'sometimes' I should be inclined to substitute 'often'.)

Summarized in two words our ideals, both now and later, must be *responsible parenthood*. And this after all is no more than an extension of the ideal of *planned parenthood*. In ending I return to my theme of education. The young – and indeed the old – need a consistent code. But they must choose it themselves.

(II) THE VERY YOUNG MOTHER
DONALD GOUGH

'Why has it happened?' and 'What can we do about it?' are questions asked by everyone concerned with a schoolgirl pregnancy. Many of these girls are making obvious and sometimes frantic appeals for help with long-standing problems. Although a feeling of parental deprivation is always present, the unconscious motives of schoolgirl pregnancy are infinitely complex and individual.

---

13. M. Schofield, *op. cit.*, p. 257.

A schoolgirl pregnancy is a tragedy in our society, because it cannot be happy for the girl, her baby, her boy friend, her parents or her friends. Ultimately it is unhappy for the country itself because it is often doubtful whether the children can be assured the provisions for normal emotional development which will enable them to become emotionally healthy citizens. In each individual case 'Why has it happened?' and 'What can we do about it now?' are questions asked by everyone concerned with a schoolgirl pregnancy. They are questions which haunt the girl and her parents. Most people feel that it is no good crying over spilt milk, that the first question is by now rather an academic one, and that the only thing to be done is to clear up the mess and forget it as soon as possible. The main objection to this way of tackling the difficulty is that it does not work, and I think we ought to discuss both these questions as fully as possible. I am better qualified to talk about the problems of an individual case than sociological factors, but I am sure that socio-economic pressures are of vast importance and I cannot avoid saying something about them. I also want to stress that my experience of unmarried mothers has been mainly with those who have found shelter in institutions, and it is important to remember that such girls represent only a small proportion of the single girls who become pregnant. It is also important to remember that, when discussing unmarried mothers, schoolgirl or otherwise, we are talking about a very special group of girls who have not only 'got into trouble' while indulging in premarital intercourse but who have failed to adopt any of the alternatives (savoury or unsavoury) to unmarried motherhood.

FOUR QUESTIONS

Let us try, a trifle artificially, to separate the questions:

1. Why has a schoolgirl become pregnant?

2. What could have been done to prevent this schoolgirl pregnancy?

3. What is the most helpful thing to do about a schoolgirl pregnancy?

4. How can we help the girl to avoid a similar unhappiness in the future?

When we start with our first question, 'Why has a schoolgirl become pregnant?' we realize at once that there are a multitude of causative factors rather than a single factor which can be identified, and when we go on to ask 'What could have been done to prevent it happening?' we find that there are many things which would have helped a proportion of the girls, but that there is no answer that would have helped all of them, except of course being happier in themselves and in their families. It is too simple to try to blame only the girl, or her parents, or the boy, or commercial advertising or any one factor, however important that may be. It is also too simple to think that we have explained the whole difficulty if we say that sexual activity is biologically natural and exciting and that our young people are now maturing physically much earlier than before, and have a great deal more freedom. These are very important facts which our society as a whole does not seem to have faced fully, although commercial advertisers and the managers of entertainment are cashing in on them very successfully.

CRAVING TO BE LOVED

There is one common feature of the very young mothers that I have seen and that is an extreme craving to be loved. They have all shown in a variety of ways that they felt deprived of love and attention somewhere within their immediate family. They have also shown a strong unconscious desire for motherhood as well as a more conscious need for sensual gratification. They hoped to satisfy their wish to feel needed, loved and good, not only in the arms of their boy friends, but also through their babies' need and love of them, through the compassion and interest which they hoped their new motherhood would arouse, and through the reassurance that they would get from producing a healthy and good baby. There is a criticism of those who stress the unconscious motivation of illegitimate pregnancy by people who feel that we are saying that single girls who become pregnant are no longer to be considered. It is feared that it is simply a more subtle form of stigmatizing and persecution. This is not the point at all. If you do not acknowledge or know what is the real difficulty of the girl whom you are trying to help, you cannot begin to help her adequately. Many of these girls are making obvious and frantic appeals for understanding help with longstanding problems and we have let them down if we fail to realize and respond to this. Although a feeling of parental deprivation is always present, the unconcious motives of schoolgirl pregnancy are infinitely complex and individual.

CASE HISTORIES

Study of the circumstances in which individual schoolgirls have become pregnant gives some idea of the complex factors which underlie the pregnancies. Marion was twelve when she had her baby. Her emotional development was blighted by the fact that her mother, who was unmarried, had placed her in a residential nursery, and then for fostering, until she was able to marry and offer her a home. This took six years, and by this time mother and child found themselves incapable of living together. The child returned to her foster home until the pregnancy was discovered. The foster parents will not have her back and she plans to keep her baby, placing her in a residential nursery until she is able to make a home for herself. She told me that she had not wanted a girl baby because girls only bring trouble on their mothers in the way that she had done.

Joan conceived her baby at her fourteenth birthday party in her parents' home. She was so homesick in the mother-and-baby home and her behaviour was so frantic that the staff feared that she was schizophrenic. Yet her mother said that she could not understand why her daughter was being such a nuisance. She was perfectly willing to have her back with the baby but she said that she could not have her back just yet because she would have to give up temporarily a job in a café which she enjoyed. Finally Joan had to return home before she had her baby and was taken each day to sit in the café where the mother worked.

Joan had conceived soon after a sister-in-law with a young baby had come to live in her mother's home and both received a great deal of attention. She told me in one of her quieter moments that she wanted to stay at the home for the usual six weeks after the baby was born so that she could learn to look after him, 'otherwise Mum will take him over.'

Sheila told me that there was no problem about her baby's future. She was going to take him home to Mum. She said that Mum had been talking of adopting a baby for the last eighteen months, ever since the doctor told her that she could have no more children of her own.

Waiting to Marry

Margaret came from Jamaica three years ago. She is thirteen. Her parents have been separated for some time and her mother who is in Barbados with several other children sent her to stay with an aunt and to be educated in England. She became pregnant by a West Indian who lived at the house of a child with whom she used to be sent to play. She will probably follow the usual practice of the West Indian children and 'keep' her baby. That will mean having him fostered by the local council and seeing him only occasionally.

June is fifteen. She has taken her baby home and is now waiting until she is old enough to be allowed to marry the child's father. This young man is four years older than June. He was sent to prison for three months because he acknowledged his responsibility for the girl's condition and refused to promise that he would never see her again. They are still keen to marry and are going to do so as soon as June is sixteen.

These stories are typical of some of the commonest backgrounds to schoolgirl pregnancy. Many girls are alas re-enacting the unhappy circumstances of their own births and childhoods. Their need to do so is largely due to their wish to understand and excuse their mother's behaviour towards themselves. I am glad to say that perhaps contrary to expectation most of them emerge from the experience of pregnancy and motherhood with a much improved relationship with their parents.

CARELESS PARENTS

A number of children have been coerced by adult males. In other cases the parents seem to have been so careless of their daughter's 'virtue' as to appear to almost encourage her to have intercourse. Quite a number of girls produce a baby as a 'present' for mother, or sometimes for father, and the babies are taken home and tacked on to the end of the mother's family. Perhaps a quarter of the children have been conceived in the course of a serious love affair. I think that if they were older a considerable number of these girls would have married before the child was born. It is a very distressing and disturbing fact that in such cases the boy is often punished by the court for sticking by the girl, when a denial would easily have secured his freedom.

What could have been done to prevent this schoolgirl pregnancy? The ideal answer to this problem is laughably easy to say and cruelly difficult to organize. This ideal answer is that we should try to insure a happy emotional development for all our children, because I am convinced that this problem of schoolgirl motherhood does not occur in truly happy families. The schoolgirl pregnancy is a sign of unhappiness as well as a cause of unhappiness. There are, however, many other possible answers to our questions, which I will list and try to discuss.

LOCK UP OUR DAUGHTERS?

Should we lock up our daughters? I believe that to a certain extent the answer is yes. Of course the full application of this principle is far from possible today and is highly undesirable anyway, but the truth which many parents have difficulty in seeing these days is that the young adolescent feels the need of a measure of control and sees it as a sign of concern and love. In case this suggestion is thought to be too smug and 'square', I should like to put it the other way round and say that young people deeply resent parents who shirk the responsibility of passing on acceptable standards of behaviour to their children and who dare not commit themselves. If they are healthy they will test the validity of any standards imposed and will probe the sincerity of their elders, but they cannot do this if the parents have abdicated and 'left it up to them'. All that they can do then is to despise the parents' weakness and make increasingly desperate attempts to get them to commit themselves.

WOULD IMPROVED SEX EDUCATION HELP?

There is no doubt that the possibility of freer mature discussion about sexual matters between adults and children would be of enormous benefit to children. The trouble is that there are deep psychological reasons why both sides are extremely embarrassed even at the thought of such discussion. It is again up to the adults to take the greater share of the responsibility and to do what they can do to pass on their knowledge and experience to their children. Schoolgirl mothers whom I have met have been ill-prepared for the tumult of modern adolescence. They have had practically no helpful guidance on sexual matters and what instruction they have had has been more concerned with facts about biology than guidance about feelings. Many of them have a strong moral sense but are enormously confused about sexual morality. Improved, wiser sex education in schools would go some way towards meeting the children's needs, but what is needed is a climate of opinion and feeling in which the subject of sex can be discussed spontaneously with adults from the earliest days. In fact there is no full substitute for mature and loving parents, although it may be easier for others to do those things which the parents find particularly difficult.

THE PILL AT PUBERTY

Should schoolgirls have free access to contraceptives and be instructed in their use?

Greater understanding and freer access to contraceptives would certainly help a small number of girls to avoid an unwanted pregnancy, but this is a very complex question. It is largely true that their boy friends have free access to contraceptives and it does not seem much for the girl to ask of her sexual partner that he should be concerned to protect her from being harmed by their mutual act. What I am trying to say is that the girl's choice of boy friend is of great significance, and tells us a great deal about her. That if she had chosen wisely she might have avoided harm, and that the girl's use of contraceptives is not her most important protection against an unhappy outcome to sexual activity; the quality of her relationship with the male is far more important. In discussion the pregnant schoolgirls totally reject contraception as an answer in retrospect or as a wise precaution in the future. One girl in a group discussion said that their mothers could not have thought much of them if they had considered putting them on the pill at puberty. She was unshaken when another girl commented, 'They would have been right, wouldn't they?' They cling to their personal responsibility even when they have failed to live up to it, and the problem is how to respect this while trying to help them avoid similar unhappiness in the future.

Incidentally, the schoolgirl mothers that I have met have been singularly reluctant to blame anyone but themselves for their condition although there are often many people trying to persuade them to put the blame elsewhere. Another odd fact, which they agree is odd, is that it never occurred to any of them that they might become pregnant. This makes me wonder whether freer access to contraceptives would make much difference.

ATTITUDES TO PREGNANCY

What is the most helpful thing to do about a schoolgirl pregnancy? Utter condemnation and the complete rejection intended by the phrase 'never darken these doors again' is in a sense meant to be the ultimate deterrent to a daughter's unchastity. The trouble with this ultimate deterrent, as with another one, is that you have to mean it if it is to be effective, and that if you ever have to use it, it is too late. In this context I do not think that it is an effective deterrent and it is most sad if the parents' rejection is increased by the unwelcome pregnancy.

LEGAL ABORTION

Legal abortion as a solution for unwanted pregnancies has been discussed lately. A small proportion of the pregnant schoolgirls that I have seen would have been greatly helped if legal termination of their pregnancies had been readily available. The Danes, who seem to order these matters much better than most people, consider it a disgrace to our society and an unnecessary cruelty that we allow so many schoolgirl pregnancies to go to term. It is again a very complex issue, and there is a slight danger of a new cruelty being inflicted upon a schoolgirl in the form of an unwanted abortion forced upon her in the name of progress and freedom. Many would get pregnant again and many would conceal their pregnancies until it was dangerous to intervene. Basically, however, there is no doubt that greater access to legal termination of pregnancy would lessen the sum total of human unhappiness and could be one of the most helpful things to do about some schoolgirl pregnancies.

We can give support during pregnancy and after the birth of the child. There are some cases in which the girl and her family will be able to make great use of skilled psychological help and this should always be available. Every case deserves and needs much human understanding. In terms of everyday life the hardest time for most schoolgirl unmarried mothers is while they are waiting for the baby to be born. The majority of them have to go away from home and feel shut off from their families and friends. During pregnancy the girls become dependent and in need of mothering to a much greater extent than older unmarried mothers. They tire very easily and are greatly distressed by the symptoms and discomforts of pregnancy and by the distortion of their shape. They seem to be more prone than older girls to complications in their pregnancy and labour, but they appear to tolerate the strain and discomfort of child-birth equally well.

Although it is such a great relief when the baby has been born safe and sound after all the months of anxious waiting, they are usually profoundly depressed just below the surface. They have a great need for help and understanding at this time, because the experience of seeing the baby as a living thing puts them in touch with all the feelings that led to the pregnancy and with all the difficulties about parting from the baby that now have to be faced. How can we help the girl to avoid a similar unhappiness in the future? The most important influence on the individual girl's future is the quality of the care which she receives over the period of her pregnancy and confinement. The quality of this care will also greatly affect the wisdom of her plans for her baby's future.

THE BABY'S FUTURE

It has been argued that a girl whose baby has been adopted should be spared the temptations and torments of seeing the child. I believe that the too-ready acceptance of a pregnant girl's decision about the future of her baby is a great disservice to the girl and deep down will be very much resented. When she is in contact with the baby as a real person and a living reality we can follow and help her in her fluctuations and indecisions. Having explored with her the many aspects of her feelings, we may hope to help her reach a decision which she is able to honour because she feels that it is truly her own. She will need skilled help if she is to find her pregnancy and contact with the baby a maturing experience. But all too often the mother and baby are just stuck together and left to get on with it. This tends to produce either a disastrously unsatisfactory nursing couple or a 'tender trap' in which it is very difficult for the mother to see things clearly.

There are many cases in which things seem to be going seriously wrong with an infant's development and response to mothering, as the result of endless battles with a young mother who was incapable of providing 'good enough' mothering but who was nevertheless compelled to go on tending him for six more weeks. If such grossly unsatisfactory nursing situations are allowed to go on, there is not only much unnecessary suffering and possible damage for mother and child but the adoptive mother is presented with a 'difficult baby'; a circumstance which may well endanger the success of the adoption.

The girls are nearly all eager to look after their babies at least for a short while. Even girls whose babies are to be adopted are incredulous at the idea that they might wish to be separated from the baby at birth although they are keenly aware that the parting from a child that they have come to know and love will be very difficult. Their ability to mother their babies varies considerably with their age, temperament and intelligence, but most of them soon learn to be very competent little mothers. The fact that there seems to be a lack of real depth and an air of make-believe about their mothering may very well be due to their knowledge that someone else will soon be taking over their mother role.

If a mother gives her baby for adoption she has a need to mourn his loss almost as though she had lost him by death. Very much depends on her ability to do this successfully and she can be tremendously helped in this by a professional worker whom she has come to trust through the months of her pregnancy. If we can help her to come to terms with her real feelings about this terrible parting and with her many conflicts about her pregnancy and her baby, then the crisis in her life may resolve more happily and not be a solely painful and deeply damaging experience.

When the girls return to their homes, there is often not the difficulty and hostility that we might expect. They very seldom return to the same school, and although there are very unfortunate exceptions, their new schools are frequently more satisfactory and understanding than their earlier ones. On the surface it is a very happy time for the schoolgirl when her family and friends welcome her home with open arms after months of exile. Deep down, however, this is the most difficult and painful time for her. While she is trying to respond to their welcome and forgiveness she is still struggling with her own anxieties and is in most cases trying to mourn the baby which she has just placed for adoption.

Her family and friends too often fail to understand that the girl has a need to come to terms with her feelings about her pregnancy and her baby, and they underestimate her ability to do so. Social workers who are in contact with these schoolgirls can offer much more than supportive help to the girl and her family because they are able to help them face and understand deep and important feelings, which in this crisis are only just below the surface.

The schoolgirl pregnancy is a challenge to all concerned with preventive mental health, and adequate help for the girl at this time may profoundly influence her future emotional health, the quality of her mothering and the wisdom of her plans for her baby. These in turn will greatly affect the emotional development of her child.

(III) WHAT IS SEX EDUCATION?

FAITH SPICER

People who know little about sex education are often dogmatically disapproving about the whole subject. Those who are actually trying to meet a need are more diffident and perhaps more concerned to find out who needs what sort of help.

A difficulty in discussing sex education is that it tends to be dragged out of its context, out of the pattern of normal living. The happiness people expect from life is no more due to their attitude to sex than to their work. Human beings are a complex outcome of innumerable influences reacting upon their basic personalities. What a person makes of his potentialities will be due to his social situation, his parents' attitude towards him, his education and the chance happenings of fate. Is it worth while then to give special talks on sex education? Should one not give talks on the whole subject of child development? Is it worth doing anything? Will the child not grow up just as well if left to his parents?

LOVING AND HATING SIMULTANEOUSLY

Dr Bowlby and others have shown the enormous importance of the parent in the child's development; how he not only receives food and warmth from his mother, but security and love which teach him in turn how to give and receive love. The struggles of the growing child to understand his environment can be very upsetting, both for him and for his parents. The child learns by finding out for himself, but he must be prevented from harming himself. He needs to be independent, yet he must conform to rules set by his parents. If he hurts himself, he will need comfort, but if his mother overwhelms him with sympathy he cannot learn to take the inevitable pains of childhood and later life. His mother loves him, but can be furious with him when he does something awful. The child loves and needs his mother, but can feel hatred of her when he is thwarted, or left alone or superseded by a younger brother. The most difficult lesson learnt in childhood may be that it is possible to hate and love someone almost simultaneously. But the experience of living in a family is so necessary that children deprived of it for long find it difficult or impossible to make good and lasting relationships in later life. In childhood one learns about facts, about how to behave, how to talk, and one also learns from living with a family how to live, how to be a person, a wife, a mother. The experience of dealing with rage and jealousy in childhood may determine how an individual will cope with comparable difficulties in later life.

EARLY DIFFICULTIES OF THE NEUROTIC

People who deal with the casualties of living, with neurotic individuals, with delinquents, with unhappy marriages, find that often the difficulties appear to stem from childhood. The psychopath, who loves no man, has never known love as a child; the man many times married was brought up in a broken home; the unmarried mother was never told the truth about sex; the frigid wife was brought up by a mother who believed that all inquiry into sex was disgusting. These are all over-simplifications but they illustrate some of the dangers of faulty upbringing.

Everybody feels strongly about sex. Both in childhood and adolescence it is a subject of wonder and exploration, just as it is in adult life. How a parent deals with his child's interest in sex is of tremendous importance. A child will want to know about sex, he will not only want to know the answers to formulated questions about his organs and about reproduction, but he will need to be helped to understand his feelings about them. There are thus several roles that the parents will have to fulfil simultaneously. They must have understanding of their child's need to explore, so that they are not horrified when the child feels his penis or compares himself with other children. Masturbation in a child is not a sign of depravity, but a seeking for self-comfort, in itself harmless, like thumbsucking, but suggestive of loneliness. When the child is old enough to ask questions, from two years onwards, parents should be willing and able to answer simply and without embarrassment any question. Yet parents' replies to questions on sex and birth are bound to be coloured by their own feelings about them. A woman who is scared of sex and not used to talking about it may find herself very upset by her child's questions. Her reply may show the child that this is a dangerous and unhappy subject, best left alone.

PREVENTING MARRIAGE DISASTERS

An organization that declares itself interested in marriage welfare should not only help to save marriages that are foundering but should prevent these disasters. It seems to me that the great tradition of the Family Planning Association, of offering a chance of happiness to couples by providing a service that gives safe birth-control advice, can best be carried forward if we continue to work in the field of prevention.

There is a great deal said about the decline in morals in this generation, there is far less said of the thirst for information in the general public; people want to know how best to help their children and we should be ready to help them to do so. The parents of older children are more concerned with how to deal with their children's own feelings about sex. They are very aware of the dangers of adolescence, and want to know how much protection is helpful. Adolescents themselves, if familiar with the facts, are eager to discuss their lives and feelings, want to know how to manage their boy friends, how to choose a husband, how to plan their families; they are in fact interested in all the things that will form the experiences of their life. Girls who have not had a good upbringing, who have very little knowledge of sex and reproduction, are very hesitant to ask for knowedge, find discussion about sex painful and embarrassing, and yet need information badly. Although talks to girls and boys at school and in youth clubs are helpful the greatest need is to teach the parents of young children how important they are in their children's development, and how much they can give their children merely by enjoying each other's company in marriage.

(IV) THE SEXUAL BEHAVIOUR OF YOUNG PEOPLE

MICHAEL SCHOFIELD

Until the Nuffield Foundation supported Michael Schofield's work as director of research for the Central Council for Health Education in 1966, information about sexual behaviour of young people was based on much imaginative opinion and little seasoned information. The survey, condensed here, was as good as time, money and knowledge could make it. By nineteen only one third of the boys and one quarter of the girls were sexually experienced – a picture which differs from popular belief.

SURVEY

About 350,000 boys and girls in England under twenty have had premarital sexual intercourse. They lack good parental influence; the boys are gregarious and outgoing but are not misfits, while the girls though they have a strong desire for independence and freedom from the family are not debauched.

Many of these 350,000 are running the risk of becoming parents. Some would take precautions if contraceptives were more readily available, but the majority are either not aware of the risks or do not consider the consequences of an unwanted pregnancy. Half of them are anxious to receive the good sex education, which the majority now lack.

THE INTERVIEWED AND THE INTERVIEWERS

Nearly two thousand (1,873) young people (934 boys and 939 girls) from seven areas, aged from fifteen to nineteen, were interviewed. Their interviewers were young graduates chosen for their ability to get on with young people and specially trained to distinguish between the genuine reply and attempts to confuse.

PREMARITAL INTERCOURSE

Premarital intercourse between teenagers is 'the exception rather than the rule'. Over three quarters had never engaged in sexual intercourse (79 per cent of the boys and 89 per cent of the girls).

Age is of course a very important factor as the following table shows:

	Have had intercourse (%)	
Age	Boys	Girls
Before 13	0.9	0.1
14	2.3	0.4
15	4	6
16	8	7
17	25	11
18	32	12
19	37	23

So before 14 only 1 in the 1,000 girls and 9 in the 1,000 boys have had intercourse, and at 16 the figures are still less than one in ten for both boys and girls. By 17 a quarter of all boys have had sexual experience, but less than one eighth of the girls. By 19 one in three of the boys and nearly a quarter of the girls are sexually experienced. Premarital sexual relations among teenagers are therefore not uncommon, but are confined to a minority.

CIRCUMSTANCES – PARTNER AND PLACE

Over 80 per cent of the girls said that their first experience was with their steady boy friend, 16 per cent with an acquaintance and 3 per cent with a pick up.

The boys' answers were more equally spread over the three categories – probably because their idea of what constitutes a 'steady' differs from the girls'. Forty-five per cent said that their first experience was with their 'steady', 34 per cent with an acquaintance, and 16 per cent with a pick-up.

In general there seemed 'no particular place where young people go to find sexual partners; commonly the first experience was at the parental home of the partner'.

Place	Boys (%)	Girls (%)
Partner's home	50	43
Own home	13	15
Flat, digs	0	12
Party	7	9
Park	10	3
Car	3	7
Other, not known	17	11

REASONS

The answers to the question 'Have you any idea why it happened?' were naturally fairly confused – but they fell into categories which showed that the first intercourse was nearly always unpremeditated.

Reasons	Boys (%)	Girls (%)
Sexual appetite	46	16
In love	10	42
Curiosity	25	13
Drunk	3	9
Others	4	8
Don't know	12	12

Over a third of the girls and over a quarter of the boys had intercourse again within a week. Less than half the boys and less than a third of the girls felt their experience had been a success.

The results of the survey suggest that a large number of the teenagers who are sexually experienced have intercourse only with very close friends and often with the person they eventually marry.

DIFFERENCES BETWEEN EXPERIENCED AND INEXPERIENCED

Part of the research was designed to find out whether there are any personality differences between those teenagers who are sexually experienced and those who are not. The picture which emerged does not resemble the popular image of the crazy, fast-living, immoral young.

Social class made little difference, membership of a youth club was not very influential and there was no connection with a disturbed childhood. Grammar-school children were less likely to be experienced, and early-maturers and party-goers (the longer the party the higher the rate of experience) were slightly more likely to be experienced.

The most important difference between the experienced and the inexperienced was the extent of the parents' interest, concern with them and amount of time they spent together.

SEX EDUCATION

Sixty-two per cent of boys and 44 per cent of girls learnt the facts about contraception from their friends, usually unpleasantly. Slightly over a quarter (27 per cent) learnt from their mothers – fathers seem to do little educating either for sons or daughters. Teachers are probably the most important source of accurate information for both boys (12 per cent) and girls (18 per cent), but those who learn from teachers are more likely not to get their information until fourteen or later. Middle-class adolescents learn about contraception slightly earlier than do working-class – this is contrary to popular belief. But over two thirds of the boys and over a quarter of the girls said that they had never at any time had advice about sex from their parents, and over half the boys said they had never had any kind of sex education at school.

Eight out of ten girls receive some kind of sex education at school, whether the school is state or private. Nearly half the boys (47 per cent) and girls (43 per cent) felt they wanted more sex education at school. They are anxious for sex education provided it is given with assurance backed by knowledge and a proper understanding of their particular problem.

USE OF CONTRACEPTIVES

All the sexually experienced teenagers were asked if they took birth-control precautions. Less than half the boys always used some form of birth control and a quarter had never used any. About a third of the experienced girls always insisted that their partners took precautions; nearly half did not insist and the others sometimes did. So apparently the majority of girls neither took precautions themselves nor insisted that their partners should do so.

Extent used	Boys (%)	Girls (%)
Always	43	20
Sometimes	25	13
Once or twice	5	3
Never	25	61
Don't know	2	3

Nearly a third (28 per cent) of the sexually experienced boys have never possessed a contraceptive.

UNMARRIED PARENTS

There were of course very few unmarried fathers in the sample of 1,873,[14] and still fewer girls who had been pregnant, but an attempt was made to get their reaction to the possibility of

14. The illegitimate birth rate over the whole of the country is seven per cent.

pregnancy. Though more than a quarter would offer marriage, less than half the boys had any clear idea what they would do, but over a third (38 per cent) of the girls felt they would turn to their mothers.

The replies in the table below show that abortion and adoption are not a solution for many girls.

Girls' replies to the question: What would you do if you were going to have a baby?

	%
Tell parents	38
Try to marry father	20
Make arrangements to keep it	18
Try to have it adopted	9
Get rid of it	7
Other	2
Don't know/couldn't happen	6
Total	100%

(V) A SMALL EXPERIMENT

MICHAEL DUANE

When Michael Duane started answering any questions in his large school in a depressed part of London, and published his answers with the questions, many people were upset and angry. Today his technique is used in most discussion groups in the field of sex education.

The class was of fourteen-year-old boys of less than average ability due to leave school within nine months. The school had been formed eighteen months earlier by the amalgamation of four schools in a grim and depressed area. The neighbourhood was a litter of new blocks of flats, small leather, furniture and engineering factories scattered about the dingy relics of a once prosperous and elegant eighteenth-century suburb with a very popular market and dozens of low-grade cafés, fish-and-chip shops, pubs and cheapjack stores within a couple of hundred yards of the school.

The population was a mixture of a few old-established families and new postwar provincial families attracted to the city, and also Greek and Turkish Cypriot, Indian, West Indian and African families, a high proportion of whom spoke little or no English. Alongside the school itself were streets where occasional and very questionable clubs were opened for short periods, closed by the police and re-opened soon afterwards under new names. Some of the local women, white and coloured, several of them mothers of children attending the school, were known as 'slags' or 'slacks' the local name for prostitutes.

None of the boys or girls so far as I could discover by questioning had previously received any recognized sex education in school and without exception all those whom I spoke to said they would not dream of asking their parents about such things. They would be told that they were 'dirty' and not to be discussed. From the first week after the formation of the new school and for the next four terms the school was wracked by truancy, hooliganism in the form of fights between gangs from the school that had been situated in the very grimmest part of the area and the prefects who had been in the main chosen from the school which had kept its boys to a later age; wanton damage to the furniture and fabric of the building; disregard for the normal attitudes to school, work, personal property and the accepted code of relations between teachers and pupils.

To children hitherto brought up in the old buildings designed for ease of supervision and control the attractions of a modern building on an open plan entailing much movement from block to block, easily accessible from the near-by streets, close to the market and shops, proved too strong. Corporal punishment had been rejected by the staff and the control by parents both of whom were too often out at work until late in the evening could not be relied on by the school.

IMMEDIATE CAUSE OF THE EXPERIMENT

For several weeks after the beginning of the autumn term, 1961, I had been taking groups of adolescent boys for discussions. My aim was to try to get to know them in the slightly more informal atmosphere of such discussions better than was possible in a series of lessons more tightly bound to a set syllabus. It was clear from the first that discussions were a bore. They were not interested in jobs or the H-bomb or current affairs for more than a few moments at a time. The horses died and remained very dead no matter how hard I flogged them.

One day I overheard a girl telling a friend what her Mum had said about the daughter of a neighbour alleged to be about to have a baby by a schoolboy. I broke in and asked what the father had said. They looked startled that I had heard and that I asked the question, but replied that the father had nearly killed her.

They followed this up by asking me what I would do if my own daughter, aged fourteen, told me that she was going to have a baby: 'Well only one thing would really test what I would do, but I hope I would have the sense to realize that she must have passed through a very unhappy time of worry, doubt and fear of discovery. I would try therefore to make her realize that her mother and I would be there to help and that she should not waste time and energy in regrets. What would happen to the baby would only be decided when she was in a calm frame of mind and would depend on all kinds of things such as her feelings for the young man, on his age, on her feelings for the baby and so on.'

By this time the girls were all ears and plainly astonished that there should be anyone who could regard such an event with anything but horrified shock. The end of that lesson followed soon after and I was not able to pursue it. That same afternoon I had a double lesson with the boys. It should have been maths but I wanted to follow up the idea that had occurred to me while talking to the girls. I told the boys what had been said during the morning, and then said:

'It's very clear that you find our discussions dull. Now ask me any question you like and I will promise to answer it truthfully.' At this there were some incredulous sniggers and muffled whispers.

'Any question?'

'Yes.' Not a move apart from giggles and further whispers.

I realized that they were afraid of the isolation demanded by asking a question.

'If you prefer you may write the question on a piece of paper and you needn't write your name. I will go out of the room for a few minutes. Put the papers on the desk before I return.' When I returned there was a pile of papers on the desk. I read out each question and answered it directly.

QUESTIONS AND ANSWERS

Except that I have corrected grammar and spelling to make them intelligible, the questions that follow are exactly as framed by the boys, and the answers as nearly verbatim as memory will allow.

'What is a —?'

'The common or vulgar word for the outer part of the female sex organs.'

'Is — a swear word?'

'This is what your mother and father did to produce you, my father and mother did to produce me, and all fathers and mothers do to produce any baby. Because nowadays we have got to the unhappy state that we speak of — as if it were something dirty or evil instead of what it is, a normal and natural act, we use the word to shock people or to make them embarrassed, and so it is used as a swear word.'

This statement was punctuated by titters, guffaws and plain roars of laughter, but the boys were staring at me with a new interest. I went on: 'Naturally you will find it embarrassing to speak plainly about things that are commonly regarded as improper or rude or bad, but if you feel like laughing, do so; I shall understand.'

'Is it bad to take yourself in hand?'

'I take it you mean "masturbate", that is to cause sexual excitement by rubbing the penis with the hand. You have probably heard a lot of old wives' tales about masturbation making you unwell or weak, or even driving you mad. That is not only rubbish, it is harmful rubbish because it makes boys nervous and anxious about the possible results, or it makes them feel guilty and ashamed about what is a harmless act. If I found that a boy was practising it a great deal I should be inclined to think that his life at home was lacking in the ordinary affection that a boy should find there, or that he had not enough friends among boys and girls of his own age, or interesting enough things to do in his spare time.'

'Why do girls have periods?'

I gave them a simple explanation with diagrams on the board, of the menstrual cycle and its function. This was interrupted by various questions about details of my explanation. By now all the boys were absolutely serious and could scarcely wait to ask their supplementary questions.

'How does a woman have a baby?'

Again, a simple and illustrated explanation. At one point I was explaining the function of the testicles and saw a look of puzzlement pass over their faces at the word 'testicles'.

'You probably know them as "balls".'

At this they became speechless with laughter. One boy had tears rolling down his cheeks and some were literally doubled up. I was a little taken aback. I had certainly expected them to smile or laugh but I was not ready for the extreme form of their amusement.

When I could get a word in, I asked they why they had found my remark so funny.

'We've never heard anyone like you say a word like that.'

'What is a bastard?'

'Strictly speaking a person who has no legal father, though he must of course have had an actual father. Because a bastard could not inherit the property of his father and could not take his place as a normal child of his father, it became a term of abuse and so a swear word.'

'What is sexual intercourse?'

'The act of inserting the penis into the vagina and releasing the sperm into the vagina.'

This was followed by many questions about the words used and the details of the act of sexual intercourse.

'Why does a boy get the "horn"?'

'The "horn" or the erection of the penis is necessary to make sure that the sperm is placed well inside the body of the woman. Since the sperm and the egg are so delicate and will only join and make a human being if the conditions of temperature, moisture, supply of blood with food, oxygen and so on are exactly right, and since those conditions are possible only in the sheltered place we know as the womb, then it is obvious that the erection of the penis is a method that has evolved to ensure that the sperm is brought close to the womb.'

'What is a homo?'

'A person who has strong feelings of sexual attraction towards people of the same sex instead of towards people of the opposite sex. It may be caused by the normal balance of chemicals in the body being disturbed, or by the child having been brought up by only one parent and by people of the same sex as that parent so that the child cannot experience affection for people of both sexes. People do not choose to be "homo" so it is wrong and foolish to punish them for what they cannot help. Some people like this have been great artists or very kind and brave in helping others.'

'What is —?'

'It is sometimes used to mean copulate and sometimes to mean "masturbate".'

'What is a ponce?'

'A man who employs women to go to bed with men for money. He takes the money in return for paying them some wages and "protecting" them or making sure that no rival women interfere with them.'

'What is love-juice?'

'The liquid produced in the vagina of a woman when she is sexually excited. It has the function of making it easy for the penis to enter the vagina.'

'What is VD?'

'VD stands for venereal disease and, strictly speaking, refers to any disease affecting the sex organs, but it normally is taken to refer to one particular disease which if not recognized and treated in the early stages, may lead to complete breakdown of the nervous system and death.'

'Can VD be caught from a toilet?'

'That is very unlikely unless you have a sore place or a cut through which the germs could enter your blood stream directly. However, this is one more reason for being fussy about the cleanliness of cups and glasses used in cafés and restaurants, and about the cleanliness of toilets.'

'What is a lesie (lesbian)?'

'Roughly a female homo.'

The number of questions relating to the less normal or more perverted manifestations of sex is a sad reflection of the unhealthy surroundings in which so many of these young people are compelled to spend their youth, and where they are too often brought into contact with attitudes that are unhealthy, depraved or merely financially determined.

'What is the difference between a pro and a whore?'

'Not much. A pro usually does it for a living whether she enjoys it or not. A whore does it for enjoyment. The words are, however, often interchanged since neither base their activities on anything we would normally call love or affection.'

'How long do you keep your prick in the girl?'

'Since the actual ejaculation lasts only for a matter of seconds it is strictly necessary to have the penis in the vagina only for the time during which this occurs, but if the man and the woman care for each other at all they will normally enjoy being together before and after the ejaculation and will wish to give each other the greatest possible degree of pleasure.'

IMMEDIATE RESULTS

By the time the double lesson had come to an end the attitude of the boys had undergone a dramatic change. Whereas at the beginning they were restless, ready for a 'lark' or a 'muck-about' or a 'giggle', horsing about, overfull of undisciplined energy, loud in volume and manner, by the end they were quiet in a way I had not hitherto experienced, leaning forward intent on every word, listening carefully (this a remarkable change!) to questions asked by other boys, and in general displaying a self-control such as I had not observed in them during other lessons. On other occasions I had had to bully them into making the desks tidy, into picking up the odd scraps of paper from the floor, and into leaving the room in a reasonable state for the incoming class. On this occasion to my surprise they did these things without being asked. Further, they went out of the room in a relaxed and quiet manner, said 'Cheerio, Sir' and walked down the corridor instead of galumphing. One boy found an excuse to loiter after the others had left and asked me whether long hair prevented intercourse. I checked that he referred to pubic hair and told him that I had not heard of such a thing.

Some days later George, a notorious dodger with a long record of appearances in court for truancy and violence, backward and idle, with two older brothers in prison for assault, with an aggressive bully for a father, went to the Second Master and asked to see me. He was told that I was busy at that moment, but he insisted on trying to see me. Eventually the Second Master persuaded him to tell him what was the matter:

'Can sperms cause a baby?'

'Of course, nitwit, what do you think they are for?'

'Yes, but in a boy of my age?'

'Certainly.'

'Oh, Gord!'

For the few days immediately after the first lesson the boys wanted to have questions in every lesson and I agreed. The questions were largely repetitive of the earlier ones but I thought I detected a wish to reassure themselves that I was serious in my attempts to satisfy their needs for reliable information, and particularly to be certain that I would not suddenly turn on them and denounce their questions as 'dirty' or 'wicked'. Gradually the questions died down and normal lessons were resumed. Now only occasionally does a boy ask a question and when I reply that I will deal with it at the end of the lesson he seems content to wait.

The change of attitude that began on the first day has continued. I had to revert to my daily bullying to get the room tidy, but I found that attendance at my lessons improved and has continued to remain good, that the boys will listen more attentively to the routine material of teaching, that they seem to feel less resentment when spoken to sharply for poor work or carelessness. In general there seems to be an air of greater relaxation and less tension in the normal lessons. The boys smile more easily, they seem to be less anxious to impress me or their fellows with how big or tough they are. They are clearly more amenable. As a result I am able to cover more ground in the syllabus more easily.

A few days ago I heard one of the boys shout abuse at another which included the word —. I told him that I did not like to hear a good word misused and made him write it out six hundred times after school. He appears to bear little resentment. I hope that I have not damaged his sex life irretrievably.

SEX EDUCATION – ONE DEFINITION

Clearly the lifebelt operation described here and carried out in what I considered to be a state of emergency in view of the little school time left for these boys could in no real sense be held to be 'sex education'. It was designed merely to begin to break down the barrier that I have found too often to exist between the adolescents and our middle-aged generation. Sex education is not something learnt from books or lectures. It should in my view embrace a wide range of experiences and activities including all the following:

1. The answering of all questions posed by children from their earliest years in the fullest and frankest manner possible consonant with the ability of the child to understand intellectually and imaginatively and to absorb emotionally.

2. The bringing up of children in a family atmosphere of affection and happiness where curiosity and plain speech are not restricted and where natural modesty is respected.

3. The instruction of school children in the rudiments of anatomy and biology including the processes of reproduction in animals and humans.

4. The discussion at home and at school of the personal social and ethical problems raised by sex in modern life, and of the structure of family relationships, material and social and

psychological, and their bearing on the development of a healthy and autonomous individual.

5. The study from the beginning of adolescence of literature dealing with the relationships of men and women and of works of art in all media inspired by such experiences. Study to include acting and singing in mixed groups.

6. The expression by adolescents of their own feelings in writing, painting, sculpture, dance, music or any other medium felt to be relevant by the young artist.

7. The sharing from their earliest years of experiences in work and play by boys and girls under both men and women teachers.

8. The freedom for boys and girls at all ages to form friendships without interference.

(VI) BROOK ADVISORY CENTRES

HELEN BROOK

In the last five years a number of clinics have been started in different parts of the country to advise young people on personal problems of sex and contraception. Judging by their success there has been a large unmet need for this service.

The idea that young people with problems of sexual relationship might need professional help began to develop in the spring of 1959. Work in the birth-control clinic at the Marie Stopes Memorial Foundation had shown the size of the need in London, and in the autumn of 1963 the board decided also to allow birth-control advice to be given at sessions for young people at the doctors' discretion.

By 1964 with the backing of an anonymous donor, who had independently recognized the need to offer help, Brook Advisory Centres were registered as a charity with the following objects: the prevention and mitigation of the suffering caused by unwanted pregnancy and illegal abortion by educating young persons in matters of sex and contraception, and developing among them a sense of responsibility in regard to sexual behaviour. The Centres exist to provide, furnish and set up all necessary equipment, and to staff, manage and maintain in London and elsewhere a centre or centres or clinic or clinics for giving to young persons on payment or otherwise, professional advice on scientific methods of contraception, birth control and family planning, and on physical and emotional problems arising from the relationship between the sexes.

At the official opening of the centre in January 1966 the late Lord Brain, president of the Royal College of Physicians, and president of the FPA, said:

> This is a new adventure in social service, and by social service I do not mean doing something for a society as a whole: I mean doing something to help individuals in need. And the first and basic justification for the existence of this centre and of others, which we hope will follow, is that it fulfils a need. So we hope that people who agree with us will not only welcome this centre, but also support us financially so that we can establish centres elsewhere and help the many whose problems seem to them so overwhelming and whose need is therefore so great.

In June 1967 the National Council of the Family Planning Association 'agreed to cooperate as closely as possible with the Brook Advisory Centres, and to underwrite the administrative costs'. The Association now works closely with the Brook Centres and provides free accommodation for the central office at 223 Tottenham Court Road, London w1. By 1969 there were two Brook Advisory Centres in London, one at 233 Tottenham Court Road, w1, and the other at 55 Dawes Street, se17, each open every day from nine to six with additional evening sessions.

Since the passing of the 1967 act, many Family Planning Association and local authority clinics advise unmarried women; but because girls under twenty often have special problems and may need more than a half-hour interview, Brook Advisory Centres – with ten years' experience – have much to contribute in helping the young. Several thousand young people (average age eighteen) have been seen in the London clinics: those under eighteen are usually introduced by social workers. The great majority of the girls are intelligent and responsible, and many are anxious to take the opportunity to discuss their anxieties.

Though plans are being developed to cooperate with the FPA in research, very little formal research has yet been attempted. A recent analysis of the occupations of fifty consecutive girls showed that seventeen were students, four schoolgirls, two teachers, three nurses, two laboratory assistants, and ten secretaries; the rest included a boutique owner, a journalist and a computer programmer. This represents a shift from a mainly student clientele over the past two years. As yet the low-income, low-intelligence group are infrequently represented; they are usually referred by local authorities and do not come on their own initiative. Just under a quarter of the girls were either engaged or had definite marriage plans; they tended to have fewer problems than girls with no marriage plans at all. Six per cent came with boy friends, five per cent had had abortions or an illegitimate child and four per cent were considered promiscuous. About one girl in ten has special problems. Each girl has a fifty-minute interview and is seen as many times as is necessary to make a diagnosis and select the best method of helping her. She may then be referred to other agencies for long-term psychotherapy, or treated at the clinic if this can be done in three or four consultations. Because of the heavy demand, four visits is the maximum that can be allowed to a patient.

Sixteen thousand new patients have used Brook Advisory Centres since the opening of the first clinic for the unmarried in 1963, and other centres have started in Birmingham, Cambridge, Edinburgh, Bristol, Liverpool, Merseyside and Glasgow: in many other towns sessions for young people are run on the same lines by the FPA.

The help provided by doctors at the Brook Advisory Centres, and the relationship which develops in discussions between patient and doctor offer a young woman the security of a good mother figure with the skill of a highly qualified doctor; the resulting relief which is often demonstrated is rewarding to both participants and a justification for the whole project.

8
Religion and Birth Control

We are accustomed to think of church opposition to birth control as coming only from Roman Catholics. This is far from true – the Anglican Church was hostile or indifferent before the Lambeth Conference of 1958, but it is now favourable. The most striking change has, however, been in the Roman Catholic attitude; the church is in a ferment mainly because of this issue. The official attitude may not have changed but this is not true for a large number of otherwise loyal members of the church. The majority of Catholics now favour – and practise – 'artificial' methods of family planning.

(I) THE NON-ROMAN VIEW

G. R. DUNSTAN

All things are finally worked out in the body; all mysteries are there manifested, even if still as mysteries. It is the only crucible of the great experiment: its innocent, even if debased, purity endures the most difficult transmutations of the soul.[1]

Charles Williams, who wrote these words – poet, novelist, mystic, perfectionist – wrote what he saw of the perfection of relationships; of relationships between God and all his creatures; and so of relationships between the creatures themselves. The perfection of human relationships, itself a mystery, he saw among people (as we all might see it) only in rare flashes, brief but unmistakable, attained and therefore attainable. The perfection touches the body; it belongs to the body, requires the body; yet is not tied to or imprisoned within the body; it dances above and about it like a light spirit flame. Love, which we reckon to be the most characteristically human of relationships (because it is most characteristically divine) seeks and expresses its perfection in different modes of consummation;

1. Charles Williams, *The Forgiveness of Sins*, London, 1942, p. 182.

there are different *ways* of loving, as relationships differ in their nature and in their purpose. One way of loving is consummated in marriage. Or, to put it another way, marriage is one way (among others) of seeking perfection in relationship. Within marriage occurs the consummation of one particular relationship, the sexual. So the pursuit of perfection in sexual relationship is part of the pursuit of perfection in marriage. In marriage the body becomes an instrument for the creating of a perfection which dances like a pure spirit flame above it – and is as elusive. Charles Williams called the body a crucible, and so it is. The body of a man, made one with the body of a woman, is a vessel in which – the conditions being apt for the action – two substances are fused, inseparably; two personalities become one person.

This is the Christian understanding of marriage. From time to time the Christian tradition has carried strains which preferred to think of marriage without the bodily union, without the crucible of the flesh. St Paul was the first, perhaps, in the Church to warn *against* this strain, to declare it a deviation.[2] Since then the tradition has known its debates about whether celibacy, virginity, is a 'higher' state than marriage – debates often begun and therefore continued in misleading terms. But about marriage itself, for those who choose it, the tradition is firm: the consummation of marital love in the flesh is an integral part of holy matrimony, as holy as the rest of it, as purposive, as natural, as desirable, as enjoyable, as proper an object of mutual consideration and care. So the Church has stood, and stands, to safeguard the integrity of the act of sexual union: by opposing those, on the one hand, who have sought to devalue it as a material debasement of a supposed purely 'spiritual' relationship in marriage; by opposing those, on the other hand, who would trivialize it by taking it out of its marital context, out of a context of two totally committed lives. If the substances in the crucible are to fuse, the conditions must be apt.

Within the tradition the meaning and purpose of marriage have been seen to have three ingredients; the discussion of them is far, far older than the modern discussion of birth control, but

2. 1 Corinthians vii, 3–5.

it shines with relevance again as soon as birth control comes into question. Indeed there can still be no Christian discourse about birth control without them. Let us call them for convenience, *part 1, part 2* and *part 3*, though insisting that we separate them only to ease our discussion, as we might split white light into the colours of the spectrum.

Part 1 is the desire for companionship, which develops into a will towards a total union, between the man and the woman, the husband and the wife. This union has many ingredients: it involves the engaging together of emotions, minds, affections, social identities, economic prospects, cultural interests, and more besides: families too in many cultures, more in some than in others. There is infinite variety in the range, depth and quality of these engagements. Sometimes they can not only be complicated but also complicating, binding the spouses to a life of *conflict* rather than of harmony or of good marital counterpoint.[3] But the point is that they *bind*. The sexual union is one of these ingredients, these binding forces. Where it is successful in itself and well integrated with other elements in the developing union, it has strong cohesive power, incomparable in the subtlety and beauty of the feeling to which it gives expression. (Where it fails, particularly in integration, it can bind the two together in resentment, frustration and discord. But at all events, it *binds*.) This part, or purpose, of marriage then is concerned with the growth of the union between the spouses themselves and of their common life: with what the French call *la communauté conjugale*; what the English Book of Common Prayer calls 'the mutual society, help and comfort, that the one ought to have of the other, both in prosperity and adversity'; what the encyclical of Pius XI, *Casti Connubii*, described as 'this mutual inward moulding of husband and wife, this determined effort to perfect each other', and as 'the blending of life as a whole and the mutual interchange and sharing thereof'.

Part 2 is a product of realism, of facing the facts about ourselves. The sexual drive in our nature is necessarily strong and

3. At the emotional or psychic level they are admirably described by Dr J. Dominian in *Marital Breakdown*, Penguin Books, 1968.

demanding. At best its desire for satisfaction has to be ordered, integrated with the rest of personality and with the demands of social living. At worst, since it is deep and fundamental, and since its development is inseparable from the earliest satisfactions and dissatisfactions of life, it can be the worst rebel element in personality, a strong power for the disordering of life. Marriage is the normal institution for the maturing of adult sexuality, for integrating it with personality and personal love, and for harnessing its power for the social good. And sexuality is wider than its simple physical expression: it includes all that is complementary in the emotional and imaginative life of men and women as such. Marriage concentrates the full power of this in a committed relationship of husband and wife; it gives it a fixed object upon which to grow. Marriage provides a second chance for the completion of what in childhood may or may not have been well begun. (When the psychic scars left by inadequate or distorted childhood relationships are too deep, marriage may fail to heal them; these are the roots of marital breakdown, when more is being asked of marriage than it can achieve.) This integrating, ordering and remedial function or aspect of marriage, which is now well to the fore in the literature of marital counselling and of psychotherapy, has had its place, variously expressed, in the Christian tradition. The old English Prayer Book said of marriage that 'it was ordained for a remedy against sin, and to avoid fornication; that such persons as have not the gift of continency might marry, and keep themselves undefiled members of Christ's body'. The new version of this, in the 1928 revision, uses more words, cloudier words, but to the same effect: marriage was 'ordained in order that the natural instincts and affections, implanted by God, should be hallowed and directed aright; that those who are called of God to this holy estate, should continue therein in pureness of living'. No one sensitive to language would claim finality for either statement; but without *some* statement of this sort, the description of marriage would be incomplete.

Part 3 of the discourse describes marriage in terms of its issue: children. Marriage exists, not only for their begetting but also for their upbringing, to give them a stable relationship of family, father and mother, within which to grow. Human societies have produced many different patterns of family structure and arrangement; they have produced no alternative to it as the best means of giving the child the security he needs, from his days at the breast to the taking of adult responsibilities of his own. This function of marriage is so obvious that it comes first in the traditional statement. So the Prayer Book again says of marriage, 'First, it was ordained for the procreation of children, to be brought up in the fear and nurture of the Lord, and to the praise of his holy name'; and *Casti Connubii* writes of it as 'instituted for the proper conception and education of the child'.

Now it is in terms of these three aspects, or functions, of marriage that the Christian discussion of contraception has been, and must be, conducted. The Christian concern, which is an undeniably human concern, is to do justice to all three. In the discussion non-Roman Christianity has reached a breathing-space to which the Roman Catholic Church perhaps still aspires. The strength of the Roman Catholic position stands in its insistence on maintaining the integrity of the act of marital union, and on a refusal to separate the three aspects or functions of marriage. The strength of the non-Roman position stands in its recognition from experience that the integrity of the union need not in fact be violated by contraception, and a separation between the function or purposes of any one act of union by no means involves a separation of the function or purposes of the marriage itself. The non-Roman position is strong also in the degree of personal liberty and responsibility which it recognizes in the spouses themselves; the Roman Catholic position is strong in its expression of a corporate concern for all the members of that Church, and of a common pursuit of a defined way to a given goal. There is evidence that the two traditions are in fact coming closer together.

The Churches have by no means always thought about contraception in terms of theology. The emotions of fear and repugnance have played their part; so have aesthetic judgements; so have considerations of population prospects and of medical possibilities. The history of the relation between population and resources is long and complicated. We err if we simplify too much, if we suppose that in no century before our own was there social or economic pressure to limit the size of families. The new factors entering western civilization in the last century have been the increase of medical skill, which has kept many more children alive in the first year of life; the increase of medical, social and nutritional care, which has prolonged the life of parents, particularly mothers, into old age; and the increase in scientific knowledge and its ingenious application, which has made contraception a practical possibility for all who want to employ it and are prepared to take the trouble. By the beginning of the twentieth century the spread of the practice, particularly in the middle classes, was evident in the declining fertility rates, and in the statistical predictions of a drastic reduction of population in western countries. It was this aspect of the question which most troubled the Lambeth Conference of 1908, the first Anglican body to give the question serious consideration. Restriction on population was considered by a committee of the conference. It wrote in its report that 'there is the world danger that the great English-speaking peoples, diminished in number and weakened in moral force, should commit the crowning infamy of race suicide, and so fail to fulfil the high destiny to which in the Providence of God they have been manifestly called'. Statistics were quoted to support the contention. Medical witnesses were quoted also, associating the most frightening physical and nervous diseases with 'the practice of prevention', a practice 'demoralizing to character and hostile to national welfare'. Doctors were called upon to have nothing to do with it. And, looking back now, we may say that that was plain tragedy.

The Christian and professional withdrawal from the question left it where it had perforce begun, under the advocacy of the *avant-garde*, the rebel, the avowedly anti-religious; it left the practice to subterfuge, associating it shamefully with the frowned upon and the illicit; it deprived the whole movement in its early days of the tutelage of medical and pharmaceutical control; it drove the supply of materials underground, literally underground, to the public lavatories of the railway stations and city centres. This was a great pity, a deplorable price to pay for the emotional repugnance with which the leaders of public life and opinion, in medicine as in religion, viewed a practice which they had little cause to try to understand. (Only later did the professions turn to help the cause: when it was becoming 'respectable'.) The personal suffering which resulted from this in the years of economic depression, between the two world wars, must have been acute. Where there was no work and little or no wages, the birth of another child could be faced only with dread. Yet where there was no work, there was also no satisfaction in life, no fulfilment – except in the marriage, in the flesh, in the very act of bodily union which, of itself, might produce the child. This is the dilemma of the poor in the poorest parts of the world still.

Steadily people taught their leaders by their practice. The Lambeth Conference of 1920, though once again it was set the task of responding to 'the decline of the birth rate throughout the civilized world', first went to the root of principle, in looking at the purposes of marriage as we have just looked at them; first broke with silence, and called for education upon sex in the home, the school and the pulpit, and in the parsonage in preparation for marriage. In its understanding of marriage it placed our *part 2* of marriage, 'the hallowing and control of natural sexual instincts', first and not second as in the Book of Common Prayer. And of this the Committee wrote, 'We recognize that the physical union of husband and wife has a sacramental value, by which is expressed and strengthened the love that the one ought to have for the other.' 'Deliberate and thoughtful self-control' were of paramount importance, and a warning was uttered against 'unnatural means by which conception is frustrated'; but a seed of truth had been implanted, and it would grow. By 1930 the pressure for advance was strong enough in the Lambeth Conference to bring it to a division. Resolution 15 of 1930, as carried by 193 votes against sixty-seven, affirmed:

Where there is clearly felt moral obligation to limit or avoid parenthood, the method must be decided on Christian principles.

The Non-Roman View

The primary and obvious method is complete abstinence from intercourse (as far as may be necessary) in a life of discipline and self-control lived in the power of the Holy Spirit. Nevertheless in those cases where there is such a clearly felt moral obligation to limit or avoid parenthood, and where there is a morally sound reason for avoiding complete abstinence, the Conference agrees that other methods may be used, provided that this is done in the light of the same Christian principles. The Conference records its strong condemnation of the use of any methods of conception-control from motives of selfishness, luxury, or mere convenience.

In direct reply to this came Pius XI's encyclical; while explicitly forbidding the practice of contraception to Roman Catholics in any circumstances, it nevertheless contained its own seed for future growth, in that remarkable statement of paragraph 24, of 'the mutual inward moulding of husband and wife' as 'the chief reason and purpose of matrimony, provided matrimony be looked at, not in the restricted sense as instituted for the proper conception and education of the child, but more widely as the blending of life as a whole and the mutual interchange and sharing thereof'. Though this paragraph 24 was omitted without explanation from early American editions and from at least one authorized English translation and commentary on the encyclical, it was the ground on which the Roman Catholic Church could advance also, twenty years later, to an admission that conception *may* be regulated, though by limited means.

Since 1930 the Anglican Church, and other churches with it, has learned more and moved again. The real advance was made by people themselves, honest, sincere Christian husbands and wives who could not in their consciences judge themselves wrong to do what their reason said it was right for them to do, and what aesthetically and emotionally they could bring themselves to accept. Thus what is called a *consensus fidelium* was formed, a concerted witness of the faithful Christian mind, that the practice was acceptable. Theological expression and moral justification of that judgement was worked out by a small but distinguished band of theologians, pastors and lay people brought together under the auspices of one of the most valuable councils which the Church of England has had in this century, the Church of England Moral Welfare Council. It included Canon Tom Pym, and his lay friends A. G. Pyte and A. P. Pelly, the first a draftsman of a highly successful and pioneering little pamphlet, *The Threshold of Marriage*;[4] Canon Hugh Warner, who in word and in print gave ordinary parents, teachers in schools, and boys and girls themselves the language, the verbal symbols, in which sex education could sensitively be undertaken; and Dr D. Sherwin Bailey, who opened up the study of sexual relations in a highly influential early book, *The Mystery of Love and Marriage*,[5] and – after numerous other publications – wrote his mature thought a decade later in *The Man-Woman Relationship in Christian Thought*.[6] Thus was formed the mind and thus were prepared the materials which made it inevitable that the Lambeth Conference of 1958 should recognize and validate the position which Anglican Christians, and many others with them, had already achieved.

The decisive recognition of the Church's change of view came with the Lambeth Conference of 1958. The preparatory work was entrusted by the then Archbishop of Canterbury, Dr Geoffrey Fisher, to a committee convened by the staff of the Moral Welfare Council. The committee included members distinguished in demography, sociology and social administration as well as in theology. Its report, *The Family in Contemporary Society*,[7] stated the case quite simply in thirty-one pages; it backed it with 200 pages of documentation, taking account of all the significant changes which made a reversal of the earlier condemnations imperative. Here, however, a balance must be kept. The report did reverse the argument on population growth: in the West the decline in population growth had been arrested, while in the Third World, because of the dramatic reduction of death rates, especially infant death rates,

4. First published 1932. A revised edition is obtainable from the Church Information Office.

5. S.C.M. Press, 1952.

6. Longmans, 1959. The inspiration of the group, in these postwar years, was Miss Ena Steel, OBE, General Secretary of the Council. Her personal influence was profound, and ought to be recorded.

7. SPCK, 1958.

since about 1930 what is now widely called 'the population explosion' was well under way with increasing poverty and starvation in its train. The report did also reverse the argument on medical fears: the early assertions about the adverse effects of contraception on physical health had no evidence to support them. But it was not on these two grounds alone that the case for responsible parenthood was argued. The case was grounded as firmly on a changed understanding of marriage and parenthood itself, and particularly of the ends or purposes of sexual union within the marriage. It was on the last factor that the *consensus fidelium*, the moral witness of conscientious, sensitive, Christian and Church people, had become established.

Simply put, it is that sexual union within marriage has two relevant ends, or purposes, not one only. It is to serve the growth of the unity, the common bond, between the husband and wife; and it is for the procreation of children. It has a unitive, or relational function, as well as its biological function. Modern methods of contraception place at the disposal of the partners a relatively simple means of separating these two ends on any given occasion. The report argued that it was licit for them to use these means responsibly: to accept the liberty to give one another the pleasure and satisfaction of the union at times when it would be not only undesirable but also irresponsible for another child to be conceived. The 'procreative' function of the union was served, sometimes – on chosen occasions – specifically in the begetting of a child. It was served on other occasions indirectly, or generally, in the consolidating of the marital and parental bond, which would beneficially affect the growth and upbringing of the existing children of the marriage.

In short, the order of primacy in the ends or purposes of marriage, as set out in the Book of Common Prayer, was turned round. The Prayer Book said *'first'* the procreation of children; *'secondly'* the integrating of the sexual drive; *'thirdly'* the building up of the common life. The new understanding reversed the order, so that it came as it was stated earlier in this chapter: the unity, the common bond, of the spouses is primary: if this is well grounded, sex becomes less of a problem and more of a blessing, and children are born into and brought up in an environment proper for growth. (It should be added that, historically speaking, it remains an open question whether the order given in the Prayer Book was a dogmatic, logical order or merely a didactic one: whether, that is, *'first'* meant *primary*, in the sense that it was logically prior and necessary to the validity of the *second* and *third*; or whether it was a simple teaching order, a counting on the fingers, so to speak, in which the procreative end happened to come first.)

The Lambeth Conference of bishops from throughout the Anglican Communion considered the report. It appointed a committee of its own members, Committee Five, and this produced its own report, accepting and re-stating the arguments and conclusions of *The Family in Contemporary Society*. The result was that Resolution 115 of the whole conference asserted the *duty* of responsible parenthood (not merely a *permission* to use contraceptive means), leaving to the spouses themselves a *liberty* to employ the means of their choice. The resolution runs as follows:

115. The Conference believes that the responsibility for deciding upon the number and frequency of children has been laid by God upon the consciences of parents everywhere: that this planning, in such ways as are mutually acceptable to husband and wife in Christian conscience, is a right and important factor in Christian family life and should be the result of positive choice before God. Such responsible parenthood, built on obedience to all the duties of marriage, requires a wise stewardship of the resources and abilities of the family as well as a thoughtful consideration of the varying population needs and problems of society and the claims of future generations.[8]

In order to read this resolution fairly in its context, two other resolutions should be quoted as well.

112. The Conference records its profound conviction that the idea of the human family is rooted in the Godhead and that consequently all problems of sex relations, the procreation of children, and the organization of family life must be related, consciously and directly, to the creative, redemptive, and sanctifying power of God.
113. The Conference affirms that marriage is a vocation to holi-

8. The Lambeth Conference, 1958, SPCK.

ness, through which men and women may share in the love and creative purpose of God. The sins of self-indulgence and sensuality, born of selfishness and a refusal to accept marriage as a divine vocation, destroy its true nature and depth, and the right fullness and balance of the relationship between men and women. Christians need always to remember that sexual love is not an end in itself nor a means to self-gratification, and that self-discipline and restraint are essential conditions of the responsible freedom of marriage and family planning.

These conclusions of the Lambeth Conference were aptly summarized in a paragraph in its Encyclical Letter:

It has long been held that a primary obligation of Christian marriage is that children may be born within the supporting framework of parental love and family concern, with a right to an opportunity for a full and spiritually wholesome life. Yet we believe that the procreation of children is not the sole purpose of Christian marriage. Implicit within the bond between husband and wife is the relationship of love with its sacramental expression in physical union. Because these two great purposes of Christian marriage illumine each other and form the focal points of constructive home life, we believe that family planning, in such ways as are mutually acceptable to husband and wife in Christian conscience, and secure from the corruptions of sensuality and selfishness, is a right and important factor in Christian family life[9]

The paragraph is important because its statement about contraception is founded on its statement about marriage: its relation to regions of population pressure was treated separately on the following page, in the assertion that:

Abortion and infanticide are to be condemned, but methods of control, medically endorsed and morally acceptable, may help people of those lands so to plan family life that children may be born without a likelihood of starvation.

The Lambeth Conference of 1968, meeting at the time when Pope Paul VI published his encyclical, *Humanae Vitae*, replied courteously but firmly in resolution 22, which quoted and

9. ibid., p. 22.

endorsed resolutions 112, 113, and 115 of the earlier conference, as given above.[10]

Methodist Christians had received some workable guidance rather earlier. In 1939 the Methodist Conference adopted a resolution in these terms:

> The Conference declares that for Christian people the determining issues are moral and spiritual. These can only be decided by the individual conscience in the sight of God. The use of a contraceptive method can only be justified if the marriage bond and married love are thereby truly honoured and not debased, if the obligation to parenthood is the better fulfilled and not evaded, if family life is enriched and not impoverished, and if increase and not diminution of good comes to society.[11]

The judgements and advice of other Christian Churches are collected and discussed by Dr Richard M. Fagley in *The Population Explosion and Christian Responsibility*.[12]

The work of the Lambeth Conference of 1958, and of the preparatory committee which produced *The Family in Contemporary Society*, had considerable influence on Christian thinking everywhere within the Roman Catholic Church and outside it. In April 1959 officers of the World Council of Churches and of the International Missionary Council convened a study group of members of churches from all over the world, including the Orthodox Churches, at Mansfield College, Oxford. The report of this group, entitled *Responsible Parenthood and the Population Problem*, was published by the World Council of Churches, and subsequently reprinted by Dr Fagley as an appendix to his book. It endorsed and amplified the Lambeth position. When documents from the Papal Commission on Birth Control were published unofficially in the spring of 1967, one headed 'III: The Argument for Reform',

10. *The Lambeth Conference 1968: Resolutions and Reports*, SPCK, 1968, p. 36. The Resolutions and the Report of Committee 5 of 1958 are reprinted together in *What the Bishops have said about Marriage*, SPCK, 1968.

11. G. R. Dunstan, *A Declaration of the Methodist Church on the Christian View of Marriage and the Family*, London, 1939, p. 21.

12. Oxford University Press, 1960.

set out a case which would have made it possible for the Commission to recommend something like a Lambeth position in its recognition, first of 'the obligation in conscience' not to generate another child in violation of the right of the child, and of existing children, to a 'community of life and unity' adequate to its proper nurture and education; and secondly that sexuality has a unitive end as well as the procreative.

> In some cases intercourse can be required as a manifestation of self-giving love, directed to the good of the other person or of the community, while at the same time a new life cannot be received [sic].[13]

This document had three distinguished signatories, and it was reported to have been approved by a majority of theologians on the commission. Both the World Council of Churches document and the Roman Catholic document went with Lambeth in insisting that 'nature' is to a certain extent under man's dominion, man's responsible control: he has a duty to use his powers over nature conscientiously to serve the human good, not merely to submit to what is often no more than hazard or chance. The procreation of children, the creation of new life, is too great a matter to be left to chance. Advance in the understanding of this truth is aptly described by Dr J. Dominian, a Roman Catholic psychiatrist, in his recent study, *Marital Breakdown*.[14] Society is gradually reaching the position of appreciating that the primary purpose of sexual intercourse is a union of love between the spouses, which becomes fruitful on specific occasions when the partners are ready to create a new life and bestow upon it unconditionally the love it needs.

In the West few Christians having given the matter due thought and consideration would dissent from this, though Roman Catholic Christians, remaining faithful to the formal teaching of their Church, still enjoy rather less liberty than others in the choice of means. Of Eastern and Russian Orthodox Christianity this author cannot speak; the evidence given by Dr Fagley in the 1960 edition of *The Population Explosion*

---

13. *The Tablet*, 6 May 1967, p. 513.
14. Penguin Books, 1968.

and Christian Responsibility suggests that the Orthodox do not yet share the growing consensus of the Roman, Anglican, Protestant and Reformed traditions; procreation is, or was then, still vigorously asserted as the primary Christian duty in marriage, and means to prevent conception were as vigorously discouraged.

This account of the Christian attitude to contraception has been set out in narrative form, in order to show that the pastoral teaching now given by the clergy in preparation for marriage, and on other normal occasions of Christian education, rests upon an authority of two sorts. It rests on the authority of a common Christian mind, developed over sixty years or more within Christian marriages, lay and clerical, as husbands and wives have decided on the best advice available what is the right thing for them to do. It rests also on the authority of careful and deliberate statements by Church bodies, acting formally on occasions when they are expected to give morally authoritative guidance on matters of Christian concern. For many people this double authority is found to be both weighty and valuable when they come to decide their own way.

Authority, however, is not the end of the matter. Not everyone who approaches the question 'reasonably' would think of examining it 'theologically' as well. For many people it is uppermost a matter of 'feeling': they may not 'like' (they would say) the thought of 'interference', preferring the expression of their love to be as simple and uncomplicated as possible; they may not 'like' the use of contraceptive appliances, some disliking the sort used by the wife, some disliking the sort used by the husband. Most people would rather be without both. For people of this sort the contraceptive pill may appear to be a relief. But then they need medical assurance, not only that the pill will do the wife no harm, but that it will not do harm to any children who may later be born. They may wish to know what any particular sort of pill – or the intra-uterine device – actually effects. Some see no moral problem in contraception pure and simple, effected by preventing the meeting of ovum and sperm. Some are less easy about the wisdom, as well as the propriety, of preventing ovulation over a long space of time. Some have moral scruples about the deliberate destruction of the ovum once it has been fertilized, taking the view that the potential for a fully human life has then begun; though of these some would see less difficulty in preventing the implanting of the morula, the fertilized ovum, in the womb – before which its potential cannot even begin to develop – than in its destruction once implanted; they would distinguish, that is, between an ovicide or an anti-nidation device and an abortifacient. Feelings, fears and scruples of this sort cannot be over-borne by authority, or even by mere argument. The counsellor or pastor must be highly sensitive to the people before him, respecting them fully with their feelings, scruples and fears, and helping them only so to be at liberty that they can make the best decision of which they are jointly capable.

The growing possibilities of genetic knowledge bring new factors into consideration. Genetic counselling is now a possibility – though still a rare one – for people in whose families there is a history or calculable risk of genetic defect. When information or reliable prediction of this sort is available, it may well be necessary – as it is certainly wise – for persons intending marriage to consider very carefully what risks attend their having children, and to determine their contraceptive practice accordingly. The implications of adverse genetic indications were considered in a useful study published by a Church of England committee, entitled *Sterilization: An Ethical Enquiry*.[15]

In general I regard it a sound rule not to consider the moral or religious implications of any question in isolation from the consideration of all their empirical features, from the facts of the case. It may well be that this chapter confirms the wisdom of this general rule. The facts are important, for the body is important: the love of which I write is worked out in the body,

---

15. Church Information Office, 1962, pp. 34–7. For a discussion of abortion, for the termination of a pregnancy complicated by rubella or by other risks of genetic defect, see the report of the same Church committee, entitled *Abortion: An Ethical Discussion*, Church Information Office, 1965, especially pp. 36 ff.

perhaps in the creation of a new body. The love is of the body, yet transcends it. Love calls for reason, wisdom, prudence in its exercise; yet transcends them all; and yet may suffer if they lack. Perhaps only poetry can express the paradox. John Donne, once dean of St Paul's, wrote:

> Our bodies are ours, though they are not we;
> We are the intelligences, they the spheres.

(II) THE ROMAN CATHOLIC VIEW
DENIS RICE

On Monday, 29 July 1968, the Roman Catholic Pope, Paul VI, issued an encyclical letter. Its Latin title was *Humanae Vitae*; the English version, published by the Catholic Truth Society, was called *On the Regulation of Birth*. Whatever its title the letter will assuredly be remembered as the birth-control encyclical.

The primary aim of the encyclical was to reaffirm the official Roman Catholic position on birth control. It was a response to questioning and criticism which had become especially loud within the Church since 1964. In this chapter I will state, with some explanation, the official Roman teaching on contraception. As a Catholic I will make criticisms of this teaching and will comment on some of the discussion of the last four years. I will conclude with some thoughts for the future of the Catholic debate on contraception, particularly in the light of Pope Paul's encyclical. For convenience throughout the chapter, I will use the word 'Catholic' to mean 'Roman Catholic'.

The Catholic Church holds that the proper context for the human sexual act is stable, monogamous marriage. The primary purpose of the sexual act is held to be procreation. It is now recognized, though it was not always clear, that the act has other praiseworthy purposes: an expression and strengthening of the love and unity of the married couple in the mutual joy, refreshment, and support which the sexual act offers. But the official Catholic emphasis is that the sexual act is clearly designed to deposit semen in the vagina, whence it may move to fertilize any available ovum. This observed design is talked of as the 'nature' of the act. The design is God's; the nature of the act is inviolable, because that is the way God intends the act to be used. Any interference with the nature of the sexual act is therefore 'unnatural', an offence against God, a sin. The sin is generally spoken of as 'mortal'. It is the sort of sin which puts a soul at risk for the eternal punishment of Hell.

Artificial contraception courts such a fate because, it is held, it interferes with the nature of the sexual act. *Coitus interruptus*, or a sheathed penis prevents the semen being deposited as designed. Differently – and the distinction is often blurred – a barrier in the vagina prevents the act being completed in the natural progress of the seed. The contraceptive pill and the intra-uterine device raise different problems because the act is carried through normally without any immediate alteration. They are forbidden, however, in that they render the act morally wrong by preventing 'the development of its natural consequences'. Surgical sterilization of women is discussed in other terms, and will be excluded from consideration here.

Though contraception is forbidden by the official Catholic position, birth control is permitted. Total abstinence is available; or the safe period or rhythm method offers a more popular, less drastic formula. It is taught that the use of the sexual act in safe, or infertile, periods is morally acceptable. The nature of the act is respected; it is intact from start to finish because no interference is introduced – mechanical, chemical or pharmaceutical. It is asserted that in the female menstrual cycle, with its fertile and infertile stages, a natural, God-given method of birth control can be read off. By observing the cycle one can use one's sexuality in a way detached from procreation. It is a way which respects the integrity of the act.

It must be noted that this rather developed argument from nature emerged later. In the first instance the safe period was used as an answer to contraception, not primarily as an argument to show that nature approved of birth control. The safe period was not always advocated with as much Catholic enthusiasm and energy, as was the attack on contraception. Use of the rhythm method without grave reason counted as, and still counts as, sin. One detects here the defensiveness which characterizes much Catholic argument. It has led to some less than fair, not to say unscientific, statements about contraception.

Contraceptive acts, it is argued by some Catholics, are unaesthetic – even Freud can be quoted in support of this. It should be noticed first, the side-issue character of the argument about aesthetics – 'our method is nicer than yours' – which is a symptom of defensiveness. Secondly, it must surely be recognized that if contraceptive sex can be ugly, so can safe-period sex. Just as contraceptive preparations can interrupt the spontaneity of the sexual act, so can infertility calculations. There has been a Catholic tendency to compare the best in safe-period practice with the worst in contraceptive practice. Limited to aesthetics and spontaneity alone, there seems little enough to choose between intelligent use of sheath and cap, and intelligent use of calendar and thermometer. In this vein of argument Pope Paul's encyclical goes further – to a point which has rightly attracted strong criticism from many, including Catholics. Without evidence contraception is linked in paragraph 17 with 'conjugal infidelity', and 'the general lowering of morality'. We are cautioned that 'the man ... may finally lose respect for the woman, and no longer caring for her physical and psychological equilibrium, may come to the point of considering her as a mere instrument of selfish enjoyment, and no longer as his respected and beloved companion'.

As a contribution to genuine understanding the example of a selfish contracepting husband is as unhelpful as the example of the selfish Catholic husband who produces an annual pregnancy.

With claims not unlike the Pope's, Catholic defenders have sometimes argued that the safe period leads to more self-control than contraception. Even before the time of pills this could be answered by suggesting that the availability of contraception can make self-control *more* likely. The decision to renounce the act is made by the couple, and not by the calendar! But in the pill era a further point seems to escape many Catholics. They speak of a more precise safe period, determined possibly by a pill which would pin-point ovulation. Is this not

The Roman Catholic View

open to all the threats and cautions which are usually set against contraception? Economically cheaper it will doubtless be open to much wider 'abuse' than contraceptives.

Quite apart from the references to Pope Paul's encyclical it has been worthwhile looking at these somewhat peripheral arguments. Any full review of the debate between Catholics and contraceptors has to face the fact that not all the Catholic arguments have been central to the main issue. Nor have they always reflected great security in the quality of the official Catholic case. It is not too much to allege that sometimes the Catholic argument has pursued a personal tactic: if you cannot get the argument get the man. The plan often seemed to be: if you cannot convince your opponent intellectually, convict him morally. Thus he supports contraception because he is sex-mad, weak-willed, abuses his wife, is selfish or is guilty of unnatural practices. Broadcasting on the day that the encyclical was issued an English Catholic bishop was anxious to show that the encyclical was not new teaching. He quoted St Augustine's view that the husband who prevented births was no better than an *adulterer*, his wife no better than a *prostitute*.

Other Catholic apologists eschew peripheral discussion of this type, and simply concentrate on the official position: contraception against the natural law is morally wrong. Argument at this level becomes at once more central; more difficult too, but more fruitful. In 1964 Archbishop Roberts' published questions about the core of the official teaching finally spread the birth-control debate through English Catholicism.

The Catholic Church teaching that contraception is wrong makes two utterances, though they may not always be expressed distinctly. First it makes the statement that contraception is against the natural law, and as such is against God's law. Second it issues the instruction or directive, 'do not contracept'. It was this double utterance, and not sheer dishonesty, that enabled some Catholics to stay obedient to the directive, while disbelieving the statement about its grounds.

One is not concerned with the truth or falsehood of an order or directive. Logically the order 'stand up' is neither true nor false. It is to be obeyed or ignored. So with 'do not contracept'.

But 'contraception is against the law of God' is a statement. Its truth or falsehood is a matter for concern. The Church teaching it must offer the ground for the teaching.

Nobody now reputably claims that the grounds are scriptural. Despite the *Sunday Telegraph* of 4 August 1968, the famous Onan quotation from Genesis xxxviii, 7–10 is irrelevant. The claim for the certainty of Catholic teaching on contraception cannot be based in the inspired revelation of the Bible.

The statement that contraception is against God's law could be claimed as infallible on the basis of solemn definition by a council of bishops or by the Pope. There has been no sustained argument to show that the statement has been so defined. Were such an argument available, it would doubtless have been well circulated in the years of discussion before Paul's encyclical, and would have appeared in the encyclical itself. It must be emphasized that a papal encyclical does not carry the guarantee of infallibility. Encyclicals can and do make mistakes. Historians of the Church will point to papal letters of which the only thing that can be said is that they are dead letters. The limited and fallible nature of most papal statements is important in considering the next point of the tradition in the teaching about contraception. It is quite reasonably argued that encyclicals may express part of the Church's tradition. It cannot be argued that encyclicals give that tradition an infallible character. This is equally true of the encyclical of Pius XI on marriage (1930), and of the address of Pius XII to the Catholic Union of Midwives (1951), both still much quoted in solemn justifications of the official Catholic position.

The statement 'contraception is against God's law' could be guaranteed as infallible in one other way. It would have to be demonstrated that the statement was part of the consistent teaching and belief of the Church. This would ground the official position towards contraception in what is known as the ordinary *magisterium* of the Church. Less technically it would claim to show that the statement was part of the Church's traditional teaching. Catholics who maintain the official position that contraception is against God's law do so in the belief that the teaching is part of the Church's tradition. They see it as guaranteed by the consistent teaching and belief of the Church. Clearly this guarantee is vaguer, more elusive than that of a formal definition. Much depends on how one defines 'consistent', and on the quantity and quality of a teaching which gives it the character of 'tradition'. In the Church's history there have been changes of more or less consistent teaching – this was one of Archbishop Roberts' early contributions to the debate. As a Catholic I believe that change can and ought to be made in the Church's teaching that contraception is against God's law. I find the teaching unsatisfactory. Pope Paul's encyclical did not cause me to change this finding.

The official Catholic position carelessly tears sexual acts out of their context – I might almost say out of their 'natural' context. The official teaching looks at each sexual act separately as a distinct unit. The context of human sexuality is marriage. Sexuality is for marriage, is used throughout marriage, and is best judged in terms of the total marriage. A couple dedicated to procreation and life produce children if able. They respect the primary purpose of their marriage by generative acts. They respect the other purposes of their marriage by these and all other sexual acts. I have used here the official 'primary, secondary' jargon, but unwillingly. These very terms are unnatural. They divide an indivisible. A marriage is a whole. A man and a woman in a marriage build a complete relationship. Loving use of sex contributes to each spouse, and to their total physical and spiritual communion. Even when for good reasons sexual acts are contraceptive, they contribute to the overall generative purpose of marriage in that they inspire and deepen the love and relationships within which off-spring are nurtured.

When the official Catholic position says that contraception is anti-life, it ignores that many marriages using contraceptives are quite manifestly dedicated to life. The intention of such couples is not judged in terms of individual acts, but in terms of a total, responsible use of their marriage. It distorts reality to judge their use of sexuality by examination of each act distinctly. This distortion, consequent on the official view, has been rightly called a 'mechanical' or 'biological' approach to human sexuality.

The official Catholic position replies that an act evil *in itself* cannot be made good by a worthy intention. My first reaction to this is that I do not accept the begged question that contraceptive acts are evil. My second reaction raises wider questions of ethics and is necessarily something of an over-simplification. But glib official statements of the Catholic position, neglectful of counter arguments, are perhaps only amenable to over-simplified objections. So I reply to the official Catholic position that I do not quite know what is meant by an act 'in itself'. Such an act *would* be 'unnatural'. The only acts I know, the only 'natural' acts, are those done by individual persons, in particular contexts, under special pressures, with mixed motives and complex intentions. This is the real context of an act, the context in which an act is properly judged morally. There is literally no such thing as a contraceptive act *in itself*. Who did it? Where and why? There is a sense of unreality about judging contraceptive acts as wrong in themselves. It is the unreality of an abstraction used without due ethical understanding.

I am not excluding considered use of 'abstract' thinking in moral discussion. I am suggesting that in the official Catholic position about contraception, the level of abstraction needs scrutiny. If the law against contraception had been given directly by God, that for the believer would have been the end of the matter. But in the absence of that or the other guarantees mentioned above, we are entitled to ask the official spokesman how the absolute rule against contraception arose.

If it arose, for example, to prevent the human race from becoming extinct, one could well appreciate its purpose. In that situation the law against contraception would be protective of life in particular conditions – short expectation of life, high infantile mortality, uncontrolled disease. Notice, the 'abstract' or absolute rule is not, *thou shalt not contracept*, but is, *your actions should be life-directed*. The law against contraception is thus an application in particular circumstances of a 'higher' moral rule. In new circumstances the 'lower' or derived rule is mistakenly being quoted as the absolute, as the abstract law incapable of being changed. I would rather wish to emphasize the new circumstances – control of death, infantile mortality and disease. I would argue that to retain the old applied law is to offend against the higher value that actions should be life-directed. Whether the official Catholic spokesman would accept my example or not is less important than facing him with this question: what were the reasons which led to the rule against contraception ever being taught? This probing approach is valid nonetheless for its being unfamiliar in Catholic discussion. The too common atmosphere of blind or unquestioning obedience to directives and statements leads to uncritical thinking about morality.

The sense of unreality in the official Catholic position about contraception has, I believe, another root. In Catholic teaching the whole field of sexual morality appears to have a detached place, and an unfortunate history. How much this is a result of a celibate clergy and a male-dominated theology can only be decided by historians and psychologists. Research should be done too on the effects of a theology of virginity, and of the Virgin Mary in particular, which has not always done honour to creation or to the Mother of God. But whatever the effects of these influences, many Catholics have heard much more about the evils of sex than about other evils. They have tended to hear much more about fornication and divorce, than about love and marriage. Sermons about marriage are too often sermons about contraception. Most Catholics know that contraception is a sin; too few realize that the sacrament of marriage is conferred not by the priest in church, but by man and wife on one another, and in the marriage bed.

However ignorant Catholics may be about theology, most of them have learned that sexual sins are to be regarded as serious.

It is at this point that as a Catholic I want to emphasize an oft-ignored fact about the nature of the tradition of the official Catholic teaching about contraception. Pope Paul's encyclical made much of the tradition of what he was reaffirming. The theme was also strong in the many bishops' letters which hastily underlined and toelined the official teaching in the succeeding weeks. It should be squarely recognized that this 'tradition' contained some quite disgusting, almost incredible elements. It has not always been the fine-sounding tradition which Catholics are now fed. The posture against contraception grew in a tradition which at one time regarded any pleasure in married sex as a sin. This matter should be fully explored in a reading of *Birth Regulation and Catholic Belief*[16] by a Catholic priest. His book is notable as a thorough criticism of the official Catholic position. It is especially relevant here as an introduction to what I carefully name the cesspool of traditional Catholic teaching on sex. All too often debate is silenced when minds bow reverently at the word 'tradition', without awareness of what all the ingredients of that tradition were.

In the same way, without apology, I must underline the logic – accepted by the moral theologians – of the official Catholic position on contraception. Sometimes an infertile husband much wanting children is asked for a semen sample for medical examination. To use a sheath (unpunctured) in an act of coitus for this purpose is gravely wrong being a contraceptive act. The child-directed intention does not, even here, save the act. At this point objectors to the official Catholic position are understandably nonplussed or hilarious. If they press their point they very quickly move into another more serious area of objection to the official Catholic position. They ask about killing, against which there is a fairly consistent tradition in the Church. In the case of killing, certain circumstances and a good intention may for Catholics turn a forbidden act into a permissible one; it may even make killing a duty. But there are *no* exceptions for contraception. Again the objector observes that while Catholics are certain about the wrongness of every contraceptive act, they are still uncertain about the hydrogen bomb. These contradictions, be they real or imaginary, are a matter of scandal to the non-Romans. The scandal has other elements. In the eyes of good and sympathetic people the Catholic Church appears more concerned to save its traditional face, than to turn that face to the personal agony of

16. Stanislas De Lestapis, translated by R. Prevett, G. Egner, Sheed & Ward, 1966.

married couples and to the social agony of poverty and starvation. This impression is deep. The warmth in word or intention of Pope Paul's encyclical, or of other restatements of the official Catholic position on contraception, only seem to compound the sense of unreality, if not of hypocrisy. Such non-Roman reactions may be illogical. They may hurt or offend my fellow Catholics. But we should readily understand why any papal or Catholic statement on population and world resources can seem totally irrelevant. They come from a Church which officially forbids all artificial contraception with a conviction not evident in its teaching about weapons of mass destruction.

A semi-defence of the Catholic authorities at this point can, I think, be asserted. It was the facts of world population and human suffering, which served as the pressure background to the last few years' review of the official Catholic teaching on contraception. Another important factor was the arrival of the contraceptive pill, associated in many people's minds with the name of Dr John Rock, a Catholic doctor. I believed in 1964, and still believe, that the specific argument about the pill is important. But it is secondary to general discussion about the morality of contraception as such. Concentration on discussion of the pill was not only because it was new. It also seemed to some to offer a ready way of both allowing contraception and forbidding, in traditional terms, any interference with the process of the sexual act. Perhaps a pill, unlike an appliance, respects the integrity of the sexual act.

Pope Paul's encyclical, however, gave no relaxation in the ban on contraceptive use of the pill. Its use as a regulative boost to the safe period seems well established. The constant risk of confusion in the arguments was well illustrated in the post-encyclical weeks. The Pope was defended on the grounds that it might turn out that the pill was medically harmful. This is a distraction. The moral status of contraception, which was the business of the encyclical, cannot be solved in terms of the medical status of the pill; or in terms of the Pope's non-medical foresight (if so it turns out).

There are Catholics who would object to my saying above that there had been a 'review' of the official teaching. Some stated that the Pope's encyclical, in the very strength of its reaffirmation of traditional teaching, shows that the matter had never been in doubt. Quite apart from the dubious logic of this position, a brief look at the years 1963 to 1968 shows that 'review' is an accurate word.

In 1963 Pope John set up a secret commission to advise the Church on questions of population. It would not be accurate to say that the commission was at its founding a birth-control commission. But as its study progressed, as it recruited more members and was confirmed in being by Pope Paul, it became clear that a thorough examination of official Catholic teaching on contraception was engaging the commission. It reported in 1966 and some of its important findings were leaked and printed in several countries. Allowing for problems of interpreting a non-official translation, the direction of the report was clear. It made an impressive case for change of official Catholic teaching on contraception. The tendency of the report was towards allowing extended contraceptive measures to married Catholics. The majority report gave great satisfaction to many who had been engaged in the contraception debate. Its arguments and insights were the same as those which many Catholics had gained for themselves. The minority report was sincere but had an atmosphere of being rooted not *in* the past but *to* the past. It was described by an eminent American theologian as revealing a mentality of 'classicism' rather than one of 'historical consciousness'. An English doctor member of the commission noted that 'the minority group acknowledged they could not demonstrate the intrinsic evil of contraception on the basis of natural law'.

The sense of review was also heightened by outstanding speeches from four leading prelates at the Vatican Council in 1964. Even earlier, in 1963, another bishop, Bekkers of Holland, had given a broadcast and written an article, which was to English ears startlingly open to new attitudes on contraception. Nor were lay people unheard. Two addresses to the hierarchy of the whole Church were drawn up and signed by eminent Catholics from all over the world (1964 and 1966). In October 1967 the World Congress of Catholic Laity, meeting in Rome, voted in favour of leaving the decision about contraception to the consciences of married couples. The flow of articles and books at times seemed endless. To read even a few was to be impressed. Authors, deeply loyal to their Church, working independently of one another, were coming to see that the official teaching on contraception was unsatisfactory. Two dramatic events in English Catholicism highlighted the urgency of the review of official teaching on contraception. Charles Davis left the priesthood in 1966, and Father Herbert McCabe wrote a comment in 1967 which lost him an editorship. Both these cases were front-page news; both involved discussion of the Catholic position on contraception.

Against that background the apparently one-man decision taken by the Pope is inevitably open to criticism. His decision was in the face of an impressive body of witness to the contrary. It is not just that the Pope did not follow this witness. It is much more that a statement of the official teaching was made with resounding certainty yet without much evidence that impressive witness against had been sufficiently weighed. This is more a question about authority than one about contraception.

Before going further into it, I would like to consider what other courses were open to the Pope besides that of reaffirming the official teaching:

1. He might have repeated the official rules, but have stated that the contraceptive pill was not open to the same objections as other contraceptive measures. Such a decision might have been put forward not as a modification of former teaching, but as a ruling on a new scientific situation.

2. The Pope might have ruled that all contraception in marriage is morally permissible. This would have represented a change of official teaching.

3. The Pope might have spoken to married people somewhat as follows: 'In your use of marriage you have a responsibility not only to produce children, but to decide prudently what number of children you can rear. You also have a duty to preserve the love in your marriage which creates the atmosphere of family life and home in which children can most happily develop. Modern man has discovered several methods of

regulating births. As married people you must make your individual decision about how best to carry out your responsibility to parenthood, to your children, to one another, and to the world. At this moment the Church cannot offer you a clear 'do' and 'don't' about contraceptive measures. From the experience and witness of you married members, the Church may yet see things more clearly.'

As I deplore the decision to reaffirm the official position, so I would reject the first and second possibilities detailed above. I do this because I believe the teaching of the Church *is* in doubt, and that this ought to be stated. It is for this reason that I also reject the possibility suggested by some that the Pope could have said nothing at all.

I have an added reason for rejecting all but the third possibility. It brings me again to the discussion of authority. I would not like the laying down of a rule *against* contraception to be replaced by the laying down of a precise rule *for* contraception. In the present life of the Church, not only in the present situation of doubt about contraception, I think the issuing of a precise rule would be unfortunate. I have two reasons. First, the Church at the Council has been given the opportunity to do much more work at all levels on how authority in the Church is held, worked out and expressed. In simple terms is there a place today in the Church for a one-man statement by the Pope which does not and is not clearly seen to stem from thorough discussion with and in the College of Bishops? Some of the episcopal letters supporting Pope Paul's encyclical read very much as though they were pre-Council documents. They read as though no decision had been made in the Council about the teaching function and authority of the bishops in Council. My second reason is that I question the appropriateness of offering specific guidance in moral questions in papal documents. I question it educationally, morally and theologically. It is unlikely to lead to the working out of an adult moral awareness in the members of the Church. It locates the responsibility for moral decision and witness in only one element of the Church. It encourages moral laziness and over-dependence.

If this sounds like arrogance, I can argue further. After

Pope Paul's encyclical many people spoke as if the matter were settled; so settled that it would be wrong to ask any questions, make any criticisms of the encyclical. Some Catholic authorities hold that the encyclical requires the intellectual and moral assent of the Church member. Fortunately some authoritative theologians have begun to question what possible meaning can be given to saying that a papal statement demands 'intellectual and moral assent'. But that point apart, why should it be considered virtuous to give uncritical assent to a document about which there are some unknowns? Did the Pope write it? Was it written for him by someone else – if so, by whom? Was the documentation favouring change submitted in full to him – if so, by whom? Was this documentation understood? Were those in favour of change allowed to explain their views face to face with the Pope? Were others given a more favoured ear? Was the Pope swayed not so much by arguments about contraception, as by his fears about misunderstanding of the Church's authority if there was a change? Why do the arguments for change not get the hearing or the footnote documentation which the traditional position gets? Was the Pope confused, overtired, emotionally exhausted, unwell when he considered and decided to issue the letter?

These are not the questions of someone who wants to explain away the encyclical on a conspiracy theory. They are and must be the questions of an adult person who believes in and cares about God and his Church. They must be the questions of one who is asked to give assent with mind and will to a document issued personally, and from on high.

The future of the Catholic debate about contraception is unclear, if what I have suggested earlier is true, and real debate will be about the nature of authority in the Church. As one aspect of this there will be more open discussion about the special status, if any, within that authority of a papal statement. As a contribution to this debate I would like to offer one possible insight. It is a mark of human groups to set someone up, push him into a role and then punish him for taking it. Sometimes this phenomenon is expressed by saying that there is collusion between the group and the individual to allow him to behave in a particular way. There is collusion even though the group may protest loudly about the individual's behaviour.

The Pope has been attacked and criticized (including by me) for making an individual decision on the contraceptive issue. But the facts are that the decision about contraception was taken out of the bishops' hands in the Vatican Council in 1964. In other words for some years the bishops, the Papal Commission, theologians and we lay people have colluded with the Pope's solitary decision. Our collusion may be partly explained by the belief of many that the decision would be in favour of contraception. But that is beside the point – a decision in favour would still have been a solitary decision because we had allowed it to be so. The time to protest more loudly about the solitary decision was not after the encyclical perhaps, so much as when the matter was first taken from the Council, and while the decision was being papally pondered. I feel certain that social psychologists may yet accuse even the radicals of collusion with the situation which allowed Pope Paul's authoritarian encyclical to appear.

In more specific terms one could certainly accuse the bishops of not taking their collegiate status seriously. After this point had been made in Council, they did not ask for the contraception question to be returned for full discussion by the bishops. I would support this again by reference to the bishop's letters which came out after Pope Paul's encyclical. They seemed to sigh with relief not only that a decision had been made about contraception, not only that the decision was as many of them had wanted, but also that they had been spared the logic or realities by their college. On other matters it was reported of the Council that bishops had a habit of speaking and writing as if they had not read, or had not fully realized the import of the documents they had passed at earlier sessions.

Finally, what of the practical level of the Catholic view? I believe that in the time of the review many Catholics formed not only a habit of contraception but, much more importantly, came to see that there were moral matters on which they must follow their consciences. To that extent the reaffirmation of the official teaching will not drive all the 'rebels' out of the Church. Some *will* leave. Others will stay believing, I think rightly, that membership of the Catholic Church does not involve a belief that contraception is morally evil.

There are many others who because of indoctrination and ignorance and the atrophy of any adult moral awareness, will not find their decisions so easy. Much will depend on the contributions made by the priests who hear confessions and who preach.

It is concern for inarticulate Catholics and for the countless human beings in underdeveloped countries that convinces me of one thing. There must be sustained Catholic criticism of Pope Paul's encyclical, and so of the official Roman teaching on contraception. If at some future time that encyclical is quoted in support of 'tradition', equally clearly recorded must be the substantial witness of loyal Catholics against both the content and the manner of the encyclical's rulings.

I am hopeful that before too long thought and talk in Catholic circles will not be about the nature of individual sexual acts. The talk will be about the nature of human freedom, the nature of the human mind, the nature of human love in all senses. I believe we shall emerge from the distracting trivialities of the debate about contraceptives. At that point we Catholics may become of much more use to our contemporaries.

It is because of that belief, that promise, that I have assumed that non-Roman readers will be interested in yet another piece of agonizing about Catholicism and contraception.

If my hope is wrong, there will be a crisis in Catholicism. It will not be a crisis of contraception or of authority. It will be the much worse crisis of relevance: of relevance to the world and to the service of humanity. That service does have a long and consistent tradition as the way to serve the Creator.

ROMAN CATHOLIC DOCTORS AND BIRTH CONTROL

Results of a survey of 654 Catholic doctors (published in the *Guardian*, 10 September 1965) show big majorities against the official Roman Catholic policy on birth control. Results of answers to five of the eight questions are given here.

	Yes	No	Uncertain
In your experience do Catholics practise contraceptions?	536	60	58
In your experience is the rhythm method successful?	242	325	87
Do you think that a drug which temporarily suspends ovulation or spermatogenesis is a contraceptive?	469	158	27
Do you in your own conscience regard contraception, within the bonds of marriage, as against natural law?	246	381	27
Do you in your own conscience think that contraception within the bonds of marriage should be permitted in circumstances such as:			
(a) to prevent the break-up of a marriage;	440	197	17
(b) for medical reasons	487	150	17
(c) for economic reasons	415	219	20

9
Wider Consequences of Planning

The idea of human improvement began to take firm shape in the seventeenth century, and by the nineteenth century men like Francis Galton were beginning to ask if heredity might not be controlled in such a way as to enrich our inborn endowments and give us a better start in life. Sir Peter Medawar and Dr Fraser Roberts show that there are grave and perhaps insuperable obstacles in the way of achieving this ambition. This does not mean that nothing can be done to improve our hereditary condition. A modest and scientifically well-founded policy of negative eugenics – 'piecemeal genetic engineering' – could do much to control certain grave defects of the genetic constitution and thus reduce the burden of human distress.

(I) PRINCIPLE AND PARADOX

PETER MEDAWAR

'Eugenics', said Sir Francis Galton, founder of the subject, 'is the science which deals with all the influence that improves the inborn qualities of a race; also with those that develop them to the utmost advantage.' So he wrote in 1904. And again in 1908,

> Man is gifted with pity and other kindly feelings; he has also the power of preventing many kinds of suffering. I conceive it to fall well within his province to replace natural selection by other processes that are more merciful and not less effective. That is precisely the aim of eugenics.

These are honourable and humane ambitions; what prevents our trying to realize them forthwith? A first difficulty is that two ambitions are expressed by these quotations; they may not be fully reconcilable, and the policies that serve one may not necessarily serve the other. Galton declares his concern for the welfare of the race, of the human species, of mankind considered collectively; but, being a humane man, he is also deeply concerned with the happiness and welfare of the individual. At first sight it seems obvious that what is best for each member of the population considered individually must be best for the race considered as a whole.

NEED FOR ADAPTABILITY

This is not necessarily so. It might be so if we lived, and had always lived, in a uniform and unchanging environment, in which natural selection could, as it were, devise some one best genetic solution of the problem of remaining alive and perpetuating our kind. In real life, however, the environment changes from time to time and from place to place, and it is therefore unconditionally necessary that a free-living population should always contain at least some members that can cope with new environments, new climates, and new enemies and infections.

This puts a certain high premium on genetic inequality or diversity. Some geneticists believe that free-living outbreeding populations such as our own are armed with an in-built genetic device which enforces genetic diversity, which makes sure that not all its individual members are genetically identical. This device is one in which predominantly hybrid (or rather, heterozygous) animals leave the most offspring, i.e. are the fittest in the Darwinian sense. Genetical diversity is ensured by the fact that hybrid animals do not 'breed true': their progeny differ from themselves and from one another. So far as present evidence goes (though some geneticists dispute it) it seems that the genetic make-up of outbreeding populations is a compromise between getting the best performance out of particular individuals and at the same time making sure that the population contains a great variety of individuals of different genetic types. It is a compromise between adaptedness and adaptability.

If this interpretation is true, it implies that the genetical system of human beings cannot be reconciled with the utopian conception of the older eugenicists with the belief that by adapting one genetic policy or another it is in principle possible to arrive at a population of uniformly excellent individuals who 'breed true', i.e. whose progeny have the same genetic make-up as themselves.

It may be argued that livestock breeders have already achieved this very thing in establishing 'pure breeds' that answer their preconceived requirements; that they have mastered the arts of applied genetics and that it is therefore open to us, in principle, to apply their knowledge to man. Unfortunately, they have done nothing of the kind. Livestock breeding is still a matter of empiricism and opportunism. One great branch of the livestock industry is moving rapidly towards the policy of crossbreeding – a frank abandonment of the utopian goal represented by the pure-breeding animal which in itself embodies the characteristics that the breeder seeks. We are not nearly as well informed about evolutionary genetics as we may like to think.

GENETICS AND HOMOSEXUALITY

Consider for a moment Dr Evelyn Hutchinson's amusing paradox about the genetical background of the paraphilias – of abnormal sexual preferences, homosexuality for example. Let us assume that paraphilic tendencies are deeply grounded in the genetic constitution; and let us also assume (what is very likely, though it has not been proved) that on the average paraphilics are less fertile than normal people – less fertile in the demographer's sense of leaving fewer children, and of making, therefore, a smaller contribution to the population of the future. If these assumptions are true, then natural selection should act in such a way as to eradicate the genetic constitutions that predispose towards paraphilia. Yet very evidently it has not done so. Either then we simply do not understand the pattern of inheritance of sexual tastes; or alternatively we must conclude that these tastes are not under any significant degree of genetical control, in which case the influence of genetic make-up on our behaviour has been greatly exaggerated.

In my opinion current genetical knowledge will simply not sustain a utopian genetics of race, of species, or of man in the abstract. What we must attempt to do is to replace this grandiose and heroic eugenics by a much more humble policy, which by a piece of gross plagiarism from Professor Karl Popper I propose to call 'piecemeal genetical engineering' – in the words of William Blake, 'the policy of doing good in minute particulars'.

HARMFUL ACCIDENTS

Before I turn to consider the ways in which the more humble policy I advocate might be put into effect, let us consider the principles that justify our belief in eugenics as a humane, rational and practicable enterprise. The first is that defects of the genetic constitution have a simple and particular basis, though they do not always have simple and particular consequences. This is self-evident. All geneticists believe that 'fitness' in its most general sense depends upon a nicely balanced co-ordination and interaction of particular genetic factors, itself the laborious product of evolutionary adjustment.

It is inconceivable, indeed self-contradictory, that an animal should evolve into the possession of some complex pattern of cooperation between genes that put it at a disadvantage, or made it inefficient or unfit. Breakdowns or ineptitudes of the genetic apparatus are therefore adventitious in character, or, as philosophers would say, accidental. Mutations and chromosomal accidents may be so described, and so also the unlucky genetic conjunctions that bring together a pair of harmful recessive genes within one individual.

The point then is that many genetic defects are, in principle, manageable; that even when the somatic consequences of a particular genetic defect are manifold and widespread, we can still in principle entertain the possibility of prevention or of cure.

NO 'CONGENITAL GENIUS'

It is a lay superstition that congenital afflictions are incurable. The very word 'congenital' has a dire sound, because it is used only in a pejorative sense: one hears of congenital imbeciles but never of congenital geniuses. It is quite untrue to say that the congenital diseases cannot be cured. Phenylketonuria and galactosaemia will be cured in the foreseeable future.[1] It is true that if one cures a condition like phenylketonuria by making certain adjustments of diet, a genetical defect remains; but the important thing to remember is that the genetical defect that remains is not phenylketonuria – it is a genetic disability that debars its victims from eating what they choose. In other words it is a genetical disability which leads to a restriction of freedom. Certainly it is worse than the sort of disability which obliges quite a number of unfortunate people to wear spectacles, but not so much worse that we should be content to see its victims die.

There are some inborn genetical disorders for which it is very difficult to envisage the possibility of a cure. The most important of them is mongolism, an important source of human wastage and distress. In 1959 three French geneticists demonstrated that mongolism is the result of a genetical accident involving a whole chromosome – the triplication of a chomosome which in normal individuals exists only in duplicate. Fortunately most forms of mongolism do not raise a eugenical problem; most mongols are either actually or effectively infertile.

Here I think one must take comfort from the fact that there

1. Phenylketonuria is a 'biochemical' disease whose victims cannot break down the compound phenylalanine: gross mental defect is the most conspicuous of its many consequences. The victims of galactosaemia are unable to break down a derivative of milk sugar. Among its consequences are retardation of growth, cataract and mental deficiency. Both these diseases have single particular biochemical causes and both are due to the conjunction of particular recessive genes. In both treatment turns on early diagnosis followed by withholding phenylalanine or lactose from the diet.

are certain widespread demographic tendencies which in themselves will reduce the incidence of mongolism. One of them is the tendency, already apparent in the United States and the United Kingdom, for married couples to complete their families a good deal earlier in married life than they would have done fifty or a hundred years ago. The frequency of mongolism in children rises very sharply with the age of their mothers, and the tendency towards an early completion of families is therefore bound to lower its incidence.

When we turn to the particular forms a policy of 'piecemeal genetical engineering' might take, I think we shall find a great measure of agreement among geneticists, for the rancour and bitterness that have disfigured the history of eugenics have risen mainly out of matters of grand genetic policy.

LETHAL DOMINANTS

Consider first what are loosely called the 'dominant' inborn diseases, diseases attributable to harmful genes which have been inherited from only one parent, or have arisen by mutation in only one gamete. There must be many such afflictions, and they may account for much of the unexplained balance of human mortality before birth. The most merciful, paradoxically enough, are those so rapid and devastating in their effects that they destroy the embryo early in pre-natal life, perhaps shortly after conception. They may cause no more distress than an early miscarriage or a missed menstrual period.

Afflictions of this kind are self-limiting and raise no great eugenic problem; the genes responsible for them must have arisen by mutation, and disappear with their possessors. But grave eugenic problems are raised by dominant afflictions which, like achondroplastic dwarfism, cause grave damage short of death, or which do not make themselves apparent until later on in life. Among the latter are Huntington's chorea and familial intestinal polyposis, leading to cancer. The average age of incidence of both is about thirty-five, so that parents who are to be victims of the disease can have children before it becomes manifest.

I think most geneticists would agree that the humane and rational policy here is to warn the future victims of these diseases, if they can be identified, of the consequences of their having children; to warn them that, on the average, half of any children they may have will be afflicted as they were themselves. No humane parent would have children at such a high risk of their being exposed to acute physical and moral distress. When one of the potential parents is himself or herself the child of a victim of the disease, the problem will be to identify the disease early enough in life for the warning to be effective. The task will be much more difficult, though not insuperable, when the offending gene has arisen by mutation, so that there is no family history to forewarn the parents that it may appear. But if all the future victims of Huntington's chorea and familial intestinal polyposis could be identified in good time, and if all foreswore having children, then the incidence of the disease would be reduced to the very low rate at which it is introduced into the community by mutation.

HAEMOPHILIA

As Professor J. B. S. Haldane has pointed out, much the same argument applies, *mutatis mutandis*, to sex-linked recessive diseases like haemophilia. With very rare exceptions only males are afflicted. A male parent cannot transmit the gene responsible for it to his sons, but he transmits it to all his daughters, with the effect that, on the average, half his daughters' sons will be afflicted by haemophilia and half his daughters' daughters, like their mothers, will be carriers. Here, too, a victim of haemophilia should be warned of the consequences of his having children. Where there is a history of haemophilia in a family it would of course be of the utmost advantage to identify those women who are carriers of the gene, but this is not yet possible.

The gravest eugenical problems arise over the 'inherited' diseases that are collectively the most numerous: the so-called 'recessive diseases', produced by genes that must be inherited from both parents (or which must be carried by both the gametes that unite to form a fertilized egg) if they are to exercise a damaging effect. In such a context the parents are carriers of (i.e. are heterozygous for) the gene, though they are not harmed by its presence. Among recessive diseases are fibrocystic disease of the pancreas, which is said to afflict approximately one child in 2,500 (a very high figure for any one such disease), and phenylketonuria and galactosaemia, which have been referred to.

AVOIDING MARRIAGE BETWEEN CARRIERS

What is to be done here? The policy of sterilizing the afflicted has been discredited, for those in whom the disease makes itself manifest are a very small fraction of those who in the genetical sense 'carry' it. To discourage childbearing by the carriers of harmful recessive genes would be to commit racial suicide, for all of us carry such genes. Some think that each one of us may carry as many as eight. A third policy, advocated by Professor Haldane, depends for its success on being able to identify the carriers of harmful recessive genes, usually by their possession of some very mild and in itself trivial disorder biochemically akin to the full recessive form of the disease. If the carriers of single particular harmful recessive genes could be identified, they should be warned of the consequences of marrying each other and having children – for, on the average, one quarter of their children will be victims of the disease and one half carriers.

The proportion of marriages 'contra-indicated' by this policy would not be large: if the incidence of the disease were one in 40,000 (which is high), only about one marriage in 10,000 would be a marriage between its carriers, to be advised against for that reason. In these days of blood grouping, very few people would object to the performance of simple biochemical tests that might do so much to secure the welfare of their future children, and there will be no insuperable difficulty in applying such tests when a family history gives grounds for suspecting that a future parent may carry a particular recessive gene.

Principle and Paradox

A THEORETICAL DANGER

The wholesale application of such a policy (when we are technically equipped to put it into practice) would reduce the overt incidence of particular recessive diseases to a very low level indeed. This would be a symptomatic solution of the eugenic problem. If our ambition is to eradicate the disease, this policy will put it in our power to do so. There is only the danger to be considered. The frequency of the occurrence of a lethal or incapacitating recessive disease represents an equilibrium between the rate at which the gene responsible for it is introduced into the population by mutation and the rate at which the gene is lost by the death or infertility of those in whom its effects appear. This is simply natural selection at work.

It is to be assumed that, where carriers of particular recessive genes have been dissuaded from marrying each other, they will marry other, normal people, and have children by them. The gene will therefore be propagated in the population, and natural selection will be unable to prevent its slow but progressive increase by mutation – for by preventing the genetic conjunction that brings two such genes together, we are denying natural selection its opportunity to reduce their number. In the very long run the carriers of particular genes must have children by each other if they are to have children at all.

This is a danger of principle only, and I use it merely to illustrate the antithesis between 'symptomatic' eugenics and eugenics of a more radical kind. It does however point the moral that ultimately in a humane society the only formula that will meet the problem of damaging recessive diseases is 'study and cure'.

SLOWNESS OF EVOLUTION

The problems first raised by Sir Francis Galton are becoming slowly and progressively more urgent. I say 'slowly' because, after all, the unit of the time scale of human evolution is a generation of some twenty or thirty years. This is a most reassuring fact, because (if I may compare obviously incommensurable quantities) the rate of accession of knowledge of human genetics is enormously greater than the rate of human evolution. Not much human evolution has happened in the last five years, yet in that period the causes of at least one human polymorphism, that responsible for sickle cell disease, have been elucidated. Great progress has been made in identifying the carriers of harmful recessive genes. A new class of inborn disorders has been disclosed by the study of human chromosomes. Much has been learnt about the genetical effects of radiation on whole animals or cells. Progress has been made with the study of the most difficult problems of genetics, the inheritance of differences controlled not by one or a few, but by a multitude of cooperating and interacting genes. And it is important to remember that, on this time scale, the proposals that we may make today about safeguarding the genetic welfare of human beings are not binding upon us in perpetuity; they are not irreversible, and if they turn out to be faulty they can be revised.

I say 'progressively' because, of those children who still die in infancy or are afflicted by disease a steadily increasing proportion is afflicted by 'inborn' disorders. I emphasize that it is a matter of proportion, not of absolute numbers: the inborn disorders take a larger toll because the infective and metabolic diseases take a lesser. In any event the generalization is true only of advanced industrial countries. In the world as a whole the inherited disorders are still of minor importance. Some 250 million people are said to be afflicted by malaria in the world today, of whom some $2\frac{1}{2}$ million die each year; and no one knows the number of deaths that can be attributed directly or indirectly to nutritional diseases, above all to protein-deficiency diseases.

CONCLUSION

In summary, then, I have drawn a distinction between on the one hand a heroic eugenics whose ultimate ambition is to reshape the genetic constitution of mankind; and on the other hand a 'piecemeal genetical engineering' dedicated to the welfare of individual men and women and content with the policy of doing good in minute particulars. I propose that we forswear the heroic eugenics and blood and soil and species and race, since it may be faulty in principle, and since neither our knowledge nor our humane inclinations will run to it.

I began with two quotations from Galton: let me enlist him as my ally with a third: 'It is above all needful for the successful progress of eugenics that its advocates should move discreetly and claim no more efficacy on its behalf than the future will confirm; otherwise a reaction will be invited.'

(II) GENETIC ADVICE FOR POTENTIAL PARENTS
JOHN FRASER ROBERTS

Some people fear, sometimes rightly, but often wrongly, that they run a serious risk of having an abnormal child. Maybe there is something in the family history which raises doubts. The great majority of inquiries, however, come from couples who have already had an abnormal child and who want to know what the risk of having another is. In the greater proportion of these cases there was nothing, before the disaster happened, that could have warned the parents or anyone else of what was to come. Routine premarital investigation of family histories can do little good and may well encourage the neurotic. Couples should not be unduly concerned about common diseases which have some genetic element in their causation – few families are free of such things. If it is not hypertension, it may be asthma, or some other allergy, gout, ischaemic heart disease, or many other such things, and it is best that couples should go ahead without worrying too much about the future.

DEFINITE RISKS

What may legitimately cause worry are the definite and considerable risks. The proportion of couples really needing genetic advice is relatively small, but those who do need advice need it badly. The problems are difficult, and deep-seated feelings are aroused: whether to risk having another child, whether to accept deprivation or whether to adopt a child. It is not a question of doctor's advice or nothing. Unfortunately the whole subject of the welfare of the unborn child and of the prospective child has collected through the ages a great mass of superstitions and old wives' tales; and, it must be said quite bluntly, these superstitions are of the most senseless and useless kind, usually of a gloomy and alarming character. Then there are the feelings of guilt, sometimes open, sometimes concealed, but nearly always ill founded. Sometimes there is the question as to which side of the family is responsible or the tacit assumption of many women that they alone are 'to blame'.

Fortunately there is now a large and growing body of medical knowledge. Sometimes the risk of recurrence can be specified precisely; sometimes a useful approximate estimate can be made. Often, though the genetics are obscure and uncertainties remain, it is reasonably certain that the risk of recurrence is low.

RISKS OF RECURRENCE

In assessing the importance of the risk of recurrence it is useful to have a yardstick in mind. The approximate one I use is that the chance that any pregnancy will end with some severe malformation or other, or that some serious error of development will manifest itself in early life, is about one in forty. If a particular couple's own special risk does not greatly exceed this amount, then it seems a good risk, a risk of an order that most sensible people, knowing the facts, might feel it reasonable to run. Big risks of recurrence on the other hand, say risks exceeding about one in ten, might be called bad risks, for many couples would feel that this was too great a chance to take, and would prefer to limit their families or to adopt a child. It is a fortunate fact that the great majority of risks do group themselves into these two regions, either worse than one in ten, or else better, and sometimes very much better, than one in forty.

BAD RISKS

In the great majority of instances the bad risks involve simple, straightforward inheritance. It is here that the observer is on the surest ground and can usually specify the risk precisely. Simply inherited conditions are practically always rare or very rare, but they are important, because there are many of them. The commonest simply inherited condition in our own population is fibrocystic disease of the pancreas, with a frequency of perhaps one in 2,000 births.

In the dominant conditions, which are determined by a gene in single dose, the pattern is direct transmission from parent to child, and the affected parent has one chance in two that any child will be similarly affected. In general such malformations, as for example polydactyly, are not very important. The parent has lived with it and not been too much handicapped, and I cannot see why he, or she, should not take the chance of passing it on to a child. A few dominant conditions however, such as Huntington's chorea,[1] raise special problems. Although this is a disabling and ultimately fatal condition, the average age of onset is about thirty-five years, so that sufferers have every chance of producing a family before it becomes manifest, and of their children, half, on the average, will be similarly affected.

SEX-LINKED CONDITIONS

Sex-linked conditions are due to genes carried on the X chromosome, of which the female has two and the male only one. The numerically important sex-linked conditions in our own population are haemophilia and the commonest type of muscular dystrophy, the Duchenne type. Women who carry this gene have an abnormal gene on one X chromosome and are outwardly normal, but on the average one son in two will be affected and one daughter in two will be a carrier. The choice for the sister of affected boys is particularly difficult. She has one chance in two of being a carrier, so that on the average

1. A grave nervous disorder, superficially resembling St Vitus' dance.

there is one chance in four that any boy will be affected or any girl a carrier. It is greatly to be hoped that in due time tests will become available to determine which sisters of affected boys are in fact carriers and which have escaped.

RECESSIVE DEFECTS

In practice the most important kind of simply inherited defects are recessive, and these may illustrate some of the problems involved in trying to give genetic advice to patients when the risks are bad. With recessive defects the person who carries one abnormal gene is outwardly normal and the defect appears only when a child receives two. Thus recessive defects appear when two persons marry who chance to carry the same harmful recessive gene. Each time the father and the mother have one chance in two of passing on the harmful gene, so there is one chance in four that both will do so and the child be affected. If parents have a child suffering from one of the recessive defects one can only say that the chance is one in four that any subsequent child will be similarly affected – but there is a great deal more to add.

First, we all of us carry at least two or three seriously harmful recessive genes or their equivalents. Most of us, however, have the luck to marry someone who does not carry our own particular harmful kinds, but some quite different ones instead, and so there is no possibility of their coming together in pairs. Moreover, human families being small, it must often happen that two people happen to marry who do carry the same harmful recessive gene, but are lucky because the one-in-four chance did not come up. This will happen to three out of four couples with one-child families. The chance is nine out of 16 with two-child families, and still 27 out of 64 with three-child families. There must be many of us who do in fact carry the same harmful gene as our wife, or husband, and have had one, or two, or three, or more, normal children, and can never know the danger we so narrowly escaped. The parents of the child suffering from a recessive defect can therefore be assured that they are in no way peculiar or different from other people.

They have been unlucky in suffering a misfortune that could happen to anyone. Moreover in the vast majority of cases there is no similar instance that can be discovered in either family. It came as a bolt from the blue; nothing that was done or not done could have affected the outcome and there could have been no warning.

The normal brothers and sisters of the affected child, and the normal younger brothers and sisters of the parents, have nothing to worry about when the time comes for marriage and children. True, they may carry the gene, but the likelihood of marrying someone carrying the very same gene is remote. And, to repeat, we all carry harmful recessive genes of one kind or another.

These are the bad risks. There are a few others where the genetics are not clear but the chance of recurrence is known to be fairly high. Such instances are rare.

RELATIVELY GOOD RISKS

When we turn from simple inheritance we nearly always find ourselves in the realms of the relatively good risks. For example, if a couple have had a child with spina bifida[2] or anencephaly[3] the risk that a subsequent child will be similarly affected is about one in twenty-five. The risk is about the same when a normal couple have a child with harelip. In some of these relatively good risks the chances are considerably better, or much better, than this. It is true that the genetics are often obscure and not well understood; such conditions may fairly be called partly genetic, for with many of them it is known that other, and non-genetic, factors are involved. Many extensive surveys, however, have been carried out on a wide variety of these partly inherited malformations, and at least the risk of recurrence in a further child can be assessed approximately: it usually proves to be relatively small and not unreasonably out of proportion to the inevitable chance taken by any couple whenever they have a child. It should also be mentioned that

2. Bifurcation of the vertebral spines.
3. Absence of the highly developed parts of the brain.

these conditions, which I have referred to rather loosely as partly inherited, are much commoner in the aggregate than the simply and purely inherited conditions. There is reason for concern, of course, and it is surely wise for parents to find out what the chances for a further child may be, but it remains an encouraging fact that with the general run of genetic inquiries by parents the answer is considerably more often encouraging rather than the reverse. It may well be that the harm done by the birth of a deformed child when parents might have refrained had they known the true risk was less than the harm done by refraining from parenthood when the risk was actually very small or, for practical purposes, negligible.

Appendix

The problem of family planning and population control are world wide. In recent years there has been a great expansion in the efforts devoted towards solving them.

The United Nations has come late on to the scene. Early attempts to get the World Health Organization to take action were frustrated by Catholic countries and, until recently, opposition was still effective. George Cadbury, Chairman of the Governing Body of the IPPF, writes of the United Nations' more positive and hopeful approach.

The International Planned Parenthood Federation, which is only twenty years old now has a membership of fifty-four countries and a budget of over a million dollars; it is supported by governments and recognized by the United Nations. Sir Colville Deverell, former secretary-general of the IPPF, describes its history and functions.

(I) UNITED NATIONS – THE STATUTORY BODY

GEORGE CADBURY

It is now 1971 and the debate goes on; but with a difference. In 1963 the story had to begin with the words 'There has been a debate – the world against the Roman Catholic Church' and to end with a story of postponement of any serious decision. In 1966 the deferred resolution finally reached the General Assembly and was passed overwhelmingly. The Roman Catholics still argue. The Pope has not given any ground. The Catholics have acquired some Communist allies, but they can no longer postpone or defeat programmes in the United Nations on this subject. I will illustrate this with some examples.

One of the most important commissions in the United Nations is that on social development, and at its nineteenth session in February 1968 it gave considerable attention to the question of family planning. The crux of the debate came when a working party reported on the necessity for the inclusion of a reference to family planning in any comprehensive declaration on social development. The key paragraph that was finally adopted as one of the principles reads:

> The family as the basic unit of society and the natural environment for the growth and well-being of all its members, particularly children and youth, should be strengthened by all possible means, each family having the right to decide the number of its children.

The vote was twenty-six in favour, none against with two abstentions. Before this, however, the final phrase was only included by a vote of thirteen to twelve with three abstentions, and some of the objectors explained their votes as follows: Inam-ul-Haque (Pakistan), Pierre Sanon (Upper Volta), Nita Constantin (Romania), Abdallah B. Suedi (United Republic of Tanzania) and M. Aboul Nasr (United Arab Republic) said that the second part of the paragraph did not belong in the section dealing with principles. Mrs Fatima Hanchi (Mauritania), Z. K. Matthews (Botswana), and Mr Constantin (Romania) said that family planning should be exercised within the framework of national demographic policies. Mrs Kastalskaya (Soviet Union) said that she would have preferred that there be no reference to family planning in the draft. Family planning was not sufficiently understood, and could damage the natural *rhythm* of growth in some developing countries, she said.

The paragraph quoted above was followed by another in the section on means and methods which read as follows:

> The establishment is needed of programmes in the field of population consistent with and related to the economic, social, religious, spiritual and cultural circumstances of the respective countries, including the provision to families within the framework of national demographic policies, of the necessary knowledge and means to enable them to exercise their right to determine the number and spacing of their children.

In another resolution, sponsored by Canada, Chile, France, Iran, the Netherlands, Norway, Pakistan, the United Kingdom and the USA, dealing with the guidelines necessary for the formulation of social goals and programmes in the next decade, there is a reference to population as follows: 'Programmes should take into account the importance of rates of population growth and patterns of distribution consistent with achieving rising levels of living.'

A further document before the commission was the *Report on the World Situation* prepared by the Secretariat which read in part:

The world's population increased by approximately 290 million people between 1960 and 1965, reaching a total of 3,295 million; this represents an estimated annual rate of growth of 1·9 per cent or an increase of 0·1 per cent by comparison with the decade 1950–60. The high population growth rates prevailing in the less developed regions continued into the 1960s and there is evidence that these rates have in many countries continued to rise. Around 1960 fertility rates in less developed countries were about double those of the economically advanced countries. Crude birth rates in developing countries varied mostly between thirty-five and fifty-five per thousand.

The implications for economic and social development of this unprecedented rate of population growth have caused widespread concern and a number of countries have adopted policies in favour of family planning. In other instances governments have encouraged birth-control programmes without having formally adopted family-planning programmes.

The growth of the world's urban population, which between 1950 and 1960 was over twice as rapid as that of the world's total population, continued unabated in both the less developed and the economically advanced regions. Tentative projections suggest that by 1980 approximately one third of the world's population will live in urban localities. In the less developed countries the problem is one of a massive influx of the poor from surrounding rural areas into the towns and the consequent mushrooming of squatter settlements and shanty-towns. In the economically advanced countries urban growth is characterized by the rapid expansion of metropolitan areas which is often accompanied by a decline in the population and physical conditions in the centre of such areas. Housing continues to lag behind needs.

In their recorded comments on this report the commission

stressed the importance of the problems associated with rapid population growth in many parts of the world; it was also recognized that in some areas it was rather a lack of population, or questions of population distribution, that might be acting as an obstacle to development. In order for families to exercise the basic responsibility, that was uniquely theirs, in determining the size of the family, within the framework of national demographic policies, it was necessary for them to possess sufficient knowledge to make an informed decision. In view of the complexity of the phenomenon of population growth and its relationship to the development process, it was thought necessary to consider more comprehensive policies and to ensure in the meantime that targets for development take fully into account the factor of rapid population growth. Further study was recommended of the social causative factors of differences in fertility levels, particularly among countries at similar levels of socio-economic development.

At about the same time as the Social Commission was sitting the Commission on the Status of Women also met. As one of the principal documents before it there was an interim report from the Secretary General on *Family Planning and the Status of Women*. It is a cautious document as most Secretariat-produced documents are bound to be, but when compared with what the United Nations would have produced three or four years ago, it seems almost revolutionary, and the turning point was clearly the passage of the General Assembly resolution in 1966. This was the resolution that was so improperly delayed in 1965, when the Vatican organized its last major effort to keep the subject away from the Assembly.

Now we can read statements like these from the report:

Efforts of the international community to aid governments of developing countries in achieving social advancement and sustained economic growth, which was the goal of the United Nations Development Decade, were thwarted to a great extent by rising rates of population growth in many countries.

The deliberations at the World Population Conference convened by the Economic and Social Council in Yugoslavia in 1965 made it evident that there was widespread sentiment in favour of family planning as an integral part of national developmental planning in areas of rapid population growth.

The Council considered at its forty-third session a report of the Secretary-General on the *Development and Utilization of Human Resources in Developing Countries*. The report recommends, among other means of aiding the development and utilization of human resources, the promotion as appropriate of family planning and child-care services.

At previous meetings the Commission on the Status of Women had adopted two resolutions on this subject. In one the Commission considered that the responsibility for planning a family should be freely assumed by both spouses according to their available facilities for giving adequate care and nurture to their children and with regard to the preservation of the health of the mother. It recognized that lack of family planning may be detrimental to the welfare of the family and interfere with the mother's own advancement and with her contribution to the development of her community and the progress of her country. The Commission also considered that married couples should have access to all relevant educational information concerning family planning. It suggested that non-governmental organizations in consultative status, each in accord with its own programme, objectives and policies, study the possibility of making available the increasing fund of knowledge in this field as a source of assistance to married couples in fulfilling their parental responsibilities.

In the other the Commission expressed the belief that expanded research with regard to family planning will be of great value, and that educational information, which can be expected to result from this research, should be available to women in developed as well as in developing countries. The commission welcomed the increasing recognition of the role of United Nations agencies in providing assistance upon the request of governments, in educational programmes concerned with the planning of families.

And then at this meeting in 1968 the commission made a very strong recommendation to the Economic and Social Council of the United Nations for action about family planning and appointed a special *rapporteur* on the subject to keep continuous interest alive.

The final vote was nineteen votes to two with nine abstentions after the United Kingdom delegate (Mrs Shirley Summerskill, MP) had successfully strengthened the resolution by adding references to the treatment of sterility, the provision of maternal and child-care facilities, and the dissemination of educational information including sex education and marriage counselling. Thus was British honour redeemed after their earlier performances at the Commission.

The two negative votes were cast by Russia and Byelo Russia but the explanation of some of the abstentions is interesting. Guinea and Mauritania abstained because their countries were underpopulated; Mexico because 'hunger could not be solved by limiting the number of mouths to be fed, but by increasing the amount of food available'; Peru because family planning must develop out of a process of social and cultural change in accordance with the principles of the papal encyclical *De populorum progessio*; Hungary because the 'concept of family planning had not been clearly defined'; and Spain because 'of her country's regulations concerning the protection of the family'.

How much explanation and education still remains to be done. How strange a partnership we see between Catholic and Communists, and how happy a government like Hungary's must be to find at least one issue on which such major internal forces can unite.

The third body also meeting at this time was the Human Rights Commission, which was preparatory to the world conference which was held last year at Teheran. The subject did not loom large in this commission's meetings but it was recognized that the right to the knowledge of how to control birth should be available to all men and women.

Another United Nations body that has a real interest in all aspects of the population question is obviously the Population Commission. Composed mainly of demographers and demographic statisticians it has had a hard time in making up its mind that the implementation of its studies in action was really its concern. But here again the atmosphere has changed. The dilemma of Catholics and Communists remains, but they have been unable to use their minority position to block all action and the Population Commission at its October 1967 meeting noted that its future work programme should, *inter alia*, give due attention to the study of fertility and to all technical cooperation programmes within this field, including family planning.

Here then is the evidence of a real revolution. The Catholic and Communist minorities can no longer block progress. The official United Nations and Specialized Agencies are going to take action and to cooperate with the voluntary bodies all over the world. It is difficult to know how much their official support may mean, but coming as it does at the same time as many governments have also recognized the need for family planning it is likely to be immense. But just one word of caution: the opposition has not given up. There are signs of a major counter-attack, couched in terms of caution and delay. We must be on our guard.

(II) THE INTERNATIONAL PLANNED PARENTHOOD FEDERATION

COLVILLE DEVERELL

The International Planned Parenthood Federation (IPPF) is the organization which unites national voluntary family planning associations throughout the world. It was founded in response to a resolution of the third international conference on family planning in Bombay in 1952 under the sponsorship of the Family Planning Association of India.

The eight founder associations were drawn from Hong Kong, India, the Netherlands, Singapore, Sweden, the United Kingdom, the United States and West Germany. Its membership now exceeds fifty national associations, which for administrative convenience are grouped into five regions. These are the Europe and Near East region with headquarters in London, the South East Asia and Oceania region with headquarters in Singapore, the Western Hemisphere region, which includes both North and South America and the Caribbean, with headquarters in New York, the Western Pacific region with headquarters in Tokyo, and the Indian Ocean region with headquarters in Pakistan. Africa south of the Sahara is administered from the central IPPF office in London with a sub-regional office for East and Central Africa in Nairobi.

Each region is controlled by a regional council elected by its constituent family planning associations, which in turn elects representatives to the central governing body, and its standing management and Planning Committee, which are responsible for the policy and conduct of the Federation. The secretary-general and his staff at the central office in London are responsible for the day to day administration of the Federation in accordance with the policy approved by the governing body. Authoritative medical and basic science committees with eminent representatives drawn from all over the world advise the Federation and are responsible for the medical and scientific aspects of international conferences.

The Federation is a union of autonomous national associations which have come together to share experience and enjoy the advantages of collective representation in international circles.

In recent years the IPPF has been accorded consultative status with a number of United Nations organizations, including the Economic and Social Council, the World Health Organization, The United Nations Children's Fund, the International Labour Office, United Nations Educational, Scientific and Cultural Organization, and the Food and Agriculture Organization; and has maintained close contact with other international organizations such as the Organization for Economic Cooperation and Development, and the Organization of American States. Increasingly national and international organizations, universities and institutions come to the central office for information on the progress and technical aspects of family planning programmes, particularly in developing countries.

This central role could not have been achieved without the remarkable changes in public attitudes towards family planning which have taken place in recent years. In the 1950s international family planning was still uncoordinated, and the IPPF relied entirely on voluntary contributions for support. Up to 1964 the annual budget was less than one million dollars for its world programme. In 1968 it was over six million dollars, as more governments followed the example of Sweden, and accepted that assistance for family planning ought to be provided on the same basis as any other form of development aid. The change of attitude is best illustrated by examining the treatment of requests for family-planning aid to the United Nations. Opposition to family planning has been vehement, coming mainly from Communist and Roman Catholic Countries, and until recently this has severely limited United Nations activity in the family planning field. In one dramatic debate in 1952 at the World Health Assembly several countries, including Eire and Belgium, even hinted at resigning from the organization if an expert on family planning was sent to India as her government had requested. Opposition to United Nations' involvement has softened over the years, partly because of a general acceptance that family planning should be an essential part of maternal and child health, and partly because it is now generally accepted that a slowing down of population growth is essential in many developing countries if their expectations of economic improvement are to be realized. By 1967 Catholic countries were included among the thirty heads of state signing the United Nations Declaration on Population, which stresses that 'the opportunity to decide the number and spacing of children is a basic human right'. The United Nations and its agencies are now active in the field of population and family planning; the secretary-general of the United Nations has set up a special trust fund to finance work in this field, and requests for help from governments are being met. Among the aid-giving countries the change in attitude is typified by the action of the US Government. In 1965 American bilateral assistance in family planning was 2·3 million dollars, and provision of contraception supplies specifically excluded. In 1967 the figure was 35 million dollars, and both financial help and contraceptive supplies were given to those requesting help.

The common bond which unites the members of the IPPF is the belief (recently endorsed by the United Nations International Conference on Human Rights in Teheran) that all parents have an individual human right to access to information and to facilities to plan the size and spacing of their families, whether or not there is an additional collective or national reason to curb population growth rates for economic or social reasons.

Broadly, the objectives are to convert people everywhere to adopt a mode of life which includes the practice of family planning as an essential element in responsible parenthood; to encourage in every country the provision of indigenously controlled services facilitating the practice of family planning; and to assist in the creation of a public awareness of all the demographic and other relevant aspects such as will enable, or impel, governments to play a fully responsible role in this important aspect of modern life.

Springing from its fundamental concern for the rights and needs of the individual and the family, the IPPF believes that family planning ought to be an integral part of any comprehensive national maternal-and-child-health service, and that logically where the provision of these services is the responsibility of the state or of local authorities, they ought also to provide the family-planning element. For this reason, and because it is clear that it will be difficult to convert people to small families as long as infantile mortality remains high, the Federation strongly supports all efforts to improve maternal-and-child-health services, and regards the general weakness of these services in developing countries as one of the major obstacles to the effective promotion of family planning.

Except perhaps in small islands, or in city states, it is hardly practicable for a voluntary organization to provide an adequate structure capable of servicing a whole country. The role of the voluntary organization is rather to establish pioneer services and to create a climate of opinion which will enable the government and local authorities to assume a proper responsibility.

International Planned Parenthood Federation

The manner in which the IPPF tries to pursue its objectives is broadly as follows:

1. To stimulate the formation of national family planning associations throughout the world.

2. To provide an international presence to give expression to the aims and activities of its associations, and to cooperate with the United Nations and other international and government agencies.

3. To provide information, technical advice, training facilities and financial assistance at least until associations become viable.

4. To make regional administrative arrangements to facilitate the development of the associations.

5. To ensure adequate representation at international and regional levels, and with the United Nations.

6. To seek directly, or through the associations, to persuade governments and community leaders of the urgent need to provide family-planning facilities.

7. To endeavour through its medical, basic science and other committees to enlist the active support of the medical profession and the intelligentsia generally.

8. To stimulate public awareness all over the world through press contacts, international and regional meetings, private discussions, the employment of mass media and visual aids, and the publication of journals, handbooks, pamphlets, both centrally and locally.

9. To encourage practical experiments with new contraceptive and organizational techniques, and to make a proper evaluation of such research.

10. To enlist financial support both for the Federation and its constituent associations on conditions strictly ensuring the complete autonomy of the Federation.

While one of the main aims of the Federation is to persuade governments to assume full responsibility for providing family-planning services, it is unfortunately clear that a good many of them will not do so effectively in the near future. Their unwillingness or inability may spring from political or communal considerations, from chauvinism, or simply the weakness of their health services and lack of funds. In many countries, particularly in Latin America, Africa, and South East Asia, the work of voluntary organizations and foundations is only just beginning, and in some of them, for a variety of political and religious considerations, it may be difficult for governments to move effectively from acquiescence to active promotion. As governments increasingly accept a degree of responsibility, it will be necessary for the voluntary associations to adjust their activities so as to fulfil their aim to make the maximum possible complementary contribution to the national objective. Now we find that even when governments have made the initial vital decision to adopt a positive family-planning policy, it by no means follows that they will find it convenient to assume total responsibility for providing the services. It would not be sensible to attempt to define a role for the voluntary organizations to complement government effort which could be universally applied. But the general aim should be to try and ensure that the associations can continue to bring to the national effort the sense of dedication and vocation, and the humanizing influence, which are the traditional hallmarks of successful voluntary effort. There has been great variation in the pattern of cooperation, which may vary from a high degree of coordination of effort, as for instance in South Korea, to a virtual assumption of governmental responsibility for clinic services as in Singapore or in Fiji, where the role of the association is educational. On the other hand in Hong Kong, Mauritius and Kenya the governments have relied very largely on the associations providing most of the clinic services. In Pakistan and India massive national programmes are being mounted by the governments but clinics meet special needs for action research and demonstration.

The voluntary associations' complementary purpose may be best performed along the following broad lines:

1. By ceaselessly propounding by every possible means (including private and public discussions and the use of the mass media) the principle that 'family planning is a duty and a right', and the advantages, domestic and public, of a small family.

2. By providing an informed and responsible pressure group to sustain public support for the government programmes and to keep it under constant review.

3. By cooperating with the governments in providing training for all kinds of voluntary and part-time workers to supplement the governments' schemes.

4. By assisting all sorts of social units, such as factories, estates, large stores, government departments, chambers of commerce, trade unions, etc. to establish their own self-perpetuating family-planning services.

5. By participating in urban areas in the establishment of reporting systems to ensure that women who are not attending post-natal clinics, can be identified post-partum and be put in touch with contraceptive services.

6. By maintaining a limited number of model clinics in which new methods of contraception, training, administration, evaluation and motivation can be tested and reported to the governments.

7. By providing volunteer para-medical personnel to assist the governments' programmes in government institutions where the existing regular staff is inadequate or disinterested.

8. By keeping in touch with all kinds of family developments elsewhere through the IPPF contacts so as to bring relevant experience to the notice of governments.

9. By identifying the reasons for the temporary or permanent unpopularity of individual methods, and by demonstrating appropriate ways of countering these handicaps.

10. By testing and evaluating alternative incentives and their long-term effects.

11. By providing experienced and impartial advice in the central and regional advisory bodies.

12. By endeavouring to bridge any gap between the public and private medical sectors.

13. By attempting to secure the support of indigenous medical practitioners and midwives for the programme, which may adversely affect their vested interests.

Until recently the IPPF's activity in developing countries was largely concentrated on Asia, an area where about eighty per cent of the people now live in countries whose governments have accepted some degree of responsibility for family planning. In nearly all of these countries voluntary family planning associations have prepared the ground and influenced the governments' decisions. In the last few years great and encouraging attempts have been made to set up associations or assist institutions, groups or even individuals in Latin America and Africa.

Despite the religious difficulty in Latin America, and the relative social backwardness in many parts of Africa south of the Sahara, there has been surprisingly little organized opposition to the provision of family planning on a voluntary basis, though generally government attitudes are still permissive rather than positive. Where governments have adopted a more positive role the weakness of the medical structure, particularly in the rural areas, where most people live, is still a severe limiting factor. This is likely to be the most serious single obstacle to the expansion of effective services generally in developing countries as long as the available methods require a considerable degree of medical supervision.

Other limiting factors, particularly in Africa, are high rates of infant mortality, the belief that children's labour still has considerable economic utility in the fields, the prevalence still in many parts of the extended family system with its built-in social insurance, illiteracy and poverty, and sometimes tribal or communal chauvinism. On the other hand, at least in Africa, there is little religious or puritanical opposition to family planning, and there is a growing realization of the educational advantages of small families, and of the nutritional and other harmful effects to women with very frequent pregnancies.

Progress in Latin America, despite traditional religious opposition, has been dramatic, not only because of concern with the current very rapid rates of growth of the population in most countries, but also because of a wish to provide a more acceptable alternative to widespread abortions, which is reaching epidemic proportions in some countries. Figures on abortion are notoriously unreliable, but a Chilean study revealed that nearly half of the emergency admissions of women to

TABLE: DECLINE IN THE BIRTH RATE

	Average yearly growth rate of population 1958–66	Yearly growth rate of population 1966	Birth Rate									
			1950–54	1955–9	1960	1961	1962	1963	1964	1965	1966	1967	1968*
China (Taiwan)	3.3	2.70	43.9	42.8	39.5	38.3	37.4	36.3	34.5	32.7	32.4	28.5	
Hong Kong	3.4	1.99	34.2	36.2	36.0	34.3	33.3	32.8	30.1	27.7	24.9	23.0	22.8
S. Korea	2.8	2.5	—	44.7	40.0	—	40.0	36.3	30.1	—	29.8	25.8	23.3
Singapore	3.0	2.44	45.5	42.8	38.7	36.5	35.1	34.7	33.2	31.1	29.8	25.8	23.3

*1968 figures for first quarter only.

hospital were caused by complications of illegal abortion, and that one out of every four blood transfusions was for these cases. Seventeen out of the twenty Latin American countries now have voluntary family planning associations, all of them formed in the 1960s, and in at least twelve countries the government is providing some degree of support for family planning activities, most notably in Chile, Colombia and Honduras.

In the Caribbean widespread immigration dramatizes population pressures, and the government of Trinidad has recently joined those of Barbados and Jamaica in accepting the need for family planning. A number of the smaller islands, particularly the Windward Islands, have established voluntary associations; and the health services in Bermuda have for long provided facilities.

Family-planning programmes in these areas are either too small or too new to have any effect on the birth rate. However, as the table shows some Asian countries have experienced a rapid decline in the birth rate, some of which demographers are agreed results from the family-planning programmes.

All these countries have either government or voluntary large-scale family-planning programmes supported by their governments. It would of course be incorrect to attribute the decline exclusively to family-planning services. Other demographic factors such as changes in age distribution can play an important part, and many economic and social factors can exert influence. In Taiwan and Korea there has been extensive research to estimate what element the family-planning programme has contributed to reducing fertility. Professor Potter of the Population Council estimates the intra-uterine-device programme as having prevented 640,000 births in Korea since it started in 1964, and 238,000 in Taiwan. This compares with an annual total of a million and 420,000 births respectively. The Population Studies Centre of the University of Michigan has examined Hong Kong's falling birth rate, and concluded that from 1961 to 1965 from a third to a fifth of the fall was due to family planning. However, from 1965 to 1966 nine tenths of the decline was due to family planning, particularly to the Hong Kong Association IUD programme started in 1965. The Singapore programme has not been so closely examined, but it is one of the few programmes to use oral contraception as its main method, and has achieved the most significant fall in the birth rate since this method was used.

While it cannot be proved that effective large-scale family-planning programmes pursued by governments, or with manifest government support, can help or harm a fall in fertility, it is difficult to assess the effect which such programmes will have on bringing about the initial changes of attitude which must take place before people feel predisposed to limit their fertility. We believe that when communities have reached some imprecise stage along the road to modernization, usually characterized by a reasonable standard of literacy, a measure of industrialization, urbanization and – perhaps most important – by a weakening of rigid kinship or caste ties, a tendency towards a fall in birth rates often emerges.

If at this stage properly organized national family planning can be mounted it will almost certainly ensure a much more rapid decline in fertility. In more backward countries the immediate aims should be to provide family planning as a logical element in maternal-and-child-health services where these exist, and to endeavour to make the leaders aware of the economic and social advantages of curtailing too rapid population growth rates.

Dr Frank Notestein, then President of the Population Council, stated at IPPF's eighth international conference in Chile in 1967 that from evidence of studies of knowledge, attitude and practice concerning contraception in all parts of the world, 'men and women everywhere want to avail themselves of the benefits of family planning whenever they are informed that family planning is possible'. This does not of course mean that people generally, whether in developed or developing countries, yet accept the need to adopt a family size consistent with the objective of population stability. To give two instances: a survey in a district in Turkey revealed that though most women had seven or more children, they said that the desired family size was three or four. In Calcutta while four children were considered an ideal family size, in present circumstances only two were desired.

The part played by the IPPF and other agencies in the remarkable expansion of family planning in recent years has been possible only because of the greatly expanded financial support provided both by the public and governments. About half the IPPF's income comes from private subscriptions, largely from America, the other half coming from the governments of such countries as Denmark, Holland, Norway, Sweden, the USA and the United Kingdom, which have accepted the propriety of providing technical aid and assistance for family planning on the same principle as any other aid to developing countries. This sort of aid cannot be provided on a government to government basis until the recipient government has accepted a family-planning responsibility; where this has not yet happened, but the government's attitude is permissive, the IPPF may be able to give practical assistance in a way that others cannot. In accepting this role, and in accepting government financial support, the IPPF insists on the principle of confining such support to its own projects and programmes, which it has itself drawn up, and over which its associations exercise unfettered control.

Until new methods have been found which do not require considerable medical supervision the work of the voluntary organizations must be concerned with the training of medical and para-medical personnel and the improvement of clinic techniques and organization. But in the long term the voluntary movements' chief concern should be with the promotion of ideas – the idea that all parents should have the knowledge and means responsibly to plan the size and spacing of their families, and that responsible parents, the world over, should accept the idea of a small family in the interest of all.